World of Business

OTHER ECONOMIST BOOKS

Guide to Analysing Companies
Guide to Business Modelling
Guide to Business Planning
Guide to Economic Indicators
Guide to the European Union
Guide to Financial Management
Guide to Financial Markets
Guide to Investment Strategy
Guide to Management Ideas and Gurus
Guide to Organisation Design
Guide to Project Management
Guide to Supply Chain Management
Numbers Guide
Style Guide

Book of Obituaries
Brands and Branding
Business Consulting
Business Miscellany
Coaching and Mentoring
Dealing with Financial Risk
Economics
Emerging Markets
The Future of Technology
Headhunters and How to Use Them
Mapping the Markets
Marketing
Successful Strategy Execution
The City

Directors: an A–Z Guide
Economics: an A–Z Guide
Investment: an A–Z Guide
Negotiation: an A–Z Guide

Pocket World in Figures

The
Economist

World of Business

THE ECONOMIST IN ASSOCIATION WITH
PROFILE BOOKS LTD

Published by Profile Books Ltd
3A Exmouth House, Pine Street, London EC1R 0JH
www.profilebooks.com

Derived from a book previously published as
The Economist Business Miscellany

The greatest care has been taken in compiling this book.
However, no responsibility can be accepted by the publishers or
compilers for the accuracy of the information presented.

Where opinion is expressed it is that of the author and does not
necessarily coincide with the editorial views of
The Economist Newspaper.

Typeset by MacGuru Ltd
info@macguru.org.uk

Printed and bound in Italy by
L.E.G.O. Spa Lavis (TN)

A CIP catalogue record for this book is available
from the British Library

ISBN 978 1 84668 158 5

Contents

Contributors

Many people contributed to this book, as follows.

Sarah Dallas, former Cities Guide editor of Economist.com, and others: "Business etiquette".

Tim Hindle, former management editor of *The Economist*: "Leading management thinkers" and "Great business books".

Andrew Palmer, finance editor of *The Economist*: "Business jargon".

Bob Tricker, author of *Directors: An A–Z Guide*: "Board styles", "Roles directors play" and "Games directors play" and .

Alexander Walsh, a freelance writer and researcher: "What companies say about themselves" and "Some business giants of the past".

Simon Wright, business writer for *The Economist*: "Behind the corporate name", "Business blunders", "Some famous advertising slogans", "Bubbles that burst", "Bad boys", "In their own words", "Behind the currency name" and "Inventors and inventions". He also contributed to "Some business giants of the past".

All other material was researched and compiled by Carol Howard, former head of *The Economist* research department, Lisa Davies, Conrad Heine, Roxana Willis and Christopher Wilson, all of whom work at *The Economist*.

Business is really more agreeable than pleasure; it interests the whole mind … more deeply. But it does not look as though it did

Walter Bagehot, journalist, author and, from 1861 to 1877, editor of *The Economist*

When firms started

Year	Firm	Activity	Country
578	Kongo Gumi	Construction	Japan
1288	Stora Enso	Paper	Finland
1385	Antinori	Wine and olive oil	Italy
1526	Fabbrica D'Armi Pietro Beretta	Firearms	Italy
1630	Kikkoman	Soy sauce	Japan
1630	Sumitomo	Conglomerate	Japan
1639	Hugel & Fils	Wine	France
1642	James Lock	Hatters	UK
1672	C. Hoare & Co	Banking	UK
1698	Berry Bros & Rudd	Wine merchants	UK
1734	Taittinger	Champagne	France
1739	William Clark	Linens	UK
1748	Villeroy & Boch	Tableware	Germany
1759	Wedgwood	China	UK
1761	Faber-Castell	Pencils	Germany
1786	Molson	Brewing	Canada
1802	Du Pont	Chemicals	US
1853	Levi Strauss	Clothing	US
1860	Anheuser-Busch	Beer	US
1862	Bacardi	Rum	Cuba
1867	Standard Oil	Oil	US
1869	Goldman Sachs	Investment banking	US
1886	Coca-Cola	Soft drinks	US
1892	General Electric	Electrical equipment	US
1896	Barclays	Banking	US
1901	US Steel	Steel	US
1903	Ford Motor	Automotive	US
1909	BP (originally Anglo-Persian Oil)	Oil	UK
1916	BMW	Motor engineering	Germany
1943	IKEA	Retailing	Sweden
1946	Sony	Consumer electronics	Japan
1955	McDonald's first restaurant	Fast food	US
1962	Wal-Mart's first store	Retailing	US
1971	Starbucks	Coffee shops	US
1975	Microsoft	Software	US
1977	Apple Computer	Computers	US
1998	Google	Internet	US

Sources: Company websites; *Centuries of Success* by William T. O'Hara; *Family Business* magazine

Oldest family firms

Year est.	Company	Business	Country
718	Houshi Onsen	Innkeeping	Japan
1000	Château de Goulaine	Vineyard/museum/ butterfly collection	France
1000	Pontificia Fonderia Marinelli	Bell foundry	Italy
1141	Barone Ricasoli	Wine and olive oil	Italy
1295	Barovier & Toso	Glassmaking	Italy
1304	Hotel Pilgrim Haus	Innkeeping	Germany
1326	Richard de Bas	Paper-making	France
1369	Torrini Firenze	Goldsmiths	Italy
1385	Antinori	Wine and olive oil	Italy
1438	Camuffo	Shipbuilding	Italy
1494	Baronnie de Coussergues	Wine	France
1500	Grazia Deruta	Ceramics	Italy
1526	Fabbrica D'Armi Pietro Beretta	Firearms	Italy
1530	William Prym	Copper, brass, haberdashery	Germany
1541	John Brooke & Sons	Woollens	England
1545	Touwfabriek	Rope-making	Netherlands
1551	Codorníu	Wine	Spain
1552	Fonjallaz	Wine	Switzerland
1568	Von Poschinger	Glassmaking	Germany
1575	Hacienda Los Lingues	Wine, hotel	Chile
1590	Berenberg Bank	Banking	Germany
1591	R Durtnell & Sons	Construction	England
1594	Royal Tichelaar	Earthenware, tiles	Netherlands
1596	Eduard Meier	Shoes	Germany
pre-1600	Toraya	Confectionery	Japan

Source: www.familybusinessmagazine.com/worldsoldest.html

Oldest newspapers still in circulation

Year est.	Title	Country
1645	Post och Inrikes Tidningar*	Sweden
1656	Haarlems Dagblad	Netherlands
1664	La Gazzetta di Mantova	Italy
1665	The London Gazette	UK
1703	Wiener Zeitung	Austria
1705	Hildesheimer Allgemeine Zeitung	Germany
1709	Worcester Journal	UK
1711	The Newcastle Journal	UK
1712	The Stamford Mercury	UK
1720	The Northampton Mercury	UK
1725	Hanauer Anzeiger	Germany
1734	Lloyd's List	UK
1737	The Belfast News-Letter	UK
1738	Feuille d'Avis de Neuchâtel	Switzerland
1740	Darmstaedter Tageblatt	Germany
1747	Press & Journal	UK
1749	Berlingske Tidende	Denmark
1750	Giessener Anzeiger	Germany
1752	Leeuwarder Courant	Netherlands
1754	The Yorkshire Post	UK
1755	La Gazzetta di Parma	Italy
1758	Provinciale Zeeuwse Courant	Netherlands
1758	Norrköpings Tidningar	Sweden
1761	Saarbrücker Zeitung	Germany
1761	Schaumburger Zeitung	Germany
1762	24 heures/Feuille d'Avis de Lausanne	Switzerland

*Online edition only since February 2007.

Sources: World Association of Newspapers; companies

The business press

Beginnings

The Economist	1843
Financial Times	1888
Wall Street Journal	1889
Forbes	1917
Barron's	1921
Harvard Business Review	1922
Time	1923
BusinessWeek	1929
Fortune	1930

Circulation, paid copies per issue

	Europe	N America	Asia-Pacific	Total
BusinessWeek	...	925,820	...	...
The Economist	375,619	786,977	133,846	1,340,252
Financial Times	263,888	129,445	41,008	434,340
Forbes	...	919,742	...	...
Fortune	83,613	865,517	85,013	1,034,143
Harvard Business Review*	40,925	164,054	23,530	242,680
Time	434,899	3,578,834	264,350	4,332,391
Wall Street Journal	79,579	2,069,463	77,365	2,226,407

Note: Data for July–December 2008 except *October. Total includes other areas.
Source: Audit Bureau of Circulations

The world's biggest firms

2009*	Market capitalisation, $bn
PetroChina (China)	343.3
Exxon Mobil (US)	341.1
Microsoft (US)	211.5
China Mobile (Hong Kong)	200.8
Industrial & Commercial Bank of China (China)	199.1
Wal-Mart Stores (US)	188.8
China Construction Bank (China)	174.2
Petrobras (Brazil)	165.1
Johnson & Johnson (US)	156.5
Royal Dutch Shell (Netherlands/UK)	156.3
Procter & Gamble (US)	148.9
BP (UK)	147.5
AT&T (US)	146.6
BHP Billiton (Australia/UK)	143.8
Nestlé (US)	144.1
HSBC (UK)	143.3
Berkshire Hathaway (US)	138.1
IBM (US)	138.0
Chevron (US)	132.8
Toyota Motor (Japan)	131.2

*As of June 30th.
Source: Thomson Reuters

1993	Revenue, $bn
General Motors (US)	133.6
Ford Motor (US)	108.5
Exxon (US)	97.8
Royal Dutch Shell (Netherlands/UK)	95.1
Toyota (Japan)	85.3
Hitachi (Japan)	68.6
IBM (US)	62.7
Matsushita Electric Industrial Co. (Japan)	61.4
General Electric (US)	60.8
Daimler-Benz (Germany)	59.1
Mobil (US)	56.6

2008	Revenue, $bn
Royal Dutch Shell (Netherlands/UK)	458.4
Exxon Mobil (US)	442.9
Wal-Mart Stores (US)	405.6
BP (UK)	367.1
Chevron (US)	263.2
Total (France)	234.7
ConocoPhillips (US)	230.8
ING Group (Netherlands)	226.6
Sinopec (China)	207.8
Toyota Motor (Japan)	204.4
Japan Post Holdings (Japan)	198.7
General Electric (US)	183.2
China National Petroleum (China)	181.1
Volkswagen (Germany)	166.6
State Grid (China)	164.1
Dexia Group (Belgium)	161.3
ENI (Italy)	159.3
General Motors (US)	149.0
Ford Motor (US)	146.3
Allianz (Germany)	142.4

Sources: *Fortune*; annual reports

1993	Revenue, $bn
Nissan (Japan)	53.8
BP (UK)	52.5
Samsung (South Korea)	51.3
Philip Morris (US)	50.6
IRI (Italy)	50.5
Siemens (Germany)	50.4
Volkswagen (Germany)	46.3
Chrysler (US)	43.6
Toshiba (Japan)	42.9

Source: *Fortune*

America's biggest firms

1955 Revenue, $bn		1965 Revenue, $bn		1975 Revenue, $bn	
General Motors	9.8	General Motors	17.0	Exxon	42.1
Exxon	5.7	Exxon	10.8	General Motors	31.6
US Steel	3.3	Ford Motor	9.7	Ford Motor	23.6
General Electric	3.0	General Electric	4.9	Texaco	23.3
Esmark	2.5	Mobil	4.5	Mobil	18.9
Chrysler	2.1	Chrysler	4.3	Chevron	17.2
Armour	2.1	US Steel	4.1	Gulf Oil	16.5
Gulf Oil	1.7	Texaco	3.6	General Electric	13.4
Mobil	1.7	IBM	3.2	IBM	12.7
DuPont	1.7	Gulf Oil	3.2	ITT Industries	11.2

1985 Revenue, $bn		1995 Revenue, $bn		2005 Revenue, $bn	
Exxon	90.9	General Motors	155.0	Exxon Mobil	339.9
General Motors	83.9	Ford Motor	128.4	Wal-Mart	315.7
Mobil	56.1	Exxon	101.5	General Motors	192.6
Ford Motor	52.4	Wal-Mart	83.4	Chevron Texaco	189.5
Chevron Texaco	47.3	AT&T	75.1	Ford Motor	177.2
IBM	45.9	General Electric	64.7	ConocoPhillips	166.7
DuPont	35.9	IBM	64.1	General Electric	157.2
AT&T	33.2	Mobil	59.6	Citigroup	131.0
General Electric	28.0	Sears Roebuck	54.6	AIG	108.9
Amoco	27.0	Altria Group	53.8	IBM	91.1

2008 Revenue, $bn	
Exxon Mobil	442.9
Wal-Mart Stores	405.6
Chevron	263.2
ConocoPhillips	230.8
General Electric	183.2
General Motors	149.0
Ford Motor	146.3
AT&T	124.0
Hewlett-Packard	118.4
Valero Energy	118.3

Source: *Fortune*; annual reports

America's biggest bankruptcies

Since 1980	Assets, $bn (2008 prices)	Assets, $bn (current prices)	Date
Lehman Brothers	691	691	2008
Washington Mutual	328	328	2008
WorldCom	124	104	2002
General Motors	91	91	2009
Enron	79	66	2001
Conseco	73	61	2002
Texaco	67	35	1987
Financial Corporation of America	61	34	1988
Bank of New England Corporation	48	30	1991
Pacific Gas and Electric Company	44	36	2001
Chrysler	40	39	2009
Thornburg Mortgage	37	37	2009
Global Crossing	37	30	2002
Refco	36	33	2005
IndyMac Bancorp	33	33	2008
General Growth Properties	30	30	2009
UAL Corporation	30	25	2002
Calphine Corporation	30	27	2005
Lyondell Chemical Company	28	27	2009
New Century Financial Corporation	27	26	2007

Note: Current prices are those at the time of bankruptcy; 2008 prices are adjusted for inflation.
Source: BankruptcyData.com; US Bureau of Labour Statistics

Big firms, Big facts

- Airbus delivered 95 aircraft in 1990, Boeing 527. In 2000 Airbus delivered 311 against Boeing's 492. In 2008 Airbus delivered 483 and Boeing 375.

- Coca-Cola products are sold in more than 200 countries, more than one billion beverage servings per day.

- Exxon Mobil produced 3.9m oil-equivalent barrels of oil and gas per day in 2008; BP produced 3.8m, Royal Dutch Shell and PetroChina 3.2m.

- General Motors had 12% of the US car market in 1921, overtook Ford Motor in 1929 and reached over 50% in the early 1960s. It fell to less than 20% in the first half of 2009.

- Google searches reached almost 300m per day in May 2009.

- McDonald's has more than 30,000 local restaurants in 118 countries, serving nearly 60m customers a day.

- Microsoft's sales went over $1m in 1978; over $1 billion in 1990; over $10 billion in 1997. Revenues were $58.4 billion in the fiscal year ending June 2009.

- Samsung Electronics had 19.9% of the LCD TV market in the second quarter of 2009. LG Electronics had 12.6% and Sony 11.4%. Vizio sold most in North America.

- Starbucks are in over 11,000 locations in 44 countries; long-term target in October 2006 was 40,000 stores worldwide with at least half outside the US.

- Wal-Mart Stores employs more than 2m associates worldwide in more than 7,000 stores. More than 200m customers visit US stores every year.

Sources: Company reports; press reports

Big bucks

Profits and losses

Biggest annual profits World: Exxon Mobil's $45.2 billion in 2008. UK: Royal Dutch Shell's $31.4 billion in 2008.

Biggest annual losses, world American International Group (AIG) lost $99.3 billion in 2008, of which $61.7 billion was in the fourth quarter. It had to write down enormous losses from toxic assets and credit-default swaps – instruments intended to protect banks against defaulting loans or derivatives. The US government rescued AIG with bail-outs totalling $182.5 billion. AIG just beat AOL Time Warner's loss of $98.7 billion in 2002, after massive write-downs on the value of America Online. The $54.2 billion loss in the fourth quarter of 2002 had also been a record.

Biggest annual losses, Europe The UK's Royal Bank of Scotland broke records with a loss of £24.1 billion in 2008. Write-downs of £16.2 billion mostly stemmed from the takeover of ABN Amro the previous year. The previous record was held by Vodafone with a loss of £21.9 billion in the year to March 2006 after big write-offs of assets, particularly in Germany.

In Japan Mizuho Financial Group, once the world's biggest bank by assets, made a loss of ¥2.4 trillion ($19.5 billion) in the year beginning April 2002. In fiscal 2008, Toyota Motor made its first loss since it started publishing results in 1941, in spite of becoming the biggest carmaker, overtaking General Motors in 2008. Hitachi made a loss of ¥787 billion (over $8 billion), the biggest annual loss by a Japanese manufacturing company.

Sources: Company websites; press reports

Big bail-outs

AIG – not so well covered

American International Group (AIG), an insurance
company, was too extensively intertwined with the global
financial system to be allowed to fail according to the
American government. In September 2008 the Federal
Reserve stepped in to provide a two-year credit line of up
to $85 billion after AIG suffered huge losses largely
stemming from toxic investments related to the American
mortgage market. In return the government got a 79.9%
stake in the insurer. But AIG's troubles didn't end there
and by March 2009 the cost of the federal bail-out had
reached $182.5 billion.

Bear Stearns – gripped by a stern bear

In March 2008 Bear Stearns, the fifth-largest Wall Street
investment bank, found itself on the verge of bankruptcy
as a result of its exposure in the asset-backed securities
market, in particular collateralised debt obligations based
on subprime mortgages. Deemed beyond rescue, it was
sold in a government-brokered deal to JPMorgan Chase
for $236m. The Federal Reserve agreed to secure up to
$30 billion (later lowered to $29 billion) of Bear Stearns's
liabilities to facilitate the purchase.

Freddie and Fannie get into trouble

Freddie Mac (the Federal Home Loan Mortgage
Corporation) and Fannie Mae (the Federal National
Mortgage Association were placed in "conservatorship"
(in effect a government takeover) in September 2008 as
the turmoil in subprime mortgage market deepened. The
government-guaranteed enterprises were estimated to
have underwritten three-quarters of new mortgages in
America, repackaging them into securities that they kept
or sold on. The Treasury Department agreed to buy up to
$200 billion of newly issued senior preferred stock, which

in February 2009 was doubled to $400 billion.

Help for airlines post September 11th

Even before the attacks on the World Trade Centre and
the Pentagon on September 11th 2001, America's
domestic airline industry was struggling with huge debt
and rising fuel costs. Eleven days after the terrorist
attacks, Congress passed the Air Transport Safety and
Systems Stabilisation Act, providing $5 billion in cash and
a further $10 billion in loan guarantees, as compensation
for grounding flights, and to offset higher security costs
and underwrite extra insurance.

Saving the car makers

In December 2008 President George W. Bush announced
that the American car industry would receive $17.4
billion to fend off the threat of bankruptcy: $13.4 billion
went to General Motors and $4 billion to Chrysler (which
when previously in trouble in 1979 had secured $1.5
billion from the government in loan guarantees). By June
1st 2009 both firms had filed for Chapter 11 protection
but emerged within a few weeks leaner and shorn of
debts. Other support measures since have included
government funded car-scrappage schemes, grants given
to customers to buy new cars and scrap older models car.
In America Congress originally released $1 billion to fund
its scheme and later added another $2 billion. In Europe,
France's programme cost an estimated €220m ($280m)
when introduced in December 2008; by July 2009 it was
€390m. Germany's original €1.5 billion scheme proved so
popular it was increased to €5 billion. The British
scrappage plan, which had a budget of £300m ($440m),
differed from others in that payment of the grant was
split between the government and car retailers.

S&Ls – not thrifty enough

In 1989 America's president, George H. W. Bush, signed
the Financial Institutions Reform, Recovery and

big bail-outs *continued*

Enforcement Act to bail out the country's Savings and Loans associations (known as "thrifts"). Deregulation had encouraged the lenders, which had specialised in mortgage loans, to branch out into riskier ventures that went sour. Over 1,000 S&Ls failed between 1986 and 1995, costing taxpayers around $120 billion.

America's financial rescue package

The US Congress passed the Emergency Economic Stability Act in October 2008 to bail out the financial system and prevent systemic collapse. The act authorised the Treasury to buy up to $700 billion in mortgage-backed securities and other toxic assets, under the Troubled Asset Relief Programme (TARP). Among those who took advantage of the government relief package were Citigroup, which received $25 billion in October and $20 billion in November, and Bank of America, which received $45 billion. The government also provided billion-dollar guarantees for both banks.

Britain's bank rescue package

The British government nationalised Northern Rock in February 2008 and took over the mortgage-lending arm of Bradford & Bingley days before it announced a bail-out package for banks on October 8th 2008. It made £75 billion ($132 billion) available for financial institutions to boost capital. The package also increased the "special liquidity facility" to £200 billion from the initial £100 billion made available in April. This allowed banks to swap illiquid mortgage-backed securities for Treasury bills. It also provided loan guarantees of £250 billion to encourage banks to start lending to each other again. Five days later the government had injected £37 billion into the Royal Bank of Scotland (RBS), HBOS and Lloyds TSB. It also suspended monopoly rules to allow Lloyds TSB to

acquire HBOS. In return it took a 60% stake in RBS and
40% in what was renamed Lloyds Banking Group.

European financial rescue packages

European governments bailed out several banks in the
wake of the financial crisis that began in the summer of
2007. IKB Deutsche Industriebank, a small domestic
German lender was the first that required help. A year
later the governments of the Netherlands, Belgium and
Luxembourg bailed out Fortis €11.2 billion ($16.4 billion)
and partially nationalised it. In late September 2008, the
Icelandic government took a 75% stake in Glitnir after
injecting €600m ($876m). In October Landsbanki and
Kaupthing were also nationalised.

In the same month the Dutch government put up €200
billion ($270 billion) to guarantee interbank lending to
add to a €20 billion emergency fund to strengthen capital
positions (ING drew €10 billion). UBS, Switzerland's
biggest bank, received SFr6 billion ($5.2 billion) from the
government, which also created a $60 billion fund into
which banks could offload toxic assets. The Swedish
government announced a SKr1.5 trillion ($200 billion)
bail-out package, equivalent to almost half of its GDP,
drawing on lessons from a financial crisis of the 1990s. The
French government set aside a €360 billion bail-out fund,
including €40 billion to recapitalise its banks. Germany
announced a rescue package with state guarantees worth
€400 billion to back interbank lending, and €80 billion to
top up capital. The country's second-biggest property
lender, Hypo Real Estate, received a revised €50 billion
bail-out package and the company was later nationalised.

In November 2008 Commerzbank received €8.2 billion
($10.4 billion) and the German government took a 25%
stake. Spain announced a bank-rescue fund of up to €99
billion ($138 billion) in June 2009. Earlier in the year, a
small bank, Caja Castilla La Mancha, received a €9 billion
bail-out.

Sources: Company reports, press reports

Behind the corporate name

Adidas The German sporting-goods firm is named after its founder, Adolf (Adi) Dassler.

Adobe Named after the creek that ran past the houses of the American software firm's founders, John Warnock and Chuck Geschke.

Aldi Named after its founders, the Albrecht family, and discount: what it does.

Alfa Romeo Anonima Lombarda Fabbrica Automobili was taken over by Nicola Romeo in 1915. The first Alfa Romeo, the Torpedo 20–30hp, was made in 1920.

Amazon.com Jeff Bezos, the American online retailer's founder, originally wanted to call his firm Cadabra.com, as in abracadabra, until his lawyer advised him that it sounded too much like cadaver. So the company was renamed after the world's second-longest river, which not coincidentally also comes near the beginning of alphabetical lists.

Amstrad The British electronics company is a contraction of Alan Michael Sugar Trading, named after its founder.

Apple Steve Jobs, one of the firm's co-founders, either sought enlightenment in the orchards of a Hare Krishna commune, or tried an experimental all-fruit diet, or wanted to make a tribute to the Beatles and their business arm, Apple Corp. Apple paid the Beatles a substantial out-of-court settlement to use the name and legal disputes continue. The Apple Macintosh is named after a popular variety of American apple, the McIntosh. McIntosh Laboratory, an audio equipment firm, was also paid off for the use of its name.

Asda The British supermarket chain, now owned by Wal-Mart, is a contraction of Associated Dairies.

Aston Martin The Aston Hill races near Birmingham, where the British car company was founded, provided the inspiration for the first half of the name. This was married to the surname of the company's founder, Lionel Martin.

Atari Derives from Go, a Japanese board game. Atari is when all an opponent's stones are threatened with capture.

Audi Founded in 1909 by August Horch, who took the name from the Latin translation of Horch, meaning "hark" in English from the imperative form of *audire*, "to hear".

B&Q The British DIY chain takes its name from the initials of its founders, Richard Block and David Quayle.

BASF The German chemicals firm name is taken from Badische Anilin und Soda Fabrik. The company began by producing aniline and soda in the German state of Baden.

BMW Bayerische Motoren Werke was founded in Munich in 1917, originally to construct aircraft engines. The German car company's logo is inspired by a rotating propeller.

Bridgestone The Japanese tyremaker is named after its founder, Shojiro Ishibashi, whose surname means "stone bridge".

Canon The Precision Optical Instruments Laboratory took its new identity from the name of its first camera, the Kwannon. It also represents Kannon, the Japanese name of the Buddhist bodhisattva of mercy.

Carrefour The French-based retailer, and now one of the world's biggest, takes it name from the crossroads in Annecy, a small town in the Alps that was the location of its first shop.

Casio Derives from the name of its founder, Kashio Tadao.

behind the corporate name *continued*

Coca-Cola The name is derived from the coca leaves and kola nuts that were part of the original flavouring of the drink that was launched as a health tonic in 1885. The coca leaf, from which cocaine is produced, undoubtedly gave Coke a kick; the last traces were removed in 1929.

Daewoo Means "great universe" in Korean.

Danone The food firm began producing yogurt in Barcelona in 1919. It takes its name from the nickname of Daniel, the son of the founder, Isaac Carasso.

eBay Pierre Omidyar, founder of the online auction site, wanted to use the name of his internet consultancy, Echo Bay Technology Group. But Echo Bay Mines, a gold mining company, had registered the name already.

Exxon Mobil The New Jersey branch of Standard Oil adopted the name Esso (S-O) in 1926. But other branches of Standard Oil, broken up in an antitrust action by America's Supreme Court in 1911, contested the use of the name in several American states years later. So in 1972 the Esso brand was replaced with the similar-sounding Exxon in America (though Esso was retained in many foreign markets). The Standard Oil Company of New York (Socony), another branch, merged with Vacuum Oil (another part of the former Standard Oil conglomerate) to form the Socony-Vacuum Corporation. In 1955, the name was changed to Socony Mobil Oil Company, and later to Mobil, which merged with Exxon in 1999.

Fiat Società Anonima Fabbrica Italiana Automobili Torino was founded in 1899 in Turin.

Garmin The world's leading portable satellite-navigation company is named after its founders, Gary Burrell and Min Kao.

Google The name, taken from the word googol, a vast number represented by 1 followed by 100 noughts, started as a boast about the amount of information the search engine would be able to cover.

Häagen-Dazs The name of the premium ice-cream company founded in 1961 is, like its products, entirely confected.

Haribo The German confectioner derives its name from that of the founder and the home city of the company, Hans Riegel from Bonn.

Hasbro The American toy was founded by the Hassenfeld Brothers.

Hewlett-Packard Bill Hewlett and David Packard tossed a coin to decide whether the company they founded would be called Hewlett-Packard or Packard-Hewlett. Bill presumably won.

Hotmail The web-based e-mail service, founded in 1995, contains all the letters from HTML – the language used to write web pages. The service was first written, with selected capital letters, as HoTMaiL.

Ikea The Swedish budget furniture-maker was founded by Ingvar Kamprad whose family home was a farm called Elmtaryd, near the Swedish village of Agunnaryd.

Intel Bob Noyce and Gordon Moore had hoped to call their microchip company Moore Noyce. Improbably, a hotel chain of the same name had beaten them to it so they went for a conflation of integrated electronics.

Kodak Is called Kodak because George Eastman, the camera company's founder, thought that it sounded good.

Lego From a Danish phrase, *leg godt*, which means "play well". Although Lego also means "I construct" in Latin, the firm's name predates its introduction of construction bricks.

behind the corporate name *continued*

Lycos *Lycosidae*, the family name of wolf spiders, provided the inspiration. These spiders are excellent hunters that run after prey instead of catching it in a web.

Mattel The American toymaker's marque is a combination of the names of its founders, Harold Matson and Elliot Handler.

Mercedes-Benz The German car company founded by Gottlieb Daimler and Karl Benz took its forename from the daughter of an Austrian businessman, Emil Jellinek. In 1898 he began to sell and promote their cars to wealthy clients and in 1900 invested in the company to aid the development of a new engine called the Mercedes-Benz. Mercedes was both his daughter's name and the pseudonym he used when racing the cars.

Microsoft Bill Gates wanted a name that suggested the microcomputer software that he would manufacture. Micro-soft dropped its original hyphen and went on to rule the world.

Mitsubishi The Japanese conglomerate's name refers to its three-diamond logo. It is a combination of the words *mitsu*, meaning three, and *hishi*, meaning water chestnut, a word that denotes a diamond shape in Japanese.

Motorola The Galvin Manufacturing Company started making car radios in the 1950s. The suffix –ola was popular in America at the time (eg, Rockola jukeboxes, Victrola sound equipment) for suggesting high-quality audio reproduction. Motorola is intended to suggest sound in motion.

Nabisco The American food firm was known as the National Biscuit Company until 1971.

Nike The American sports equipment company is named after the Greek goddess of victory.

Nikon The original name of the camera company was Nippon Kogaku, meaning "Japanese optical".

Nissan The company was earlier known by the name Nippon Sangyo, meaning "Japanese industry".

Nokia Named after a small town in Finland that was home to a successful pulp and paper company that later expanded into rubber goods before hitting on the idea that mobile phones could prove popular.

Oracle Larry Ellison, Ed Oates and Bob Miner were working for the CIA as consultants on a project codenamed Oracle. The project's funding ended but the three decided to finish what they had begun and to keep the name for their software company. One of Oracle's first customers was the CIA.

Pepsi Brad's Drink, a concoction formulated by Caleb Bradham, a pharmacist, was renamed Pepsi-Cola in 1898 after the kola nuts used in the recipe and possibly to incorporate pepsin, an enzyme produced in the stomach that helps digestion.

Royal Dutch Shell Its origins go back to the Shell Transport and Trading Company. It was established by Samuel & Co as a business that sold sea shells to Victorian natural-history enthusiasts. Later, the company thought that there could be a market for oil, which it began to trade.

Saab Svenska Aeroplane Aktiebolaget, a Swedish plane manufacturer, launched its first car in 1949.

Samsung The South Korean electronics firm's name means "three stars" in Korean.

Seat Sociedad Española de Automoviles de Turismo was officially founded in 1950 in Barcelona.

Skype Founded in 2003, the company that enables free phone calls over the internet was originally named Sky peer-to-peer. This was subsequently shortened to Skyper and then Skype.

behind the corporate name *continued*

Sony The Japanese electronics firm's name is taken both from a Latin word, *sonus*, which is the root of the word sonic, and from the expression "sonny boy", popular in post-war Japan when the firm was founded. The words were meant to show that the firm was a group of young people with energy and passion.

Starbucks Named after Starbuck, the mate of the *Pequod* in Herman Melville's whaling novel, *Moby Dick*.

Subaru The Japanese car company takes its name from the Japanese for the star constellation called the *pleiades* or "Seven Sisters". The firm, with a logo incorporating seven stars, was formed by the merger of seven companies.

SunMicrosystems The firm's name originally stood for Stanford University Systems after the college where the founders designed their first workstation as students. They chose the name hoping to sell their product to Stanford. They failed to do so.

Tesco Sir Jack Cohen, founder of the British supermarket giant, began selling groceries in London's East End in 1919. Tesco first appeared on packets of tea in the 1920s. The name was based on the initials of T.E. Stockwell, a partner in the firm of tea suppliers, and the first two letters of Cohen.

Toyota Sakichi Toyoda first called his company Toyeda, but changed it after running a competition to find one that sounded better. The new name is written with eight strokes in Japanese script, an auspicious number.

Unilever The multinational that sells many of the world's best-known consumer products brands, stretching from Dove soap and Hellman's mayonnaise to Lipton tea, Sunsilk shampoo and Ben and Jerry's ice cream, was formed in 1980 by the merger of Lever Brothers, a British soapmaker, and Dutch margarine-maker Unie.

Vauxhall Vauxhall Iron Works was built on the site of "Fulk's Hall", the house of a medieval knight, Fulk le Breant, on the south bank of the Thames in London in 1894. *Vokzal* is the Russian word for a train station, a corruption of the name Vauxhall. Tsar Nicholas I visited the station while touring Britain and was clearly impressed.

Virgin Group According to Sir Richard Branson, the firm's founder, the name was suggested in the 1970s when he began one of his first ventures, a mail-order record company, as a business "virgin".

Volvo From the Latin meaning "I roll". It was originally a name for a ball bearing developed by the parent company of the Swedish carmaker founded in 1927.

Wipro The Indian IT-services giant's name derives from its more humble origins as Western India Vegetable Products.

WPP The worldwide advertising agency and PR firm tales its name from Wire and Plastics Products, a British public company acquired in 1985 as an entity on which to build the firm.

Xerox Chestor Carlson invented a revolutionary dry-copying process as an improvement on current wet-copying methods. *Xeros* is the Greek word for dry.

Yahoo! The name is an acronym for "yet another hierarchical officious oracle", but the company's founders also liked the definition of a yahoo as "rude, unsophisticated, uncouth" taken from the unpleasant and savage creatures in Jonathan Swift's *Gulliver's Travels*.

Business blunders

Amaranth and Mr Hunter

Brian Hunter, star trader at Amaranth, an American hedge fund, made big money in 2005 betting on the price of natural gas. He is reckoned to have amassed profits of over $1 billion after Hurricane Katrina swept across the southern states, sending gas prices spiralling. But the next year the weather turned against Mr Hunter. Even bigger wagers on gas-price futures turned bad after he wrongly reckoned that more storms would keep gas prices high. His weather forecasting abilities let him down – gas prices plunged. Amaranth's losses exceeded $6 billion. It parted company with Mr Hunter shortly afterwards – and a civil case was instigated by regulators against both for attempted manipulation of the natural gas markets

America Online and Time Warner

The merger of America Online and Time Warner in 2000 was hailed as a business masterstroke for its brilliant marriage of the old technology and new. Time Warner had an extensive back-catalogue of films and music, which AOL would be able to exploit through its internet distribution. AOL used its highly priced shares to create AOL Time Warner in a deal worth $180 billion, but the hoped-for cross-media synergies failed to materialise and the collapse of the dotcom bubble wiped out much of AOL's value. The firm's shares slumped. In 2002 the company suffered the biggest ever corporate loss of some $100 billion. A year later Time Warner dropped the AOL prefix from its name.

British Airways

At the height of "cool Britannia" in 1997, BA decided that it would chime with the trend-setting mood of the nation and announced that it would do away with the union flag that decorated the tailfins of its aircraft. At a cost of some

£500,000 a time, it replaced the patriotic symbol with a series of ethnic designs that represented important destinations around the world. The change was lampooned in the press, denounced by Margaret Thatcher and proved highly unpopular with British passengers (though the airline claimed that foreign travellers liked it). Virgin Airlines, a competitor, plastered Union flags all over its aircraft to the discomfort of its embattled rival. The red, white and blue tailfin motif was later restored.

The C5

Sir Clive Sinclair, a British inventor and businessman, had revolutionised the electronics industry and amassed a considerable fortune with his succession of ground-breaking yet affordable devices, including watches, calculators and microcomputers. His innovative knack deserted him in the field of personal transport. The C5, a battery-powered tricycle launched in 1985, was an unmitigated disaster. Constructed in a vacuum-cleaner factory, it seemed to offer similar levels of roadworthiness. It looked ridiculous; factors such as safety and convenience seemed to have been barely considered and very few were sold (though it was relatively cheap). The C5 became a byword for business failure. Never one to be deterred, Sir Clive suggested in 2003 that the C6 was on its way. It has yet to take to the road.

Carmakers make an unwise flight

The bosses of Detroit's "Big Three" carmakers travelled to Washington, DC, at the end of 2008 to ask the outgoing administration of George Bush for substantial bail-out funds to keep their cash-strapped companies alive. To make the journey to plead poverty, the heads of General Motors, Chrysler and Ford chose to travel separately on their companies' corporate jets. Public uproar forced the three out-of-touch executives to travel to a subsequent meeting in the greenest cars that their companies manufactured. It was all to little avail. GM and Chrysler were both forced to seek bankruptcy protection in June 2009.

business blunders *continued*

Dasani

A costly marketing push preceded Coca-Cola's launch of Dasani, its bottled water brand, in Britain in 2003. Further launches in France and Germany were stymied after press reports suggested that the "pure" water came out of a pipe in Sidcup, an unfashionable suburb on the outskirts of south-east London. Worse still, the entire British supply of some 50,000 bottles had to be taken off the shelves after a contamination scare. Despite a sophisticated purification process, the water contained high levels of bromate, a chemical linked with cancer. Although Dasani ran into trouble in Europe, it remains one of America's most popular bottled waters.

Decca Records … and another music misjudgment

Dick Rowe of Decca Records turned down the chance to sign the Beatles in 1962 saying "groups with guitars are on their way out", though the next year he made amends by signing the Rolling Stones. Sam Phillips, owner of a small recording company in Memphis, Tennessee, sold his exclusive contract with Elvis Presley to RCA Records in 1955, for $35,000. He missed out on royalties on the sale of more than a billion records.

Ford Edsel

The launch of the Ford Edsel in September 1957 was preceded by a big and expensive marketing campaign. Motorists eagerly awaited the arrival of Ford's mysterious new car after months of teasing advertisements announcing that "The Edsel is Coming" but without revealing what the new car looked like. The advertising effort had raised expectation to such a level that the potential buyers who flocked to showrooms in the first few days after the car went on sale were disappointed.

They found a fairly ordinary vehicle with unappealing bold styling. Furthermore, the extra gadgets included did not justify the high price Ford was charging compared with competing models. The Detroit giant hoped to sell some 200,000 Edsels annually but 1958 was a poor year for car sales in general. The firm sold just 64,000 in the first year. Poor quality control didn't help. Ford stopped production during the construction of the 1960 model of a vehicle which led to the mnemonic "Every Day Something Else Leaks". The firm lost $250m (equivalent to over $2 billion today) but the damage was not as severe as sometimes assumed. Ford made a profit and paid a dividend for all the time that the Edsel was produced.

Fat-finger syndrome

Fat-finger syndrome is a terrible affliction that affects those working in financial markets. In 2005, the problem, whereby hapless traders input incorrect information, hit Mizuho Securities. A cack-handed employee mistakenly typed a sell order for 610,000 shares at 1 yen in a firm called J-Com rather than one share for 610,000 yen. The Japanese financial group managed to buy back many of the shares and overall the error is estimated to have cost the firm over 40 billion yen. In 2002 a trader at Eurex in London wanted to sell one futures contract when the DAX, Germany's leading share index, hit 5,180. Unfortunately, he sold 5,180 contracts and the market plummeted. The exchange later cancelled the errant trades. In the same year, a trader at Bear Stearns, an American investment bank, entered a $4 billion sell order instead of one for $4m. He was blamed for a subsequent 100-point drop in the Dow Jones. In 2001 a trader at UBS Warburg lost the Swiss investment bank £71m in a matter of seconds while trying to sell 16 shares in Dentsu at 600,000 yen each. Instead he sold 600,000 shares in the Japanese advertising giant at 16 yen each. The bank managed to cancel most of the transactions. In 2001 Lehman Brothers was fined £20,000 after a trader,

business blunders *continued*

wishing only to sell shares worth £3m in various blue-chip companies, typed in too many noughts. He sold shares worth £300m and sent the markets into freefall, wiping 120 points and £30 billion off the FTSE 100. In 2003, a trader bought 500,000 shares in GlaxoSmithKline at £13 a time. Unfortunately the price at the time was around 70p. In 2005 a broker, attempting to sell 15,000 shares in a music publisher, EMI, at £2.80, instead placed an order for 15m in a transaction worth £41.5m.

Hoover

The consumer electronics firm came up with a scheme to shift a surplus of vacuum cleaners and washing machines in Britain. In 1992, it offered two free return flights to Europe if customers spent just £100 on any Hoover product. Restrictive rules and the sale of extras was intended to cover the costs of the promotion. While travel agents failed to cope with the overwhelming response, Hoover extended the promotion with flights to America. "Two return seats: Unbelievable" ran the ad's tagline. How true. Hoover was inundated by disgruntled customers, questions were asked in Parliament and a pressure group was formed. Customers started taking Hoover to court. The cases continued for six years. Some 220,000 people did eventually fly at a cost to Hoover of £48m and huge damage to its reputation.

The Hunt brothers' silver spree

Bunker Hunt was one of the world's richest men through the family's Texas-based oil business but he wanted more. In the early 1970s, he and his younger brother, Herbert, made some cash when, after buying 200,000 ounces of silver, prices doubled to $3 an ounce. Over the rest of the decade they purchased 59m ounces, roughly a third of the world's supply, pushing the price to $50 an ounce and earning a paper profit of about $4 billion. But the high prices led to greater supplies of scrap silver and higher mining investment. In 1980 silver prices fell by 80% in a matter of days. The Hunt brothers declared bankruptcy and in 1988 were convicted of conspiring to manipulate the market.

Louisiana Territory

In 1803, the United States purchased from France the Louisiana Territory, more than 2m sq. km of land extending from the Mississippi River to the Rocky Mountains. The price was 60m francs, about $15m. France acquired Louisiana after Napoleon swapped it with Spain for Tuscany (which Spain never got hold of).

Manhattan Island

In 1626 the Lenape Indians sold Manhattan Island to Peter Minuit, director-general of New Netherlands Colony, a Dutch settlement, for goods valued at 60 Dutch guilders, or $24. The goods are commonly identified as trinkets and beads, though this may be a later addition to the story. Minuit was also involved in the purchase of Staten Island in return for kettles, cloth, wampum and tools. These Indian chiefs did at least do better than thousands of others who got nothing for land later appropriated in America.

New Coke

In the early 1980s Coca-Cola executives decided that the way to fight the growing popularity of the Pepsi brand was a new formula for their soft drink. New Coke was first tested in 1985, and the company concluded that it was on to a winner. The public thought otherwise. Coke received thousands of complaints as soon as the drink was launched. These were dismissed as "relatively insignificant" at first. After three months and complaints from half a million irate customers the old Coke, renamed "Coke Classic", was back on the shelves. Conspiracy

business blunders *continued*

theorists argue that it was a ruse to rekindle interest in Coke. The company claimed that it wasn't clever enough to come up with an idea like that.

Perrier

In 1990 American regulators said that bottles of Perrier were contaminated with traces of benzene, a chemical linked with cancer. The French producers of the sparkling mineral water claimed it was an isolated incident caused by the mistaken use of cleaning fluids at an American bottling plant and recalled 70m bottles in America and Canada. However, Dutch and Danish authorities also found traces of the chemical in Perrier, leading to a worldwide recall. The water firm then claimed that benzene occurred naturally in carbon dioxide and later blamed employees for not changing filters at its source in France. After the scandal Perrier's worldwide sales fell by nearly half and in 1992 Nestlé, a Swiss multinational, acquired the struggling firm.

Persil Power

Unilever launched Persil Power in Britain as a washing powder containing a manganese "accelerator" that removed dirt at lower temperatures. Procter & Gamble, the Anglo-Dutch firm's biggest rival, conducted research that showed that far from cleaning favourite garments, the new powder rotted clothing away. A war of words ensued in the press and through advertising but eventually Unilever was forced to withdraw Persil Power.

Ratners

Gerald Ratner, speaking at the Institute of Directors in 1991, explained why he could sell products so cheaply in his chain of high-street jewellers. He said he "sold a pair of earrings for under a pound, which is cheaper than a prawn sandwich from Marks & Spencer, but probably wouldn't last as long". He followed up by revealing that a decanter was so cheap because it was "total crap". Reports in the media led to the company's shares losing £500m in value. Ratner resigned in 1992 and in 1993 the company was renamed Signet, since when it has reclaimed its position as one of the world's biggest jewellery firms. Mr Ratner went on to set up an online jewellery business.

South African gold

In 1886 Sors Hariezon, a gold prospector from Witwatersrand in the Transvaal, sold his South African gold claim for $20. Over the next 100 years, mines sunk on or near his claim produced over 1,000 tonnes of gold a year, 70% of the supply of the precious metal in the West.

Topman

Topman's brand chief David Shepherd said in an interview with a trade magazine that the British clothes firm's target customers were "hooligans or whatever". He carried on: "Very few of our customers have to wear suits to work ... They'll be for his first interview or first court case." Retail giant Arcadia, which owned Topman, said the remarks were taken out of context.

Venice on the cheap

When the website of the four-star Crown Plaza Venice East, where rooms cost between $150 and $250 a night, offered a two-night stay for a mere €0.01, more than 5,000 bookings were made before the mistake came to light. Luckily for those who had logged on in time, the hotel, part of the Intercontinental group, agreed to honour the bookings, a decision that cost them some $150,000 it was reported.

Xerox

In 1977 the office equipment firm showed its top managers an electronic typewriter that could display

business blunders *continued*

written correspondence on a screen, store it with a click of a button, send it around the office and print out copies. The project had taken ten years to develop but the managers were unconvinced that it had a commercial future. Meanwhile, Apple Computer emulated much of the technology and developed the personal computer. Some 35 years earlier, IBM, Kodak and General Electric had all eschewed a new technology for rapidly reproducing copies on paper.

Jerry Yang and Yahoo!

Jerry Yang's reputation for business acumen was based on his co-founding Yahoo! in 1994 while a graduate student at Stanford University. The web portal grew into one of the world's biggest internet companies but ran into increasing competition. In 2007 Mr Yang took the helm at the struggling company as it sought to fight back against Google, which had supplanted it as the world's favourite way of accessing the internet. In March 2008 Microsoft – which owned a portal similar to Yahoo!'s and a search engine even further behind Google's – made a takeover offer of $33 per share for Yahoo!, which valued the company at close to $47 billion, a healthy premium for investors. Mr Yang said "no thanks" his company would do better alone. When Microsoft walked away from the deal. Yahoo!'s share were worth less than $10. Mr Yang departed as chief executive in November 2008. In July 2009 Microsoft and Yahoo! eventually announced a tie-up that stopped short of a takeover.

The Bible

Adam gave up the rights to the Garden of Eden for an apple. Esau sold his birthright for a mess of potage, though the extent of his father's estate is unknown.

Board styles

Boards of directors vary enormously in their style.

- **The rubber-stamp board** shows little concern for either the tasks of the board or the interpersonal relationships among directors. The meetings of the board are a formality and decisions may be minuted without a meeting actually taking place. Examples of such boards can be found in the "letter-box" companies registered in offshore tax havens and in private companies where one individual is dominant and takes the decisions, or the key players see each other frequently and decisions are taken in the management context.

- **The country-club board**, in contrast, is very concerned with interpersonal relations and the issues before the board may take second place. The boards of some old-established companies and some family controlled companies fit this model. Meetings always follow the same pattern. Traditions are revered. Innovation is discouraged.

- **The representative board** places more accent on the tasks of the board than it does on board relations. It often has directors representing different stakeholders and behaves more like a parliament of diverse interests. Issues can easily become politicised. Board discussions can be adversarial. The basis and balance of power are important.

- **The professional board** shows a proper concern for both the board's tasks and directors' interpersonal relationships. A board with a successful professional style will have sound leadership from the chair. There will be tough-minded discussion among the members combined with mutual understanding and respect for each other.

Source: *Directors: An A–Z Guide*, R.I. (Bob) Tricker, The Economist/Profile Books

Roles directors play

Among the main performance roles directors play are:

- **Wise man** A director who brings accumulated knowledge and experience to bear on issues facing the board is usually much respected by his fellow directors. Accumulated wisdom can, of course, have limitations in fast-changing circumstances.

- **Specialist** Non-executive directors are often appointed for their specialist knowledge of, say, a particular market, technology or functional area. If they are to continue to be useful, specialists need to keep in touch with their area of expertise.

- **Window on the world** A director who provides relevant information, insights into market opportunities, new technologies, industry developments, and so on. A role often played by a non-executive director, and again the director's contribution remains useful only so long as he remains in touch with his sources.

- **Figurehead** The director – in large listed companies often the chairman – who represents the company at, say, trade and industry gatherings and public commissions. Likely also to have an important role in dealing with the media.

- **Contact person** Someone with useful connections with individuals and organisations. Retired senior executives, politicians and civil servants are approached with this role in mind.

- **Status provider** Someone appointed for the status they bring rather than the contribution they will make. When a company is in trouble, it can help restore confidence if a status provider with a reputation for integrity is brought on board.

Source: *Directors: An A–Z Guide*, R.I. (Bob) Tricker, The Economist/Profile Books

Games directors play

Although routinely presented as a serious, analytical and rational process, boardroom behaviour is often intensely political, involving personal rivalries and power plays. The games directors play include the following.

- **Alliance building** is played outside the boardroom for ensuring mutual support within. Allied to log rolling.

- **Coalition building** involves canvassing support for an issue informally outside the boardroom so that there is a sufficient consensus when it is discussed formally.

- **Cronyism** is supporting a director's interests even though they may not be in the best interest of the company or its shareholders. It is sometimes alleged to be the basis of corporate governance in Asia.

- **Deal making** is a classic game usually involving compromise, in which two or more directors reach a behind-the-scenes agreement to achieve a specific outcome in a board decision.

- **Divide and rule** is a dirty game, in which the player sees the chance to set one director against another, or groups of directors against each other, in order to achieve an entirely different personal aim.

- **Empire building** is the misuse of privileged access to information, people or other resources to acquire power over organisational territory. The process often involves intrigue, battles and conquests.

- **Half truths** occur if a director, although not deliberately lying, tells only one side of the issue in board deliberations.

- **Hidden agendas** involve directors' pursuit of secret goals to benefit their own empire or further their career against the interest of the organisation as a whole.

- **Log rolling** occurs when director A agrees, off the record, to support director B's interests, for mutual support when it comes to matters of interest to A.

▨ **Propaganda** is the dissemination of information to support a cause and is seen more in relationships with shareholders, stockmarkets and financial institutions than in board-level deliberations. The regulatory authorities are likely to act if propaganda becomes excessive or deliberately false.

▨ **Rival camps** is a game played when there are opposing factions on a board, in which hostilities, spies and double agents can be involved.

▨ **Scaremongering** emphasises the downside risks in a board decision, casting doubts about a situation, so that a proposal will be turned down.

▨ **Snowing** involves executive directors deluging an outside director seeking further information with masses of data confusing the situation and papering over any cracks.

▨ **Spinning** is an art form which presents a distorted view of a person or a situation, favourable to the interests of the spinner. In corporate governance, it can be carried out at the level of the board, the shareholders or the media.

▨ **Sponsorship** is support by a powerful director for another, usually for their joint benefit.

▨ **Suboptimisation** occurs when a director supports a part of the organisation to the detriment of the company as a whole. Some executive directors suffer from tunnel vision because they are too closely involved with a functional department or a subsidiary company, and from short-sighted myopia because they will be personally affected by the outcome.

▨ **Window dressing** produces a fine external show of sound corporate governance while covering up failures, as a board might present financial results in the best possible light while hiding weaknesses.

Source: *Directors: An A–Z Guide*, R.I. (Bob) Tricker, The Economist/Profile Books

The world's most valuable brands

Most valuable brands by region, $bn

United States		Europe (Ex. UK)	
Google	100.0	Vodafone	53.7
Microsoft	76.2	Nokia	35.2
Coca Cola	67.6	BMW	23.9
IBM	66.6	SAP	23.6
McDonald's	66.6	Tesco	22.9
Apple	63.1	Louis Vuitton	19.4
GE (General Electric)	59.8	HSBC	19.1
Marlboro	49.5	Porsche	17.5
Wal-Mart	41.1	Santander	16.0
BlackBerry	27.5	Mercedes	15.5
Asia		**UK**	
China Mobile	61.3	Vodafone	53.7
ICBC	38.1	Tesco	22.9
Toyota	29.9	HSBC	19.1
China Construction Bank	22.8	O2	8.6
Bank of China	21.2	Standard Chartered Bank	8.2
Nintendo	18.2	Barclays	7.0
NTT DoCoMo	15.8	Marks & Spencer	6.0
Honda	14.6	BP	5.9
Nissan	10.2	ASDA	5.4
Canon	8.8	Smirnoff	5.2

Most valuable brands by sector, $bn

Apparel			
H&M	12.1	Ralph Lauren	3.0
Nike	12.0	Puma	1.9
Zara	8.6	Next	1.7
Esprit	6.6	Gap	1.3
Adidas	4.9	Old Navy	1.0

the world's most valuable brands *continued*

Beer

Bud Light	6.7	Guinness	3.5
Budweiser	6.6	Miller Lite	2.5
Heineken	5.1	Skol	2.2
Stella Artois	4.5	Amstel	2.0
Corona	4.3	Kronenbourg 1664	2.0

Automobiles

Toyota	30.0	Nissan	10.2
BMW	23.9	Ford	5.9
Porsche	17.5	Volkswagen	5.8
Mercedes	15.4	Lexus	4.6
Honda	14.6	Chevrolet	4.3

Coffee

Nescafé	5.6	Jacobs	1.0
Nespresso	2.5	Starbucks	0.8
Folgers	1.3	Douwe Egberts	0.7
Maxwell House	1.3	Carte Noire	0.6

Financial institutions

ICBC	38.1	American Express	15.0
China Construction Bank	22.8	RBC	14.9
Bank of China	21.2	Citi	14.6
HSBC	19.1	BBVA	12.5
Visa	16.4	TD	11.0
Wells Fargo	16.2	Chase	10.6
Santander	16.0	Standard Chartered	8.2
Bank of America	15.5		

Gaming consoles

Nintendo DS	9.7	Nintendo Game Boy	0.2
Nintendo Wii	8.3	Sony PSP	0.1
Microsoft Xbox 360	4.6	Sony PlayStation 2	0.1
Sony PlayStation 3	0.3	Nintendo GameCube	0.1
Microsoft Xbox	0.3		

Luxury goods

Louis Vuitton	19.4	Hennessy	5.4
Hermès	7.9	Cartier	4.9
Gucci	7.5	Moët & Chandon	4.8
Chanel	6.2	Fendi	3.5
Rolex	5.5	Prada	2.7

Mobile communications

China Mobile	61.3	Orange	13.2
Vodafone	53.7	Movistar	10.9
AT&T	20.1	T-Mobile	10.9
Verizon Wireless	17.7	MTS	9.2
NTT DoCoMo	15.8	Beeline	8.9

Technology

Google	100.0	Cisco	18.0
Microsoft	76.2	Dell	15.4
IBM	66.6	Accenture	15.1
Apple	63.1	Siemens	13.6
Nokia	35.2	Canon	8.8
BlackBerry	27.5	Yahoo!	7.9
HP	26.7	Samsung	6.3
SAP	23.6	Sony	6.2
Intel	22.9	Baidu	5.8
Oracle	21.4	Sony Ericsson	4.8

Sources: Millward Brown Optimor

The world's most admired companies

2009	Industry	Country	Score (out of 10)
Apple Computers	Computers	US	7.07
Berkshire Hathaway	Insurance: P & C	US	7.78
Toyota Motor	Motor vehicles	Japan	6.25
Google	Internet services & retailing	US	7.72
Johnson & Johnson	Pharmaceuticals	US	7.31
Procter & Gamble	Soaps and cosmetics	US	7.69
FedEx	Delivery	US	7.56
Southwest Airlines	Airlines	US	6.89
General Electric	Electronics	US	7.44
Microsoft	Computer software	US	6.37
Wal-mart	General merchandisers	US	7.29
Coca Cola	Beverages	US	6.84
Walt Disney	Entertainment	US	8.53
Wells Fargo	Mega-banks	US	6.38
Goldman Sachs	Securities	US	7.75
Mcdonald's	Food services	US	7.72
IBM	Infotech services	US	7.55
3M	Medical & other precision equipment	US	6.96
Target	General merchandisers		6.90
JPMorgan Chase	Mega-banks	US	6.53
Pepsico	Consumer food products	US	7.47
Costco	Speciality retailers	US	6.92
Nike	Apparel	US	8.02
Nordstrom	General retailers	US	6.49
Exxon Mobil	Petroleum Refining	US	7.79
Bank of America	Mega-Banks	US	6.69
United Parcel Service	Delivery	US	7.39
BMW	Motor Vehicles	Germany	6.50
American Express	Consumer credit cards & related services	US	6.79
Hewlett-Packard	Computers	US	7.04

Source: *Fortune*

Britain's most admired companies

2008	Industry	Score (out of 90)
Diageo	Restaurants, pubs and breweries	71.88
Johnson Matthey	Chemicals	70.50
Unilever	Food producers and processors	70.30
BSkyB	Media	69.70
Tesco	Retailers (food and personal)	68.93
Stagecoach	Transport	68.49
Rolls-Royce	Engineering (aero and defence)	67.75
Man Group	Speciality and other finance	67.58
Kingspan	Building materials and merchants	67.03
3i	Speciality and other finance	66.80
BG Group	Oil and gas extractive	66.30
Serco Group	Support services	66.20
Berkeley Group	Home construction	66.20
InterContinental Hotels	Leisure and hotels	65.00
SIG	Building materials and merchants	64.60
WPP Group	Media	63.80
Capita Group	Support services	63.70
Cadbury Schweppes*	Food producers and processors	63.60
GlaxoSmithKline (GSK)	Health and household	63.50
Whitbread	Leisure and hotels	63.40
Tullow Oil	Oil and gas	63.40
Thomson Reuters*	Media	63.30
Marshalls	Building materials and merchants	63.00
Vodafone	Telecommunications	63.00
Royal Dutch Shell	Oil and gas extractive	63.00
BP	Oil and gas extractive	62.90
Sainsbury (J)	Retailers (food and personal)	62.80
Bayer (UK & Ireland)	Chemicals	62.70
Marks & Spencer	Retailers (food and personal)	62.50
SABMiller	Restaurants, pubs and breweries	62.40

*Merged, acquired or name change

Source: *Management Today*

What companies say about themselves

Anheuser Busch Our vision: Through all of our products, services and relationships, we will add to life's enjoyment.

Carlsberg Mission: Carlsberg is a dynamic, international provider of beer and beverage brands, bringing people together and adding to the enjoyment of life.

Coca-Cola Our mission is:
- to refresh the world – in mind, body and spirit;
- to inspire moments of optimism – through our brands and actions; and
- to create value and make a diffrence – everywhere we engage.

Diageo Our brands offer consumers a variety of ways to mark big events in their lives and brighten small ones.

Ericsson Our vision is to be the prime driver in an all-communicating world.

Ford Our Vision: to become the world's leading company for automotive products and services.
Our Mission: we are a global, diverse family with a proud heritage, passionately committed to providing outstanding products and services.
Our Values: we do the right thing for our people, our environment and our society, but above all for our customers.

Gillette The Gillette Company's vision is to build total brand value by innovating to deliver consumer value and customer leadership faster, better and more completely than our competition.

Goldman Sachs [Our] culture is very much in evidence helping to attract and retain the best employees and clients. [Goldman Sachs'] commitment to its clients, teamwork, integrity, professional excellence and entrepreneurial spirit has its beginnings in 1869 with Marcus Goldman.

Google Google's mission is to organise the world's information and make it universally accessible and useful. Our philosophy: Never settle for the best.
Ten things Google has found to be true

1. Focus on the user and all else will follow
2. It's best to do one thing really, really well
3. Fast is better than slow
4. Democracy on the web works
5. You don't need to be at your desk to need an answer
6. You can make money without doing evil
7. There is always more information out there
8. The need for information crosses all borders
9. You can be serious without a suit
10. Great just isn't good enough.

Heinz Our vision, quite simply, is to be "the world's premier food company, offering nutritious, superior tasting foods to people everywhere".

Honeywell Whether you're flying on a plane, driving a car, heating or cooling a home, furnishing an apartment, taking medication or playing a sport, Honeywell products touch most peoples' lives everyday. We are building a world that's safer and more secure … more comfortable and energy efficient … more innovative and productive.

Johnson & Johnson We believe our first responsibility is to the doctors, nurses and patients, to mothers and fathers and all others who use our products and services.

Lagardère Where there's a will, we pave the way.

Levi Strauss & Co Our values are fundamental to our success. They are the foundation of our company, define who we are and set us apart from the competition. They underlie our vision of the future, our business strategies and our decisions, actions and behaviours. We live by

what companies say *continued*

them. They endure. Four core values are at the heart of Levi Strauss & Co: Empathy, Originality, Integrity and Courage ...

Generations of people have worn our products as a symbol of freedom and self-expression in the face of adversity, challenge and social change. They forged a new territory called the American West. They fought in wars for peace. They instigated counterculture revolutions. They tore down the Berlin Wall. Reverent, irreverent – they all took a stand ...

People love our clothes and trust our company. We will market the most appealing and widely worn apparel brands ...

Our products define quality, style and function ...

We will clothe the world.

Microsoft At Microsoft, we work to help people and businesses throughout the world realise their potential. This is our mission. Everything we do reflects this mission and the values that make it possible.

Nokia Connecting is about helping people to feel close to what matters. Wherever, whenever, Nokia believes in communicating, sharing, and in the awesome potential in connecting the 2 billion who do with the 4 billion who don't.

Pfizer Our mission: We will become the world's most valued company to patients, customers, colleagues, investors, business partners, and the communities where we work and live.

Philip Morris International Our goal is to be the most responsible, effective and respected developer, manufacturer and marketer of consumer products, especially products intended for adults.

Procter & Gamble We will provide branded products and services of superior quality and value that improve the lives of the world's consumers. As a result, consumers will reward us with leadership sales, profit, and value creation, allowing our people, our shareholders, and the communities in which we live and work to prosper.

Royal Mail Through our trusted brands, we reach everybody every working day in mail, parcels and express services and Post Office branches. Today, we are reinventing our business to meet the changing needs of our customers and the demands of competition. Our goal is to be the world's leading postal service.

Tesco Our core purpose is to create value for customers to earn their lifetime loyalty.

Our success depends on people. The people who shop with us and the people who work with us. If our customers like what we offer, they are more likely to come back and shop with us again. If the Tesco team find what we do rewarding, they are more likely to go that extra mile to help our customers.

This is expressed as two key values:

- No one tries harder for customers, and
- Treat people as we like to be treated.

Starbucks Our mission: to inspire and nurture the human spirit – one person, one cup, and one neighbourhood at a time.

Unilever Mission: To add vitality to life. We meet everyday needs for nutrition, hygiene, and personal care with brands that help people feel good, look good and get more out of life.

Virgin We believe in making a difference. In our customers' eyes, Virgin stands for value for money, quality, innovation, fun and a sense of competitive challenge.

Source: Company websites

The most effective websites

Company	Total 2009	Website (www.)
Roche (Switzerland)	210	roche.com
Nokia (Finland)	209	nokia.com
BP (UK)	209	bp.com
Siemens (Germany)	202	siemens.com
Schlumberger (US)	198	schlumberger.com
Unilever (Netherlands/UK)	197	unilever.com
Eni (Italy)	197	eni.it
General Electric (US)	195	ge.com
IBM (US)	195	ibm.com
Royal Dutch Shell (UK/Netherlands)	195	shell.com
Novartis (Switzerland)	194	novartis.com
Nestlé (Switzerland)	194	nestle.com
Wal-Mart (US)	194	walmartstores.com
Intel (US)	194	intel.com
Cisco Systems (US)	193	cisco.com
GlaxoSmithKline (UK)	192	gsk.com
Rio Tinto (Australia/UK)	192	riotinto.com
Google (US)	191	google.com
Microsoft (US)	190	microsoft.com
Unicredito Italiano (Italy)	189	unicredit.eu
E.ON (Germany)	189	eon.com
Total (France)	187	total.com
Coca-Cola (US)	187	thecocacolacompany.com
Vodafone (UK)	187	vodafone.com
Hewlett-Packard (US)	187	hp.com
Chevron (US)	186	chevron.com
Sanofi-Aventis (France)	184	sanofiaventis.com
ArcelorMittal (Luxembourg/India)	184	arcelormittal.com
HSBC (UK)	183	hsbc.com
BHP Billiton (Australia)	182	bhpbilliton.com
Johnson & Johnson (US)	181	jnj.com
StatoilHydro (Norway)	180	statoilhydro.com
Philip Morris International (US)	174	philipmorrisinternational.com
Citigroup (US)	171	citigroup.com

Volkswagen (Germany)	171	volkswagenag.com
Exxon Mobil (US)	168	exxonmobil.com
Apple (US)	166	apple.com
ConocoPhillips (US)	163	conocophillips.com
Pfizer (US)	163	pfizer.com
Allianz (Germany)	162	allianz.com
Toyota Motor (Japan)	159	toyota.co.jp
Procter & Gamble (US)	159	pg.com
Verizon Communications (US)	158	verizon.com
JPMorgan Chase (US)	154	jpmorganchase.com
Samsung (South Korea)	153	samsung.com
NTT DoCoMo (Japan)	152	nttdocomo.com
Banco Santander (Spain)	152	santander.com
Vale (Brazil)	151	vale.com
Bank of America (US)	151	bankofamerica.com
Telefonica (Spain)	150	telefonica.com
BNP Paribas (France)	149	bnpparibas.com
Petrobras (Brazil)	149	petrobras.com
PepsiCo (US)	148	pepsico.com
Intesa Sanpaolo (Italy)	146	intesasanpaolo.com
EDF (France)	144	edf.com
Industrial & Commercial Bank of China (China)	143	icbc.com.cn
AT&T (US)	142	att.com
American International Group (US)	137	aig.com
NTT (Japan)	136	ntt.co.jp
Sberbank (Russia)	134	sbrf.ru
China Construction Bank (China)	132	ccb.com
Reliance Industries (India)	129	ril.com
Mitsubishi UFJ Financial (Japan)	128	mufg.jp
Nintendo (Japan)	128	nintendo.com
Rosneft (Russia)	127	rosneft.com
Lukoil (Russia)	127	lukoil.com
Saudi Basic Industries (Saudi Arabia)	126	sabic.com.sa
PetroChina (China)	121	petrochina.com.cn

Note: The index is based on scoring websites for the following: construction; message; contact; serving society, investors, media, jobseekers and customers.

Source: FT/Bowens Craggs Index of corporate website effectiveness

Business friendliness

Business environment index

2004–08, score out of 10

Singapore	8.87	Bahrain	7.09	Turkey	5.80
Hong Kong	8.59	South Korea	7.04	Russia	5.73
Finland	8.53	Slovenia	6.96	Argentina	5.62
Canada	8.52	Cyprus	6.93	Egypt	5.46
Switzerland	8.52	Poland	6.92	Indonesia	5.46
Denmark	8.51	Portugal	6.85	India	5.42
US	8.36	Slovakia	6.83	Sri Lanka	5.39
Netherlands	8.33	Mexico	6.78	Tunisia	5.36
Ireland	8.28	Hungary	6.73	Serbia	5.30
Sweden	8.21	Thailand	6.62	Dominican Rep.	5.20
Australia	8.20	Lithuania	6.53	Kazakhstan	5.06
New Zealand	8.19	Brazil	6.47	Ecuador	5.03
UK	8.17	Italy	6.47	Morocco	5.00
Norway	8.06	Costa Rica	6.44	Venezuela	4.99
Germany	8.04	Latvia	6.44	Vietnam	4.92
Belgium	7.99	Kuwait	6.36	Pakistan	4.81
Austria	7.95	South Africa	6.34	Bangladesh	4.74
Chile	7.83	Greece	6.26	Azerbaijan	4.60
France	7.81	Peru	6.10	Ukraine	4.59
Taiwan	7.65	Bulgaria	6.06	Algeria	4.52
Estonia	7.50	Romania	6.03	Libya	4.41
Spain	7.43	El Salvador	6.01	Nigeria	4.41
Israel	7.36	Philippines	5.98	Cuba	4.28
Czech Republic	7.29	Saudi Arabia	5.95	Kenya	4.23
Malaysia	7.28	Colombia	5.95	Iran	3.77
UAE	7.20	Croatia	5.93	Angola	3.65
Qatar	7.17	Jordan	5.84	*Average*	*6.47*
Japan	7.15	China	5.83	*Median*	*6.45*

Note: Index ranks countries on their business environments, based on opportunities for and hindrances to the conduct of business, in categories covering macroeconomic and political environment, foreign investment and trade policy, tax regime, financing, labour market and infrastructure.

Source: Economist Intelligence Unit

Offshore attractions

Tax havens

Andorra	Dominica	Panama
Anguilla	Gibraltar	St Kitts and Nevis
Antigua and Barbuda	Grenada	St Lucia
Aruba	Liberia	St Vincent & the
Bahamas	Liechtenstein	Grenadines
Bahrain	Marshall Islands	Samoa
Belize	Monaco	San Marino
Bermuda	Montserrat	Turks and Caicos
British Virgin Islands	Nauru	Islands
Cayman Islands	Netherlands Antilles	Vanuatu
Cook Islands	Niue	

Note: A tax haven has three criteria according to the OECD – no or only nominal taxes; lack of effective information exchange; inadequate transparency.

Other financial centres

Countries that have committed to the internationally agreed tax standard but have not substantially implemented it:

Austria	Chile	Singapore
Belgium	Guatemala	Switzerland
Brunei	Luxembourg	

Countries that have not committed to the internationally agreed tax standard:

Costa Rica	Malaysia	Philippines
	(Labuan)	Uruguay

Source: OECD, as at April 2nd 2009

How competitive?

Growth competitiveness index, 2008

US	5.74	Estonia	4.67
Switzerland	5.61	Czech Republic	4.62
Denmark	5.58	Thailand	4.60
Sweden	5.53	Kuwait	4.58
Singapore	5.53	Tunisia	4.58
Finland	5.50	Bahrain	4.57
Germany	5.46	Oman	4.55
Netherlands	5.41	Brunei Darussalam	4.54
Japan	5.38	Cyprus	4.53
Canada	5.37	Puerto Rico	4.51
Hong Kong	5.33	Slovenia	4.50
UK	5.30	Portugal	4.47
South Korea	5.28	Lithuania	4.45
Austria	5.23	South Africa	4.41
Norway	5.22	Slovakia	4.40
France	5.22	Barbados	4.40
Taiwan	5.22	Jordan	4.37
Australia	5.20	Italy	4.35
Belgium	5.14	India	4.33
Iceland	5.05	Russia	4.31
Malaysia	5.04	Malta	4.31
Ireland	4.99	Poland	4.28
Israel	4.97	Latvia	4.26
New Zealand	4.93	Indonesia	4.25
Luxembourg	4.85	Botswana	4.25
Qatar	4.83	Mauritius	4.25
Saudi Arabia	4.72	Panama	4.24
Chile	4.72	Costa Rica	4.23
Spain	4.72	Mexico	4.23
China	4.70	Croatia	4.22
UAE	4.68	Hungary	4.22

Note: Based on macroeconomic environment, quality of public institutions, and level of technological readiness and innovation. A higher score indicates greater competitiveness.
Source: World Economic Forum

Easy money?

Accessibility of capital to entrepreneurs, max=10, 2008

Canada	7.90	Oman	5.97
Hong Kong	7.82	Lithuania	5.87
Switzerland	7.76	Czech Republic	5.86
UK	7.70	Hungary	5.79
Singapore	7.64	Saudi Arabia	5.76
US	7.56	Panama	5.56
Netherlands	7.28	Lebanon	5.54
Norway	7.27	Slovakia	5.53
Australia	7.26	Greece	5.52
Finland	7.21	Jordan	5.51
Sweden	7.13	Poland	5.51
South Korea	7.06	Mexico	5.46
Denmark	7.03	China	5.45
Malaysia	7.03	Slovenia	5.34
Estonia	6.96	India	5.33
Japan	6.96	Bulgaria	4.97
France	6.95	Croatia	4.97
Ireland	6.95	Turkey	4.95
New Zealand	6.92	Brazil	4.92
UAE	6.92	Latvia	4.90
Israel	6.81	Tunisia	4.90
Belgium	6.76	Belarus	4.85
Germany	6.67	Egypt	4.85
Taiwan	6.63	Peru	4.84
Austria	6.49	Colombia	4.82
Portugal	6.40	Russia	4.80
Spain	6.33	Uruguay	4.63
South Africa	6.21	Costa Rica	4.61
Chile	6.19	Romania	4.60
Italy	6.11	El Salvador	4.55
Kuwait	6.10	Philippines	4.55
Thailand	6.09	Macedonia	4.53

Note: Based on over 50 measures such as strength of banking system and the diversity of financial markets.
Source: Milken Institute

Business cycles

America's ten-year expansion from March 1991 to March 2001 was the longest in the 150 years covered by the National Bureau of Economic Research's data.

America's business cycle dates, duration in months

Peak	Trough	Peak to trough	Trough to peak	Trough to trough	Peak to peak
Feb-45	Oct-45	8	80	88	93
Nov-48	Oct-49	11	37	48	45
Jul-53	May-54	10	45	55	56
Aug-57	Apr-58	8	39	47	49
Apr-60	Feb-61	10	24	34	32
Dec-69	Nov-70	11	106	117	116
Nov-73	Mar-75	16	36	52	47
Jan-80	Jul-80	6	58	64	74
Jul-81	Nov-82	16	12	28	18
Jul-90	Mar-91	8	92	100	108
Mar-01	Nov-01	8	120	128	128
Dec-07				73	

Source: National Bureau of Economic Research

- The Economic Cycle Research Institute in New York covers data for 20 countries from 1948; eg, Britain rose from a trough in August 1952 to a peak in September 1974, fell briefly to a trough 11 months later, up to a peak in June 1979, a trough in May 1981, a long expansion to a peak in May 1990 and a short fall to a trough in March 1992.

- Japan had a long expansion period from December 1954 to November 1973, contracted briefly then had another long period of growth until April 1992. After several short cycles it reached a peak in February 2008.

Business start-ups and failures

US

	Start-ups, '000	Shut-downs, '000
1995	752	650
1996	788	671
1997	789	697
1998	805	703
1999	813	737
2000	828	760
2001	810	817
2002	816	751
2003	778	730
2004	828	731
2005	868	737
2006	871	762
2007	844	805
2008 Jan–Sept	591	...

Source: US Bureau of Labour Statistics

UK

	VAT registrations, '000	VAT deregistrations, '000
1995	161.4	159.3
1996	165.1	146.4
1997	181.5	140.9
1998	180.7	139.8
1999	175.6	143.1
2000	177.8	147.7
2001	169.2	147.5
2002	176.2	154.0
2003	191.5	153.5
2004	184.0	149.7
2005	182.4	142.8
2006	182.1	144.3
2007	205.7	147.8

Note: Value-added tax threshold at the start of 2008 was an annual turnover of £67,000; 2m of the estimated 4.7m enterprises in the UK were VAT-registered.
Source: National Statistics, Small Business Service

Bribery and corruption

Most likely to engage in bribery, 2008
0 = most likely, 10 = least likely

	Index	Number of respondents
Russia	5.9	114
China	6.5	634
Mexico	6.6	123
India	6.8	257
Brazil	7.4	225
Italy	7.4	421
Taiwan	7.5	287
South Korea	7.5	231
South Africa	7.5	177
Hong Kong	7.6	288
Spain	7.9	355
US	8.1	718
Singapore	8.1	243
France	8.1	462
Australia	8.5	240
Japan	8.6	316
UK	8.6	506
Germany	8.6	513
Switzerland	8.7	256
Netherlands	8.7	255
Canada	8.8	264
Belgium	8.8	252

Note: Based on the responses of 2,742 senior business executives from companies in 26 developed
and developing countries, chosen by the volume of their imports and inflows of foreign direct
investment. Respondents were asked about the likelihood of foreign firms from countries they have
business dealings with, to engage in bribery.
Source: Transparency International

Most corrupt, 2008
0 = most corrupt

Somalia	1.0	Angola	1.9
Iraq	1.3	Gambia	1.9
Myanmar	1.3	Laos	2.0
Haiti	1.4	Ecuador	2.0
Afghanistan	1.5	Papua New Guinea	2.0
Guinea	1.6	Tajikistan	2.0
Chad	1.6	Central African Republic	2.0
Sudan	1.6	Côte d'Ivoire	2.0
Congo-Kinshasa	1.7	Belarus	2.0
Equatorial Guinea	1.7	Syria	2.1
Uzbekistan	1.8	Bangladesh	2.1
Turkmenistan	1.8	Russia	2.1
Zimbabwe	1.8	Kenya	2.1
Cambodia	1.8	Kazakhstan	2.2
Kyrgyzstan	1.8	Timor-Leste	2.2
Azerbaijan	1.9	Yemen	2.3
Burundi	1.9	Cameroon	2.3
Congo-Brazzaville	1.9	Iran	2.3
Sierra Leone	1.9	Philippines	2.3
Venezuela	1.9	Paraguay	2.4
Guinea-Bissau	1.9	Liberia	2.4

Least corrupt, 2008
10 = least corrupt

Denmark	9.3	Saint Lucia	7.1
New Zealand	9.3	Barbados	7.0
Sweden	9.3	France	6.9
Singapore	9.2	Chile	6.9
Finland	9.0	Uruguay	6.9
Switzerland	9.0	Slovenia	6.7
Iceland	8.9	Estonia	6.6
Netherlands	8.9	Spain	6.5
Australia	8.7	Qatar	6.5
Canada	8.7	Saint Vincent and the Grenadines	6.5
Luxembourg	8.3	Cyprus	6.4
Austria	8.1	Portugal	6.1
Hong Kong	8.1	Israel	6.0
Germany	7.9	Dominica	6.0
Norway	7.9	United Arab Emirates	5.9
Ireland	7.7	Botswana	5.8
UK	7.7	Puerto Rico	5.8
US	7.3	Malta	5.8
Japan	7.3	Taiwan	5.7
Belgium	7.3	South Korea	5.6

Note: Country ranking based on the degree to which corruption is perceived to exist among public officials and politicians, by business people, academics and risk analysts.

Source: Transparency International

Business ratios

These are ratios commonly used in corporate financial analysis.

Working capital

Working capital ratio = current assets/current liabilities, where current assets = stock + debtors + cash at bank and in hand + quoted investments, etc, current liabilities = creditors + overdraft at bank + taxation + dividends, etc. The ratio varies according to type of trade and conditions; a ratio from 1 to 3 is usual, with a ratio above 2 taken to be safe.

Liquidity ratio = liquid ("quick") assets/current liabilities, where liquid assets = debtors + cash at bank and in hand + quoted investments (that is, assets which can be realised within a month or so, which may not apply to all investments); current liabilities are those which may need to be repaid within the same short period, which may not necessarily include a bank overdraft where it is likely to be renewed. The liquidity ratio is sometimes referred to as the "acid test"; a ratio under 1 suggests a possibly difficult situation, while too high a ratio may mean that assets are not being usefully employed.

Turnover of working capital = sales/average working capital. The ratio varies according to type of trade; generally a low ratio can mean poor use of resources, while too high a ratio can mean overtrading. Average working capital or average stock is found by taking the opening and closing working capital or stock and dividing by 2.

Turnover of stock = sales/average stock, or (where cost of sales is known) cost of sales/average stock. The cost of sales turnover figure is to be preferred as both figures are then on the same valuation basis. This ratio can be expressed as number of times per year, or time taken for stock to be turned over once = (52/number of times) weeks. A low turnover of stock can be a sign of stocks that are difficult to move, and usually indicates adverse conditions.

Turnover of debtors = sales/average debtors. This indicates efficiency in collecting accounts. An average credit period of about one month is usual, but varies according to credit stringency conditions in the economy.

Turnover of creditors = purchases/average creditors. Average payment period is best maintained in line with turnover of debtors.

Sales

Export ratio = exports as a percentage of sales.

Sales per employee = sales/average number of employees.

Assets

Ratios of assets can vary according to the measure of assets used:

Total assets = current assets + fixed assets + other assets, where fixed assets = property + plant and machinery + motor vehicles, etc, and other assets = long-term investment + goodwill, etc.

Net assets ("net worth") = total assets − total liabilities = share capital + reserves

Turnover of net assets = sales/average net assets. As for turnover of working capital, a low ratio can mean poor use of resources.

Assets per employee = assets/average number of employees. This indicates the amount of investment backing for employees.

business ratios *continued*

Profits

Profit margin = (profit/sales) × 100 = profits as a percentage of sales; usually profits before tax.

Profitability = (profit/total assets) × 100 = profits as a percentage of total assets.

Return on capital = (profit/net assets) × 100 = profits as a percentage of net assets ("net worth" or "capital employed").

Profit per employee = profit/average number of employees.

Earnings per share (eps) = after-tax profit – minorities/average number of shares in issue.

Entrepreneurial activity

% of workforce

	2000	2001	2002	2003	2004	2005	2006	2007	2008
US	16.6	11.6	10.5	11.9	11.3	12.4	10.0	9.6	10.8
UK	6.9	7.8	5.4	6.4	6.3	6.2	5.8	5.5	6.0
France	5.6	7.4	3.2	1.6	6.0	5.4	4.4	3.2	2.8
Germany	7.5	8.0	5.2	5.2	4.5	5.4	4.2	...	4.0

Note: % of the labour force either actively involved in starting a new business or owner or manager of a business that is less than 42 months old.
Source: Global Entrepreneurship Monitor

Business costs

2007	US=100
Germany	116.8
Japan	114.3
Italy	107.9
Netherlands	107.3
UK	107.1
France	103.6
Australia	100.2
US	100.0
Canada	99.4
Mexico	79.5

Note: Based on 17 industries within manufacturing, R&D, software and corporate services; and 27 cost components grouped under labour, facilities, transportation, utility, taxes and income.
Source: Competitive Alternatives, KPMG

Office occupancy costs
Total annual rent, taxes and operating expenses

March 2009	$ per sq. metre per year
Tokyo (Inner Central)	1,976
Moscow	1,832
Hong Kong	1,619
London (West End)	1,858
Dubai	1,319
Mumbai	1,411
Paris	1,237
Singapore	891
New York (Midtown)	739
Frankfurt	735
São Paulo	622
Buenos Aires	583
Beijing	532
Sydney	456
Mexico City	423
Bangkok	240

Source: CB Richard Ellis

The changing workforce

Numbers of workers, m

	Canada	France	Germany	Italy	Japan	UK	US
1970	8.7	21.6	35.4	21.1	53.3	25.6	87.3
1980	12.1	24.0	35.4	22.2	56.4	27.4	114.2
1990	14.7	24.8	39.3	24.0	63.9	29.5	132.6
2000	16.2	26.3	40.5	23.8	67.7	29.7	149.3
2009	19.0	28.1	41.9	25.2	65.0	31.7	161.8

Unemployment trends, % of labour force

	Canada	France	Germany	Italy	Japan	UK	US
1985	10.7	10.2	…	10.3	2.6	11.3	7.2
1986	9.6	10.1	…	11.2	2.8	11.2	7.0
1987	8.8	10.6	…	12.0	2.9	10.8	6.2
1988	7.8	10.1	…	12.1	2.5	8.8	5.5
1989	7.5	9.5	…	12.1	2.2	7.2	5.3
1990	8.1	9.2	…	11.4	2.1	6.8	5.6
1991	10.3	9.0	6.6	11.0	2.1	8.4	6.8
1992	11.2	10.0	7.9	11.6	2.2	9.7	7.5
1993	11.4	11.1	9.5	10.0	2.5	10.3	6.9
1994	10.4	12.3	10.3	11.0	2.9	9.6	6.1
1995	9.4	11.6	10.1	11.4	3.2	8.6	5.6
1996	9.6	12.1	8.8	11.5	3.4	8.2	5.4
1997	9.1	12.3	9.8	11.6	3.4	7.1	4.9
1998	8.3	11.8	9.7	11.7	4.1	6.1	4.5
1999	7.6	11.7	8.8	11.4	4.7	6.0	4.2
2000	6.8	10.0	7.9	10.5	4.7	5.5	4.0
2001	7.2	8.8	7.9	9.5	5.0	4.8	4.8
2002	7.7	8.9	8.7	9.0	5.4	5.1	5.8
2003	7.6	8.5	10.0	8.7	5.3	4.8	6.0
2004	7.2	8.8	11.0	8.0	4.7	4.6	5.5
2005	6.8	8.5	11.1	7.7	4.4	5.0	5.1
2006	6.3	8.8	10.3	6.8	4.1	5.4	4.6
2007	6.0	8.0	8.6	6.1	3.9	5.3	4.6

Source: International Labour Organisation

The sex divide

	Male, m	Female, m	Male, %	Female, %
Canada				
1980	7.30	4.80	*60.3*	*39.7*
2009	10.01	8.99	*52.7*	*47.3*
% change			*-12.7*	*19.2*
France				
1980	14.38	9.59	*60.0*	*40.0*
2009	15.00	13.14	*53.3*	*46.7*
% change			*-11.1*	*16.7*
Germany				
1980	21.81	13.60	*61.6*	*38.4*
2009	22.82	19.11	*54.4*	*45.6*
% change			*-11.6*	*18.7*
Italy				
1980	14.78	7.44	*66.5*	*33.5*
2009	14.70	10.53	*58.3*	*41.7*
% change			*-12.4*	*24.7*
Japan				
1980	34.58	21.86	*61.3*	*38.7*
2009	37.78	27.18	*58.2*	*41.8*
% change			*-5.1*	*8.0*
UK				
1980	16.58	10.80	*60.6*	*39.4*
2009	17.07	14.59	*53.9*	*46.1*
% change			*-11.0*	*16.8*
US				
1980	66.94	47.21	*58.6*	*41.4*
2009	87.26	74.58	*53.9*	*46.1*
% change			*-8.1*	*11.4*

Source: International Labour Organisation

Days lost in strikes and lockouts

Man days, m

	Canada	France*	Germany	Italy	Japan	UK	US
1971	2.87	4.39	…	14.80	6.03	13.55	47.59
1972	7.75	3.76	…	19.50	5.15	23.91	27.07
1973	5.78	3.91	…	23.42	4.60	7.20	27.95
1974	9.22	3.38	…	19.47	9.66	14.75	31.81
1975	10.91	3.87	…	27.19	8.02	6.01	17.56
1976	11.61	4.05	…	25.38	3.25	3.28	23.96
1977	3.31	2.43	…	16.57	1.52	10.14	21.26
1978	7.39	2.08	…	10.18	1.36	9.41	23.77
1979	7.83	3.17	…	27.53	0.93	29.47	20.41
1980	8.98	1.52	…	16.46	1.00	11.96	20.84
1981	8.88	1.44	…	10.53	0.55	4.27	16.91
1982	5.80	2.25	…	18.56	0.54	5.31	9.06
1983	4.44	1.32	…	14.00	0.51	3.75	17.46
1984	3.88	1.32	…	8.70	0.35	27.14	8.50
1985	3.13	0.73	…	3.83	0.26	6.40	7.08
1986	7.15	0.57	…	5.64	0.25	1.92	11.86
1987	3.81	0.51	…	4.61	0.26	3.55	4.47
1988	4.90	1.09	…	3.32	0.17	3.70	4.38
1989	3.70	0.80	…	4.44	0.22	4.13	16.53
1990	5.08	0.53	…	5.18	0.14	1.90	5.93
1991	2.52	0.50	…	2.99	0.10	0.76	4.58
1992	2.11	0.36	…	2.74	0.23	0.53	3.99
1993	1.52	0.51	0.59	3.41	0.12	0.65	3.98
1994	1.61	0.50	0.23	3.37	0.09	0.28	5.02
1995	1.58	0.78	0.25	0.91	0.08	0.42	5.77
1996	3.35	0.44	0.10	1.93	0.04	1.30	4.89
1997	3.61	0.39	0.05	1.16	0.11	0.23	4.50
1998	2.44	0.35	0.02	0.58	0.10	0.28	5.12
1999	2.45	0.57	0.08	0.91	0.09	0.24	2.00
2000	1.66	0.81	0.01	0.88	0.04	0.50	20.42
2001	2.20	0.69	0.03	1.03	0.03	0.53	1.15
2002	3.03	…	0.31	4.86	0.01	1.32	0.66
2003	1.74	…	0.16	1.96	0.01	0.50	4.08
2004	3.22	…	0.05	0.70	0.00	0.90	1.02
2005	4.15	…	0.02	0.91	0.00	0.22	1.35
2006	0.81	…	0.43	0.55	0.00	0.75	2.69
2007	1.81	…	0.29	0.90	…	1.04	1.26

* Figures exclude agriculture and public administration. Series discontinued in 2002.

Source: International Labour Organisation

Labour union strength

Latest year

	Union members, m	% of workforce
Australia	1.8	20
Belgium	2.7	58
Canada	42.0	29
China	150.3	90
Colombia	1.1	29
Denmark	2.1	87
Finland	2.2	100
France	6.0	31
Germany	8.3	26
Hong Kong	0.7	21
Iceland	0.1	92
India	5.4	26
Ireland	0.5	44
Japan	10.1	19
Malaysia	0.8	10
Malta	0.1	61
Netherlands	1.9	27
New Zealand	0.4	21
Norway	1.5	72
Pakistan	0.3	16
Philippines	3.9	27
Singapore	0.4	24
Slovakia	0.7	39
South Africa	3.3	58
South Korea	1.6	10
Sri Lanka	0.3	4
Sweden	3.5	85
Switzerland	0.8	26
Taiwan	3.0	36
Turkey	2.9	58
UK	6.8	29
US	15.7	12

Source: International Labour Organisation

Changes in working hours

Average annual hours worked per employed person

	1950	2000	2005	2007
Australia	1,838	1,855	1,732	1,722
Austria	1,976	1,632	1,656	1,652
Belgium	2,283	1,545	1,565	1,566
Canada	1,967	1,766	1,738	1,736
Denmark	2,283	1,554	1,564	1,574*
Finland	2,035	1,750	1,718	1,698
France	1,926	1,592	1,550	1,561
Germany	2,316	1,468	1,435	1,433
Ireland	2,250	1,696	1,654	1,630
Italy	1,997	1,855	1,819	1,824
Japan	2,166	1,821	1,775	1,785
Netherlands	2,208	1,368	1,375	1,392
Norway	2,101	1,380	1,420	1,411
Spain	2,200	1,815	1,672	1,652
Sweden	1,951	1,625	1,607	1,562
UK	1,958	1,708	1,676	1,670
US	1,867	1,841	1,795	1,794
Czech Republic	...	...	2,002	1,985
Greece	...	...	2,053	...
Hungary	...	...	1,994	1,986
Iceland	...	...	1,794	1,807
Luxembourg	...	...	1,570	1,542
Mexico	...	...	1,909	1,871
New Zealand	...	...	1,810	1,771
Poland	...	...	1,994	1,976
Portugal	...	...	1,752	1,728
Slovakia	...	...	1,741	1,749*
South Korea	...	...	2,354	2,305*
Switzerland	...	...	1,669	1,657*
Turkey	...	...	1,918	1,918*

*2006
Source: OECD

Biggest business employers

2008

	'000
Wal-Mart Stores (US)	2,100
China National Petroleum (China)	1,618
State Grid (China)	1,537
US Postal Service (US)	765
Sinopec (China)	640
China Telecommunications (China)	498
Carrefour (France)	495
Hon Hai Precision Industry (Taiwan)	486
Gazprom (Russia)	456
Deutsche Post (Germany)	452
Agricultural Bank of China (China)	442
United Parcel Service (US)	426
Siemens (Germany)	421
Hitachi (Japan)	400
McDonald's (US)	400
IBM (US)	398
Compass Group (UK)	388
Industrial & Commercial Bank of China (China)	386
Aviation Industry Corporation of China (China)	383
Volkswagen (Germany)	370
Tesco (UK)	364
Sodexo (France)	355
Target (US)	351
HSBC Holdings (UK)	331
Kroger (US)	326
Citigroup (US)	325
Sears Holdings (US)	324
General Electric (US)	323
Hewlett-Packard (US)	321
Toyota Motor (Japan)	321

Sources: *Fortune*, company reports

Chief executive pay

United States

2008	Company	Total compensation, $m
Lawrence Ellison	Oracle	557
Ray Irani	Occidental Petroleum	233
John Hess	Hess	155
Michael Watford	Ultra Petroleum	117
Mark Papa	EOG Resources	90
William Berkley	WR Berkley	87*
Matthew Rose	Burlington Santa Fe	69
Paul Evanson	Allegheny Energy	67
Hugh Grant	Monsanto	65
Robert Lane	Deere & Co	61
Keith Hutton	XTO Energy	55†
Mark Hurd	Hewlett-Packard	52
John Hammergren	McKesson	51

* 2007
† New chief executive; compensation may be for another executive office.
Source: *Forbes*

Europe*

2008	Company	Total compensation, €m
Daniel Vasella†	Novartis	16.0
Peter Brabeck-Letmathe	Nestlé	10.8
Arun Sarin	Vodafone	10.3
Jeroen van de Veer	Royal Dutch Shell	8.2
Franz Humer	Roche	7.2
Paolo Scaroni	Eni	6.2
Michael Geoghegan	HSBC	6.1
Christophe de Margerie	Total	5.4
Tony Hayward	BP	4.3

*Chief executives at top 10 companies by market capitalisation.
†Long-term incentives included are calculated on same basis for all, resulting in higher figure than reports disclose.
Source: Hay Group

Chief executive base salary, 2007/08, €'000

	US	Europe	France	Germany	Italy	Switzerland	UK
Upper quartile	1,100	1,660	1,280	1,320	...	...	1,460
Median	930	1,280	1,150	1,150	1,930	1,840	1,310
Lower quartile	680	1,100	770	1,090	...	...	1,140

Chief executive total cash (base salary and bonus), 2007/08, €'000

	US	Europe	France	Germany	Italy	Switzerland	UK
Upper quartile	4,710	4,300	3,040	4,940	...	...	4,440
Median	3,400	3,340	2,670	4,100	3,500	3,370	2,960
Lower quartile	2,520	2,690	1,730	3,480	...	...	2,700

Chief executive total direct compensation (total cash and long-term incentives), 2007/8, €'000

	US	Europe	France	Germany	Italy	Switzerland	UK
Upper quartile	12,790	8,280	5,550	5,690	6,430	15,730	8,260
Median	9,660	5,610	4,250	5,150	6,190	10,820	6,260
Lower quartile	7,520	4,200	2,160	4,540	4,170	7,160	5,300

Source: Hay Group

Chief executive package, % of total

	US	Europe
Salary	10	27
Bonus	31	38
Long-term incentives	59	35

Note: All tables on this page based on the 50 largest European and 50 largest US companies by market capitalisation for which compensation data are disclosed.
Source: Hay Group

Disappearing CEOs

Retirement, illness, or long-expected changes, %

	North America	Europe	Japan	World
1995	7.4	1.7	…	7.1
1998	5.4	2.3	…	4.5
2000	8.2	3.2	12.3	6.4
2001	6.8	2.9	15.6	6.0
2002	5.1	4.7	5.2	5.0
2003	5.3	3.1	12.7	5.3
2004	6.4	7.2	11.5	7.7
2005	9.3	7.5	15.7	9.2
2006	6.7	5.2	11.0	6.6
2007	7.0	7.7	9.1	6.8
2008	7.1	7.1	12.9	7.2

Prompted by mergers and acquisitions, %

	North America	Europe	Japan	World
1995	1.7	0.5	…	0.8
1998	2.8	1.9	…	1.9
2000	4.3	3.9	0.6	3.2
2001	3.9	1.6	1.2	2.4
2002	1.6	1.6	0.6	1.4
2003	1.5	1.9	0.6	1.3
2004	2.9	2.5	2.2	2.5
2005	3.3	2.6	2.0	2.6
2006	4.6	4.2	0.5	3.2
2007	3.9	3.5	0.8	2.8
2008	3.5	2.5	0.9	2.2

Dismissed by board, %

	North America	Europe	Japan	World
1995	1.3	1.0	…	1.1
1998	2.4	1.9	…	2.0
2000	5.4	2.4	1.7	3.4
2001	2.8	3.7	0.3	2.4
2002	4.3	3.4	4.0	4.4
2003	3.3	4.9	0.6	3.2
2004	3.6	7.1	1.9	4.5
2005	3.7	4.7	2.0	3.6
2006	4.3	6.1	3.0	4.6
2007	4.5	5.7	0.8	4.2
2008	4.2	5.5	3.1	5.1

Dismissals by industry, %, world

	2008	1995–2008
Telecommunication services	10.3	6.2
Financials	8.8	3.4
Information technology	7.4	4.7
Energy	5.6	2.7
Consumer discretionary	4.0	3.9
Materials	3.2	2.5
Consumer staples	3.2	3.5
Health care	3.1	3.0
Industrials	2.1	2.8
Utilities	1.9	3.5

Note: Percentages are of total CEOs within a country or region and are based on the world's largest 2,500 public companies by market capitalisation.
Source: Booz & Company

Big payouts to CEOs

- Lee Raymond, chairman and chief executive of Exxon Mobil between 1993 and 2005, may have deserved his $400m compensation packet on retirement. The American oil giant posted record profits during his tenure and its market capitalisation increased from $80 billion to $360 billion. His pay-out included stock options, a $1m consulting deal, use of a company jet and other perks, and a $98m lump-sum pension payment, which he had accrued over four decades of employment.

- Home Depot, a home-improvement company, paid its chief executive of six years, Robert Nardelli, $210m when he resigned in January 2007. The company had performed poorly but the pay-out had been agreed in 2000 when markets were booming.

- Pfizer, an American drug company, sacked its boss Henry "Hank" McKinnell in the summer of 2006, after lacklustre performance by the company and a sinking share price. His compensation, for presiding over a 40% decline in Pfizer's share price during his five years as chief executive, was $99m (and a pension pot of $82m).

- When Gillette, a consumer goods company, was sold to Procter & Gamble in 2005 for $57 billion, its chief executive, James Kilts, pocketed $165m. In response to public criticism over his role in the merger, he referred to himself as "Boston's piñata" (a figurine filled with sweets that children hit) arguing he had earned his payout. In his four years in charge, Gillette's share price rose by 50%, and the flagging Duracell battery business was revived.

- Huge write-downs at Merrill Lynch, together with merger discussions that had not been authorised by the board, led to the departure of the bank's chief executive, Stan O'Neal, in October 2007. He left with a $161.5m pay-off; the bank was acquired by Bank of America the following year.

- Michael Ovitz, president of Walt Disney Company for only 14 months, left with a payout worth $140m. He was hired and fired by his long-time friend and the company's chief executive, Michael Eisner. Shareholders sued over the generous severance terms, with a pay-off worth as much as if he stayed for five years, but a Delaware court ruled against them in 2005, some ten years after Mr Ovitz was hired.

- In October 2008 Sir Fred Goodwin ("Fred the Shred" as he was widely known because of his ruthless cost cutting) resigned as chief executive of Royal Bank of Scotland (RBS). In February 2009 it was disclosed that he had walked away with a pension worth over £700,000 ($980,000) a year. RBS had suffered huge write-downs from its exposure to the American subprime mortgage market, and from its takeover of ABN Amro, a Dutch bank, in 2007. It was subsequently bailed out by the British government, which took a majority shareholding. After months of widespread criticism, Sir Fred agreed to return a third of the £16.6m package.

- Charles "Chuck" Prince had been with Citigroup for some 20 years since its merger with Travelers Group. But he had led the American financial-services giant for less than four years when he left in November 2007 with some $40m. Citi, however, suffered huge write-downs resulting from its exposure to subprime mortgages.

- Wendelin Wiedeking, boss of Porsche, agreed to stand down in July 2009 in return for €50m ($71m). Under Mr Wiedeking's leadership since October 1992, Porsche became the most profitable car company in the world and its implied market capitalisation went from $340m to $8 billion. Reportedly Wolfgang Porsche, Porsche's chairman, had proposed an even bigger compensation package, but representatives of the workforce on the board rejected it.

Sources: Company reports, press reports

Best paid hedge fund managers in the US

2008	Company	$m
James Simons	Renaissance Technologies Corporation	2,500
John Paulson	Paulson & Co.	2,000
John Arnold	Centaurus Energy	1,500
George Soros	Soros Fund Management	1,100
Raymond Dalio	Bridgewater Associates	780
Bruce Kovner	Caxton Associates	640
David Shaw	D.E. Shaw & Co.	275
Stanley Druckenmiller	Duquesne Capital Management	260
David Harding	Winton Capital Management	250
Alan Howard	Brevan Howard Asset Management	250
John Taylor Jr	FX Concepts	250
James Chanos	Kynikos Associates	225
Michael Platt	BlueCrest Capital Management	210
Roy Niederhoffer	R.G. Niederhoffer Capital Management	200
John Horseman	Horseman Capital Management	180
Paul Touradji	Touradji Capital Management	140
Henry Laufer	Renaissance Technologies Corporation	125
Kenneth Tropin	Graham Capital Management	120
Pierre Andurand	BlueGold Capital Management	90
Dennis Crema	BlueGold Capital Management	90
Christopher Rokos	Brevan Howard Asset Management	90
Christian Baha	Superfund	85
Christian Levett	Clive Capital	85
William Dunn	DUNN Capital Management	80
Andrew Hoine	Paulson & Co.	75

Source: *Alpha*, published by *Institutional Investor*

International pay comparisons

Gross salary $'000, 2008	Labourer (general)	Labourer (skilled)	Professional (junior)	Professional (senior)	Management (lower middle)	Management (upper middle)
Australia	29.9	37.5	46.7	62.3	83.2	111.0
Brazil	7.8	16.9	27.4	44.5	66.4	115.4
Canada	37.9	46.8	57.7	71.1	87.6	108.0
China*	5.5	9.5	16.2	27.8	47.6	81.5
Denmark	41.6	53.8	69.6	90.0	116.5	150.6
France	25.4	34.4	46.7	63.2	85.7	116.1
Germany	35.9	48.2	64.8	87.1	117.2	157.5
India	3.9	6.4	10.4	17.1	27.9	45.7
Italy	25.2	35.3	49.4	69.1	96.8	135.5
Japan	38.6	50.0	64.7	83.8	108.6	140.7
Mexico	6.7	13.6	21.8	34.8	57.5	98.0
Netherlands	33.4	43.4	56.3	69.3	92.6	123.7
Poland	10.8	17.1	27.1	42.8	67.6	106.8
Romania	7.4	11.3	17.3	26.5	40.5	62.1
South Korea	22.6	29.0	37.3	48.0	61.6	79.2
Spain	33.5	44.0	57.7	75.8	99.5	130.6
Sweden	...	40.1	46.9	55.0	66.9	92.5
Switzerland	48.5	64.4	85.5	113.6	150.9	200.4
UK	29.8	40.0	53.9	72.5	97.5	131.1
US	31.0	41.5	55.5	74.4	99.6	119.5

*China figures are for Beijing.
Source: Mercer Human Resource Consulting

Leading law firms

2008

Company	Head Office	Fees, $bn	Headcount
DLA Piper	UK/US	2.19	7,847
Skadden, Arps	US	2.17	5,500
Clifford Chance	UK	2.13	7,139
Linklaters	UK	2.07	5,591
Latham & Watkins	US	2.01	4,700
Freshfields Bruckhaus Deringer	UK	1.88	5,250
Baker & McKenzie	US	1.83	10,000
Allen & Overy	UK	1.63	4,694
Jones Day	US	1.44	5,040
Sidley Austin	US	1.39	3,960
White & Case	US	1.37	2,330
Kirkland & Ellis	US	1.31	3,960
Greenberg Traurig	US	1.20	4,320
Mayer Brown	US	1.18	3,630
Weil Gotshal & Manges	US	1.18	3,672
Morgan, Lewis & Bockius	US	1.03	3,795
Dewey & LeBoeuf	US	1.01	3,240
Sullivan & Cromwell	US	0.99	2,650
McDermott Will & Emery	US	0.98	2,450
Paul, Hastings, Janofsky & Walker	US	0.98	3,125
Simpson Thacher & Bartlett	US	0.97	1,631
WilmerHale	US	0.94	3,045
O'Melveny & Myers	US	0.93	2,430

Source: Managing Partners' Forum (MPF) Global 500, 2008

Leading accountancy firms

2008

Company	Head Office	Fees, $bn	Headcount
PricewaterhouseCoopers	UK/US	25.15	146,767
Deloitte	UK/US	23.10	150,000
Ernst & Young	UK/US	21.10	124,335
KPMG	Holland	19.80	113,000
BDO International	Belgium	4.70	31,576
Grant Thornton	UK	3.46	27,453
RSM International	UK	3.00	24,893
Praxity	France	2.84	26,000
Horwath International	US	2.53	19,127
Baker Tilly	UK	2.50	24,256
Nexia International	UK	2.20	18,213
Moore Stephens	UK	1.88	19,279
HLB International	UK	1.73	13,400
PKF	UK	1.72	15,000
The Leading Edge Alliance	US	1.72	13,500
Kreston International	UK	1.70	18,500
AGN International	UK	1.32	10,100
Fiducial International	France	1.24	15,100
BKR International	US	0.89	8,012
DFK International	UK	0.88	7,580
IAPA	US	0.84	9,000
IGAF	UK	0.80	5,300
CPA Associates	US	0.80	7,404

Source: Managing Partners' Forum (MPF) Global 500, 2008

Women in business

Firsts among women

1809 Mary Kies – first woman to receive
a US patent (for weaving straw in hatmaking)
1963 Katharine Graham – first woman CEO of a
Fortune 500 company (The Washington Post Co)
1967 Muriel "Mickey" Siebert – first woman to purchase
a seat on the New York Stock Exchange
1997 Marjorie Scardino – first woman CEO of a FTSE 100
company (Pearson)
1999 Carly Fiorina – first woman CEO in the 30-
company Dow Jones Industrial Average (Hewlett-Packard)
2001 Clara Furse – first woman to become CEO of the
London Stock Exchange
2002 Baroness Sarah Hogg – first chairwoman of a
FTSE 100 company (3i)
2006 Bishop Katharine Jefferts Schori – first woman
leader in the Anglican church
2009 Helen Alexander – first woman to head the
Confederation of British Industry (CBI)
2009 Ursula Burns – first African-American woman to
head a *Fortune* 500 company in the first woman-to-
woman CEO handover in a *Fortune* 500 company

Most powerful women in business in America

Indra Nooyi	PepsiCo CEO
Irene Rosenfeld	Kraft Foods CEO
Pat Woertz	Archer Daniels Midland CEO
Anne Mulcahy	Xerox CEO
Angela Braly	Wellpoint CEO
Andrea Jung	Avon Products CEO
Susan Arnold	Procter & Gamble President, Global Business Units
Oprah Winfrey	Harpo chairman
Brenda Barnes	Sara Lee CEO
Ursula Burns	Xerox President

Source: *Fortune*

Most powerful women in business outside America

Cynthia Carroll	Anglo American	UK	CEO
Gail Kelly	Westpac	Australia	CEO
Linda Cook	Shell Gas & Power, Shell Trading	Netherlands	Executive director
Ho Ching	Temasek Holdings	Singapore	Executive director, CEO
Marjorie Scardino	Pearson	UK	CEO
Anne Lauvergeon	Areva	France	CEO
Annika Falkengren	SEB	Sweden	President, CEO
Marina Berlusconi	Fininvest	Italy	Chairman
Güler Sabanci	Sabanci Holding	Turkey	Chairman, MD
Gulzhan Moldazhanova	Basic Element	Russia	CEO

Source: *Fortune*

Most powerful women working in entertainment

Oprah Winfrey	Harpo	Chairman
Anne Sweeney	The Walt Disney Company	Co-chairman of Media Networks; president of Disney-ABC Television Group
Amy Pascal	Sony Pictures Entertainment	Co-chairman; chairman Motion Picture Group
Nancy Tellem	CBS Paramount Network Television Entertainment Group	President
Stacey Snider	DreamWorks	Co-chairman, CEO
Bonnie Hammer	NBC Universal Cable Entertainment and Universal Cable Productions	President
Judy McGrath	MTV Networks	Chairman, CEO
Mary Parent	MGM Worldwide Motion Picture Group	Chairman
Dana Walden	20th Century Fox Television	Chairman
Nina Tassler	CBS Entertainment	President

Note: Most powerful women rankings are for 2008.
Source: *Hollywood Reporter*

$pending on advertising

	Total, 2008, $m	% of GDP	Per head, 2008, $
Argentina	2,147	0.65	53.8
Australia	10,177	1.03	483.0
Austria	3,848	0.93	461.4
Belgium	4,641	0.93	438.3
Brazil	11,563	0.73	60.2
Bulgaria	862	1.73	113.6
Canada	9,420	0.63	283.2
Chile	20,074	0.54	59.3
China	3,832	0.46	15.0
Colombia	3,467	1.92	85.1
Czech Republic	2,770	1.60	336.0
Denmark	646	0.81	507.2
Egypt	163	0.40	7.9
Estonia	2,061	0.70	121.4
Finland	14,946	0.76	389.0
France	27,540	0.52	240.9
Germany	3,821	0.76	334.8
Greece	3,284	1.07	343.0
Hong Kong	1,187	1.52	470.5
Hungary	4,914	0.77	118.6
India	2,873	0.39	4.2
Indonesia	2,725	0.56	12.6
Ireland	1,120	0.96	613.7
Israel	12,684	0.56	158.8
Italy	44,947	0.55	212.8
Japan	704	0.92	353.1
Kuwait	199	0.52	241.3
Latvia	776	0.59	88.1
Lithuania	1,903	1.64	233.6
Malaysia	5,428	0.86	70.5
Mexico	26	0.50	50.0
Netherlands	1,578	0.65	342.4
New Zealand	4,976	1.18	373.1
Norway	137	1.11	1,043.2
Panama	336	1.56	98.8

Peru	412	0.32	14.3
Philippines	3,861	2.29	42.7
Poland	3,218	0.61	84.5
Portugal	1,359	0.56	127.3
Puerto Rico	1,841	1.60	462.6
Romania	796	0.41	37.2
Russia	10,736	0.63	75.9
Saudi Arabia/ Pan Arab	1,174	0.27	46.6
Singapore	1,497	0.82	324.0
South Africa	4,029	1.46	81.1
South Korea	8,000	0.86	166.2
Spain	10,246	0.64	230.3
Sweden	3,493	0.73	379.2
Switzerland	3,998	0.81	530.3
Taiwan	1,533	0.37	66.9
Thailand	2,878	1.08	42.7
Turkey	2,645	0.36	35.8
UK	22,810	0.85	372.5
Uruguay	146	0.48	43.7
US	171,913	1.21	551.6
Venezuela	56	0.36	2.0
Vietnam	1,113	0.36	39.6
Total	462	0.50	5.3

Source: ZenithOptimedia

%	Television	Newspapers	Magazines	Radio	Out-of-home	Internet	Cinema
2007	37.3	26.9	12.2	8.0	6.5	8.7	0.5
2008	38.0	25.1	11.6	7.7	6.7	10.5	0.5
2009	38.6	23.4	10.5	7.6	6.8	12.6	0.5
2010	39.3	22.2	9.9	7.4	6.9	13.8	0.5
2011	39.2	21.2	9.7	7.2	7.0	15.1	0.6

Note: 2008 is estimate; 2009–11 are forecasts.
Source: ZenithOptimedia

Some famous advertising slogans

"All the news that's fit to print." *New York Times* (1896)

"Good to the last drop." Maxwell House coffee (1915)

"I'd walk a mile for a Camel." Camel (1921)

"Ask the man who owns one." Packard (1925)

"Guinness is good for you." Guinness (1929)

"Snap! Crackle! Pop!" Kellogg's Rice Krispies (1932)

"Don't be vague. Ask for Haig." Haig Scotch Whisky (1934)

"If you want to get ahead, get a hat." Hat Council (1934)

"Careless Talk Costs Lives." UK Ministry of Information (1940)

"Think." IBM (1941)

"A diamond is forever." De Beers (1948)

"A little dab'll do ya." Brylcreem (1949)

"Finger lickin' good." Kentucky Fried Chicken (1952)

"The milk chocolate melts in your mouth, not in your hand." M&Ms (1954)

"You'll wonder where the yellow went when you brush your teeth with Pepsodent." Pepsodent (1956)

"Go to work on an egg." UK Egg Marketing Board (1957)

"Drink a pinta milka day." National Milk Publicity Council (1958)

"You're never alone with a Strand." Imperial Tobacco (1959)

"Happiness is a cigar called Hamlet." Hamlet (1960)

"Think small." Volkswagen (1962)

"We try harder." Avis (1962)

"Schhh … You-Know-Who." Schweppes (1962)

"Put a tiger in your tank" Esso (1964)

"Let your fingers do the walking." Yellow Pages (1964)

"A Mars a day helps you work, rest and play." Mars (1965)

"Beanz Meanz Heinz." Heinz (1967)

"Because I'm worth it." L'Oréal (1967)

"It's the real thing." Coca-Cola (1971)

"Say it with flowers" Interflora (1971)

"Accountancy was my life until I discovered Smirnoff." Smirnoff (1971)

"Probably the best beer in the world." Carlsberg (1973)

"Lipsmackin' thirstquenchin' acetastin' motivatin' goodbuzzin' cooltalkin' highwalkin' fastlivin' evergivin' coolfizzin' Pepsi." Pepsi Cola (1973)

"Heineken refreshes the parts other beers cannot reach." Heineken (1974)

"For mash get Smash." Smash instant mashed potatoes (1974)

"Don't leave home without it." American Express (1975)

"The ultimate driving machine." BMW (1975)

"Reach out and touch someone." AT&T (1979)

"I liked it so much I bought the company." Remington shavers (1979)

"H2Eau." Perrier (1980)

"Reassuringly expensive." Stella Artois (1981)

"When it absolutely, positively, has to be there overnight." Federal Express (1982)

"The world's favourite airline." British Airways (1983)

"Vorsprung durch technik." Audi (1984)

"Australians wouldn't give a Castlemaine XXXX for anything else." (1986)

"Just do it." Nike (1988)

"It's everywhere you want to be." Visa (1988)

"Intel inside." Intel (1990)

"It's good to talk." British Telecom (1994)

"The future's bright. The future's Orange." Orange (1996)

"Absolut perfection." Absolut Vodka (1998)

"Think different." Apple Macintosh (1998)

"Be the first to know." CNN (2002)

"10,000 songs in your pocket." iPod (2004)

"Live in your world, play in ours." Sony Playstation (2004)

"Buy it. Sell it. Love it." eBay (2005)

"So where the bloody hell are you?" Australian Tourist Commission (2006)

Some business giants of the past

Carnegie, Andrew (1835–1919)

The richest man ever to come out of Dumfermline, Andrew Carnegie left Scotland for Pittsburgh, Pennsylvania, with his family in search of work after the introduction of the mechanical loom put his weaver father out of work. Carnegie's first job was as a bobbin boy in a textile factory. After later jobs as a clerk and a messenger boy, in 1853 he became assistant to Tom Scott, the superintendent of the Pennsylvania Railroad's western division. He started investing on his own behalf in iron manufacturing and other businesses, and made substantial returns. In 1859 he was promoted to the position of superintendent and in 1865 he resigned from the railroad to concentrate on business, in particular iron and steel. The civil war had fuelled demand for iron, as had the move to replace wooden bridges with iron ones and, most important of all, the expansion of the railroads. Carnegie introduced the Bessemer steel process to America, which meant that steel could be produced at greater speed and lower cost, with the result that the Carnegie Steel Company was producing a quarter of America's steel by 1900 and was making a profit of $40m. Carnegie believed that great wealth was of no value unless it was put to good use and he wrote several treatises on this theme, including the *Gospel of Wealth* in which he argued that any riches beyond those needed for the survival of one's family should be used for the good of the wider community. By the time he sold his company to J.P. Morgan in 1901 for $480m, Carnegie had already spent a great deal of money in accordance with his principles. As a self-educated but cultivated man, he was a great believer in public libraries and he spent over $50m setting up some 2,500 of them. By the time he died, he had given away $350m.

Disney, Walt Elias (1901–66)

Walt Disney was a sentimentalist whose somewhat rigid idea of America on occasions gave his work a sinister edge. The inventor and voice of Mickey Mouse also produced cheery military propaganda like *Victory Through Airpower* and in 1947 appeared before the House Committee on Un-American Activities to name employees he said were communist infiltrators: "I really feel that they ought to be smoked out for what they are so that all the liberalisms that really are American can go out without the taint of communism." Between 1942 and 1943, 95% of Disney Studios' output was on contract to the US government and Disney was particularly proud of his contribution to the tax-take after *The New Spirit* explained the importance of declaring your income for tax.

He was born in Chicago, left school to drive an ambulance for the Red Cross in France aged 16 and returned from there, having survived influenza in the great epidemic, in 1919. Walt began drawing cartoons and set up a little company, Laugh-O-Gram Films, before moving to Hollywood. There he brought Oswald the Lucky Rabbit into existence and then Mickey Mouse, who appeared with synchronised sound. Walt Disney was among the first to recognise the importance of sound for bringing cartoons, and later nature films, to life. He also pioneered Technicolor, winning an Academy Award for *Flowers and Trees* in 1932. The combination of these successes led to a feature-length cartoon and *Snow White and the Seven Dwarves* opened in 1937. The profits ran to millions and Disney set about constructing $3m offices that would churn out the now familiar Disney cartoons. He returned to bulk-making cartoons after the war, but also continued with informational films such as those about NASA which he made with the help of ex-Nazi Wernher von Braun, inventor of the V2 Rocket. Disneyland opened in 1955 in Anaheim, California, and there were other theme-parks on the horizon. These

some business giants of the past *continued*

perhaps helped formulate an idea in Walt's mind that he called EPCOT (Experimental Prototype Community of Tomorrow). But he died before he was able to see its fruition.

Ford, Henry (1863–1947)

Henry Ford is best known for the invention of the Model T Ford and the moving assembly line and less well-known as the US publisher of the notorious anti-semitic *Protocols of the Elders of Zion* (in his newspaper *The Dearborn Independent*). Ford was born to Irish immigrant parents from County Cork and left the family farm to work as a machinist in Detroit. He returned to work on the family farm in 1882 but was shortly afterwards taken on, thanks to his skills with steam engines, as a maintenance engineer in a local company. In 1891 he joined the Edison Illuminating Company but found sufficient spare time to invent, build and drive his Quadricycle which led to the creation of the Henry Ford Company. This, however, was taken over by the investors who turned it into Cadillac, so Henry Ford set up the Ford motor company in 1903 and released the Model T six years later. In 1918, half of all cars in America were Model T Fords. Ford's approach to his workers was paternalistic but combined the generous treatment of suitable workers with suppression of union activity.

Gibbs, William (1790–1875)

"Mr Gibbs made his tibbs selling turds of foreign birds." One of the sons of Anthony Gibbs, William built churches and the grand house of Tyntesfield near Bristol with money made from guano. Guano is seabird dung, rich in nitrates and phosphates, and was harvested in earnest off South America's coast from the middle of the 19th century as fertiliser. William and his brother George signed their first contract with the Peruvian government in 1842 and in 1858 imported 300,000 tons of guano to Britain. William was able to build Tyntesfield at a cost of £70,000, the profits of just one year's trade. (In 2002 the house was acquired by the National Trust for £25m.) He also paid for churches to be built elsewhere, including the chapel of Keble College, Oxford.

Kroc, Ray (1902–84)

It was Ray Kroc who persuaded Dick and Mac McDonald to expand and set up their restaurants across the United States, and to employ him to oversee this project. At the age of 15, Ray Kroc, who had lied about his age, had been destined for Europe as a Red Cross ambulance driver. He was saved by the war ending before he could leave and began instead a variety of salesman's jobs. He first met the McDonald brothers when selling mixing machines for restaurants; their purchase of eight of these machines gave him the idea for setting up identikit restaurants like theirs. Kroc prided himself on his standards of quality, service and cleanliness, and he believed that there should be no reservations, no waiting and low prices. There was no doubt, however, about his core principle – in his own words: "The definition of salesmanship is the gentle art of letting the customer have it your way." He was chairman of the McDonald's Corporation from its creation in 1955 until his death and he never stopped developing new ideas, from German taverns to theme parks. When his widow, Joan, died in 2004, she left a bequest of £800m to the Salvation Army.

Krupp, Alfred (1812–87)

Alfred Krupp was an outstanding businessman and engineer who profited from industrialisation and war in Europe. Born in Essen into a family of metal-workers, he began work in the family iron forge when his father fell ill. Together with his mother, who took control of the firm on the death of her husband in 1826, Alfred began

some business giants of the past *continued*

building on the possibilities presented by the manufacture of steel. The firm became a central element in the building of the railways and produced, among other railway components, the seamless wheel tyre. Increasingly, however, Alfred was looking to armaments for the company's survival – he had produced its first steel gun in 1847. In 1848, he became the head of the company and began in earnest the acquisition of mines, docks and collieries in order to guarantee the raw materials that he needed. By the time of his death, Krupps employed 20,200 people and had instituted a rule that the company could only be passed to a single heir. Later, the Krupps firm would produce the artillery used to shell Paris in first world war ("Big Bertha"). The Krupp whose collaboration with Adolf Hitler led to the break-up of the Krupp empire was in fact Gustav von Bohlen und Halbach, who changed his name when he married Alfred's granddaughter, Bertha.

Lever, William Hesketh (1851–1925)

Born in Bolton in the north of England, William Hesketh Lever was a pioneering manufacturer of soap who applied his wealth to a variety of good causes. In 1886, he was the founding partner in Lever Brothers with James Lever. In the course of their business, they made the discovery that soap could be made from vegetable oil instead of tallow and from that discovery came Sunlight soap – hence Port Sunlight, the model village near Liverpool that Lever built for his workers. After his purchase of the Scottish islands of Harris and Lewis in 1918, he established similar projects there, too, and spent large sums of money trying to create a gainfully employed community free from poverty. Lever is known for his art collections, which served a dual purpose, for not only did he have a passion for art and artefacts, but he also saw that certain types of

painting could be used to promote soap sales. These
tended to be illustrations of pristine clothes worn by
happy but poor people. The artists were not always happy
to find their creations used in this way. However, after his
wife's death in 1913, Lever built a gallery in her memory
where the pictures and other collections are preserved.
Lever's pre-eminence in business and social zeal were
recognised by a series of titles. He was MP for the Wirral
and was made a baronet. He was raised to the peerage as
Lord Leverhulme of Bolton-le-Moors in 1917 and became
Viscount Leverhulme of the Isles five years later. To this
day, money left by him is given to research and education
projects.

Morgan, John Pierpoint (1837–1913)

The richest man in America by 1900, John Pierpoint
Morgan made his money through the financing of debt
and the control of important US industries. He rescued
America's finances on more than one occasion, notably
helping to refinance the civil war debt and bailing out
Wall Street during its financial crisis in 1907. Born into a
banking family, Morgan travelled widely when he was
young and graduated from the University of Göttingen.
After a stretch working as an accountant for the Duncan
Sherman & Co banking house, he began working in as an
accountant for a finance house that served George
Peabody, his father's partner, in New York. His father,
Junius Spencer, subsequently succeeded Peabody and
renamed the company J.S. Morgan, which John Pierpoint
joined in 1864. In 1895, he took over the bank, and it
became J.P. Morgan. He began systematising the railroads
and gained stock in the railroad companies he
reorganised; by 1900 he controlled 5,000 miles of railroad
rights, one-sixth of the total. There followed the purchase
and consolidation of US steel manufacturing – he bought
the Carnegie Steel Company from Andrew Carnegie for
$480m and joined it to his own Federal Steel Company in
1901. The resulting US Steel Corporation was the first

some business giants of the past *continued*

company in the world to be capitalised at over $1 billion. In the meantime, he had also started the International Harvester Company, which dealt in agricultural equipment, and the International Mercantile Marine shipping company (owner of White Star Line, which built the Titanic). It was with reason that antitrust campaigners attacked him given that he controlled several industries almost in their entirety. In spite of the cathedral and churches he built, and his intervention to save Wall Street in 1907 (which eventually led to the creation of the Federal Reserve System), J.P. Morgan's reputation still hangs somewhere between "robber baron" and builder of America's economy.

Morita, Akio (1921–99)

The man who conceived the idea of the Walkman was born into a Nagoya family that traded in sake and soy sauce. Instead of working in the family firm and ignoring his father's advice that he study economics, Akio Morita chose to study electronics at Tokyo University. It was in his subsequent work in missile design that he met Masaru Ibuka with whom, in 1946, he set up Tokyo Telecommunications and Engineering Industries (Tokyo Tsushin Kogyo). Ibuku was the source of much of the company's electrical engineering success but Morita provided the business sense that underlay the greatest achievements. He wanted to destroy the image of Japan as a source of cheap and shoddy goods and started selling the company's products abroad. In 1958 he rebranded the company as Sony (a combination of *sonus* (Latin: sound) and Sonny Boy), and in 1961 Sony was the first foreign company to be listed on the New York Stock Exchange. Morita retired from Sony in 1994. Henry Kissinger said that he was probably the most effective spokesman for Japan he ever met.

Rockefeller, John Davison (1839–1937)

The wealth of the Rockefellers was created by John Davison Rockefeller through control of oil production in the United States. He began as a book-keeper in a company buying and selling futures and then moved to an oil refinery in Ohio. In 1870, with several others, Rockefeller founded Standard Oil. The company grew in power through the acquisition of competing refineries and through control of the railroads. The scale of consolidation was such that Standard Oil came under attack from the antitrust movement and in 1911 was ordered by the US Supreme Court to be broken up; many new small companies were formed from its ruins. But the Rockefeller fortune had been made. John Rockefeller was reckoned to be worth $900m in 1901 and, one of the modern age's great philanthropists, had given away $500m by the time he died; he had founded the University of Chicago, the Rockefeller Institute for Medical Research and the Rockefeller Foundation to "promote the well-being of mankind" and had supported many other organisations and institutions. It was his son, John Davison Rockefeller II, who built the Rockefeller Centre in New York.

Rothschild, Mayer Amschel (1744–1812)

"There cannot be too many Rothschilds," wrote Benjamin Disraeli, a British prime minister of the later Victorian period. Mayer Amschel Rothschild, founder of the family banking empire, made sure that there were plenty of Rothschilds to perpetuate the dynasty. Rothschilds aplenty were strategically scattered across Europe at the time of the Napoleonic wars. Mayer Amschel was born in 1744 in Frankfurt, Germany, and had five sons of significant abilities. Led by the astute Nathan Mayer in London, the brothers offered their expertise to the British and other governments in transferring subsidies and remitting funds for war. In the early days, the family fortune was made with the proceeds of smuggling, market

some business giants of the past *continued*

speculations and front-running on government commissions. By the time of Napoleon's defeat in 1815, the Rothschilds – from their bases in London, Paris, Frankfurt, Vienna and Naples – had established themselves as the leading bankers in Europe. Nathan Rothschild's issue of bonds for Prussia in 1818, denominated in sterling with dividends payable in London, laid the foundations for the family's domination of the market for foreign-bond issues for the remainder of the 19th century. Their dominant position in London and Paris made the Rothschilds the first choice for European governments seeking loans on the international market. But success did not last forever. When James, the youngest brother, died in Paris in 1868, the unity of the family began to crumble. Later Rothschilds spent more time indulging their passions for building, collecting, horse racing and natural history than in the banking halls. By the time of the first world war, American finance, led by the house of Morgan, had asserted its dominance.

Walton, Sam (1918–92)

Sam Walton's perfecting of the idea of discount shopping had made him America's richest man by the time he died in 1992. The founder of Wal-Mart, today the world's largest retailer, knew a thing or two about seeking out a bargain. He had $5 haircuts, never tipped his barber and was renowned for searching through dustbins. Rather than looking for cast-offs, this was one of the ways in which he kept an eye on his competitors: binned price tickets, for example, revealed what was selling in other shops. His stinginess, an oddly common trait in the super-rich, a fanatical attention to costs and a willingness to beg, borrow and steal ideas were at the heart of Walton's incredible success. He opened his first Wal-Mart in 1962 but, lacking the resources to compete directly with giants like Sears and Woolworth, he began by locating his stores in rural towns where local independents were his only rivals. In the following 30 years the company became such a dominant retailer in part because its founder fostered a culture of loyalty among his employees (who are called "associates") and an attention to customers that bordered on the intrusive. Walton excelled at making direct contact with his workers and jotting down their ideas on yellow notepads. They were even welcome to phone him at home.

Woolworth, Frank (1852–1919)

Frank Woolworth originally conceived the idea of selling goods at discounted and fixed prices when he observed the attraction discount stalls of leftovers held for customers. He reasoned that this was because of the price but also because people liked seeing and handling the goods. On this basis he set up the first of his stores in 1879. His misjudgment on this occasion was to sell goods at only five cents and the shop went bust. Undeterred, he proceeded to set up new stores which offered goods at both five and ten cents (hence "five and ten cents stores"). After one or two further failures the business started to grow, and by 1904 there were 120 Woolworths stores in 21 states across America. On his death in 1919, Woolworth had established more than 1,000 stores in America and elsewhere and a $65m corporation had been formed. Woolworth built the eponymous tower in New York which was the tallest in the world at the time.

The world's richest people

2009	Worth, $bn	Country/region	% change on year earlier
Bill Gates	40.0	US	-31
Warren Buffett	37.0	US	-40
Carlos Slim Helu & family	35.0	Mexico	-42
Lawrence Ellison	22.5	US	-10
Ingvar Kamprad & family	22.0	Sweden	-29
Karl Albrecht	21.5	Germany	-20
Mukesh Ambani	19.5	India	-55
Lakshmi Mittal	19.3	India	-57
Theo Albrecht	18.8	Germany	-18
Amancio Ortega	18.3	Spain	-9
Jim Walton	17.8	US	-7
Alice Walton	17.6	US	-7
Christy Walton & family	17.6	US	-8
S. Robson Walton	17.6	US	-8
Bernard Arnault	16.5	France	-35

1996	Worth, $bn	Country/region
Bill Gates	18.5	US
Warren Buffett	15.0	US
Paul Sacher, Oeri & Hoffmann, family	13.1	Switzerland
Lee Shau Kee	12.7	Hong Kong
Tsai Wan-lin, family	12.2	Taiwan
Kwok, Brothers	11.2	Hong Kong
Li Ka-shing, family	10.6	Hong Kong
Yoshiaki Tsutsumi	9.2	Japan
Theo & Karl Albrecht	9.0	Germany
Hans & Gad Rausing	9.0	Scandinavia
Johanna, Susanne & Stefan Quandt	8.1	Germany
Haniel, family	8.1	Germany
Paul Allen	7.5	US

Source: *Forbes*

Europe's richest people

2009	Country of residence	€bn	% change on a year earlier
Karl & Theo Albrecht*	Germany	31.0	12
Brenninkmeyer family	Netherlands	21.1	30
Ingvar Kamprad*	Sweden	16.9	-2
Mulliez family	France	16.9	52
Johanna Quandt*	Germany	14.4	0
Amancio Ortega	Spain	14.1	26
Bernard Arnault	France	12.7	-11
Stefan & Liselott Persson	Sweden	12.7	15
Lakshmi Mittal*	UK	12.0	-61
Liliane Bettencourt	France	10.3	-19
Michael Otto*	Germany	10.1	0
Oeri/Hoffmann family	Switzerland	9.4	-8
Herz family	Germany	8.3	-28
Roman Abramovich	UK	7.8	-40
Birgit Rausing*	Switzerland/UK	7.7	-1
Michele Ferrero*	Italy	7.3	20
Mikhail Prokhorov	Russia	7.3	-33
Duke of Westminster	UK	·7.2	-7
Fentener van Vlissingen family	Netherlands	6.3	-5
Alain & Gerard Wertheimer	France	6.1	-15
Vagit Alekperov	Russia	6.0	-17
François Pinault*	France	5.9	-38
Ernesto & Kirsty Bertarelli	UK	5.6	-11
Andreas & Thomas Strungmann	Germany	5.6	6
August von Finck	Germany	5.1	0

*Family wealth.

Source: *Sunday Times*; ECB

Philanthropy in America and Britain

America's most generous philanthropists

	Background	2004–08 given or pledged, $bn
Warren Buffett	Berkshire Hathaway CEO	40.66
Bill & Melinda Gates	Microsoft co-founder	2.63
George Kaiser	Oil and gas, banking, investments	2.38
George Soros	Investor	2.21
William Barron Hilton	Heir and former CEO of Hilton Hotels	1.70
Walton Family	Family of Wal-Mart founder	1.38
Herbert & Marion Sandler	Golden West Financial co-founders	1.33
Peter Peterson	Blackstone Group co-founder	1.17
Donald Bren	Real estate developer	0.91
Michael Bloomberg	Bloomberg founder, NYC Mayor	0.90
Jon Huntsman	Huntsman chairman	0.80
Bernard Osher	Banking, investments	0.80

Source: *BusinessWeek*

Britain's most generous philanthropists

2009*	Background	Recent donations, £m
Lord Ashcroft	Business services	885
Christopher Cooper-Hohn	Finance	463
Lord Sainsbury†	Supermarkets	405
Hans Rausing†	Inheritance	151
George Weston†	Retailing	98
Johan Eliasch	Sports goods	50
Robert Edmiston	Car sales and property	46
Arpad Busson & Uma Thurman	Finance, films	43
Sir Elton John	Music	42
Lily Safra	Inheritance	33

*Year to April.
†Family wealth.
Source: *Sunday Times*

Causes	Estimated lifetime giving, $bn	Donations as % of net worth
Health, education, humanitarian causes	40.79	82
Global health and development, education	27.60	48
Poverty in Oklahoma	2.90	24
Open and democratic societies	6.94	63
International health, children	1.70	75
Education reform, marine conservation	2.02	2
Environment, civil rights, journalism	1.39	58
Fiscal health, foreign policy, education	1.18	47
Education, environment, research	1.34	11
Health, education, arts, social services	1.50	8
Cancer, business education	1.26	70
Higher education, medicine, arts	1.00	111

Causes	Recent donations as % of net wealth
Community, education, children, military	80
HIV/Aids, education, humanitarian	544
Education, medical, arts, environment	37
Human rights, women, environment	4
Education, religion, arts, welfare	11
Environment	17
Religious, humanitarian, education	15
Children, HIV/Aids, education	41
HIV/Aids, medical, humanitarian, arts	24
Medical, children, HIV/Aids, Jewish	7

Wealth and philanthropy in China

China's richest people

2008*	Company
Huang Guangyu	Pengrun Investments
Du Shuanghua	Rizhao Steel Group
Yang Huiyan	Country Garden
Peng Xiaofeng	LDK Solar
Liu Yongxing†	East Hope Group
Rong Zhijian	Citic Pacific
Shi Zhengrong	Suntech Power
Zhang Jindong	Suning
Xu Rongmao†	Shimao
Zhang Zhixiang	Jianlong Steel
Zhu Mengyi†	Hopson Development
He Xiangjian†	Midea Group
Liu Yonghao†	New Hope Group
Lu Guanqiu†	Wanxiang Group
Chen Lihua	Fu Wah International

China's most generous philanthropists

2004–09‡	Company
Yu Pengnian	Pengnian Industries
Huang Rulun	Jinyuan Group
Zhu Mengyi	Hopson Development
Niu Gensheng	Mengniu Group
Chen Guangbiao	Huangpu Investment
Yang Guoqiang†	Country Garden
Sun Yinhuan	YiDa Group
Yang Lan & Wu Zheng	Sunmedia Investments
Huang Nubo	Zhongkun Group
Duan Yongping	BBK Group
Lu Zhiqiang	Fanhai
Xu Rongmao†	Shimao

*As of September 1st. †Includes family, ‡Up to March
Source: *Hurun Report*

Industry	Wealth, $bn
Household appliance retail, property, private equity	6.3
Steel	5.1
Property	4.9
Solar panel components	4.0
Alumina, aluminium, feed	3.7
Diversified	3.7
Solar energy	3.2
Household appliance retail, property	3.2
Property	3.1
Steel	2.9
Property	2.9
Household appliances	2.9
Finance, pig feed, property, dairy products	2.8
Auto parts, finance, property	2.7
Property, private membership club, museum	2.6

Causes	Donations, $m
Health care, education	441
Education, poverty alleviation, disaster relief, health care, culture & sports	212
Education, health care, disaster relief	169
Disaster relief, poverty alleviation, education, health care, social welfare	96
Health care, disaster relief, social welfare	92
Education, poverty alleviation, health care, disaster relief	77
Education, disaster relief, social welfare	48
Education, culture & sports	47
Education, culture & sports, social welfare, disaster relief	45
Education, disaster relief	40
Disaster relief, poverty alleviation, education	38
Education, disaster relief, social welfare, culture & sports	37

Central bankers since 1900

Bank of England governors

	Year appointed
Samuel Steuart Gladstone	1899
Sir Augustus Prevost	1901
Samuel Hope Morley	1903
Alexander Falconer Wallace	1905
William Middleton Campbell	1907
Reginald Eden Johnston	1909
Alfred Clayton Cole	1911
Walter Cunliffe	1913
Sir Brien Ibrican Cokayne	1918
Montagu Collet Norman	1920
Lord Catto of Cairncatto	1944
Cameron Fromanteel Cobbold	1949
The Earl of Cromer	1961
Leslie Kenneth O'Brien	1966
Gordon William Humphreys Richardson	1973
Robert (Robin) Leigh-Pemberton	1983
Edward Alan John George	1993
Mervyn Allister King	2003

US Federal Reserve chairmen

	Year appointed
Charles S. Hamlin	1914
W. P. G. Harding	1916
Daniel R. Crissinger	1923
Roy A. Young	1927
Eugene Meyer	1930
Eugene R. Black	1933
Marriner S. Eccles	1934
Thomas B. McCabe	1948
Wm McC Martin, Jr	1951
Arthur F. Burns	1970
G. William Miller	1978
Paul A. Volcker	1979
Alan Greenspan	1987
Ben S. Bernanke	2006

European Central Bank presidents

	Year appointed
Willem F. Duisenberg	1998
Jean-Claude Trichet	2003

Bank of Japan presidents

	Year appointed
Tatsuo Yamamoto	1898
Baron Shigeyoshi Matsuo	1903
Korekiyo Takahashi	1911
Viscount Yataro Mishima	1913
Junnosuke Inoue	1919
Otohiko Ichiki	1923
Junnosuke Inoue	1927
Hisaakira Hijikata	1928
Eigo Fukai	1935
Seihin Ikeda	1937
Toyotaro Yuki	1937
Viscount Keizo Shibusawa	1944
Eikichi Araki	1945
Hisato Ichimada	1946
Eikichi Araki	1954
Masamichi Yamagiwa	1956
Makoto Usami	1964
Tadashi Sasaki	1969
Teiichiro Morinaga	1974
Haruo Mayekawa	1979
Satoshi Sumita	1984
Yasushi Mieno	1989
Yasuo Matsushita	1994
Masaru Hayami	1998
Toshihiko Fukui	2003
Masaaki Shirakawa	2008

Sources: Central banks

Quotable quotations

◾ Business is really more agreeable than pleasure; it interests the whole mind ... more deeply. But it does not look as if it did.
Walter Bagehot, English journalist and author and early editor of *The Economist*

◾ We don't have a monopoly. We have market share. There's a difference.
Steve Ballmer, CEO of Microsoft

◾ Every young man would do well to remember that all successful business stands on the foundation of morality.
Henry Ward Beecher, 19th century American theologian

◾ Failing organisations are usually over-managed and under-led.
Warren G. Bennis, management theorist

◾ A brand for a company is like a reputation for a person. You earn reputation by trying to do hard things well.
Jeff Bezos, founder of Amazon

◾ The gambling known as business looks with austere disfavour upon the business known as gambling.
Ambrose Bierce, American satirist

◾ Corporation: An ingenious device for obtaining profit without individual responsibility.
Ambrose Bierce

◾ "Why" and "How" are words so important that they cannot be too often used.
Napoleon Bonaparte, French military and political leader, crowned emperor in 1804

◾ If you can run one business well, you can run any business well.
Sir Richard Branson, founder of Virgin group

The market, like the Lord, helps those who help themselves. But unlike the Lord, the market does not forgive those who know not what they do.

Warren Buffett, American investor

I don't try to jump over seven-foot bars. I look for one-foot bars that I can step over.

Warren Buffett

Wide diversification is only required when investors do not understand what they are doing.

Warren Buffett

In the search for companies to acquire we adopt the same attitude one might find appropriate in looking for a spouse: it pays to be active, interested and open minded, but it does not pay to be in a hurry.

Warren Buffett

To open a shop is easy, to keep it open is an art.

Chinese proverb

Be not afraid of going slowly, but only afraid of standing still.

Chinese proverb

Some regard private enterprise as if it were a predatory tiger to be shot. Others look upon it as a cow that they can milk. Only a handful see it for what it really is – the strong horse that pulls the whole cart.

Winston Churchill, British statesman

The chief business of the American people is business.

Calvin Coolidge, former American president

You can buy a person's hands but you can't buy his heart. His heart is where his enthusiasm, his loyalty is.

Stephen Covey, business writer and consultant

The way to get started is to quit talking and begin doing.

Walt Disney, founder of the Walt Disney Company

quotable quotations *continued*

Wherever you see a successful business, someone once made a courageous decision.

Peter Drucker, American management theorist

Most of what we call management consists of making it difficult for people to get their work done.

Peter Drucker

The fewer data needed, the better the information. And an overload of information, that is, anything much beyond what is truly needed, leads to information blackout. It does not enrich, but impoverishes.

Peter Drucker

There is an enormous number of managers who have retired on the job.

Peter Drucker

The measure of success is not whether you have a tough problem to deal with, but whether it's the same problem you had last year.

John Foster Dulles, US Secretary of State under President Eisenhower

The movie business has always been like the wild-catting oil business. Everyone wants a gusher.

Michael Eisner, former head of Walt Disney

Try not to become a man of success, but rather try to become a man of value.

Albert Einstein

When you innovate, you've got to be prepared for everyone telling you you're nuts.

Larry Ellison, CEO of Oracle

Ask five economists and you'll get five different answers – six if one went to Harvard.

Edgar Fiedler, economist

▨ Once I began following my own instincts, sales took off and I became a millionaire. And that, I think, is a key secret to every person's success, be they male or female, banker or pornographer: trust in your gut.

Larry Flynt, pioneering American pornographer

▨ The best vision is insight.

Malcolm S. Forbes, publisher of Forbes, which was founded by his father

▨ A business that makes nothing but money is a poor business.

Henry Ford, American carmaker

▨ Failure is simply the opportunity to begin again, this time more intelligently.

Henry Ford

▨ When everything seems to be going against you, remember that the airplane takes off against the wind, not with it.

Henry Ford

▨ A bank is a place where they lend you an umbrella in fair weather and ask for it back when it begins to rain.

Robert Frost, American poet

▨ By working faithfully eight hours a day you may eventually get to be boss and work twelve hours a day.

Robert Frost

▨ It is difficult, but not impossible, to conduct strictly honest business.

Mahatma Gandhi, political and spiritual leader

▨ Your most unhappy customers are your greatest source of learning.

Bill Gates, founder of Microsoft

▨ In this business, by the time you realise you're in trouble, it's too late to save yourself. Unless you're running scared all the time, you're gone.

Bill Gates

quotable quotations *continued*

▨ The difference between tax avoidance and tax evasion is the thickness of a prison wall.

Denis Healey, British politician

▨ Success is 99% failure.

Soichiro Honda, founder of Honda

▨ In the end, all business operations can be reduced to three words: people, product and profits. Unless you've got a good team, you can't do much with the other two.

Lee Iacocca, former CEO of Chrysler

▨ The most successful businessman is the man who holds onto the old just as long as it is good, and grabs the new just as soon as it is better.

Lee Iacocca

▨ Sometimes when you innovate, you make mistakes. It is best to admit them quickly, and get on with improving your other innovations.

Steve Jobs, founder of Apple Computer

▨ More business is lost every year through neglect than through any other cause.

Rose Kennedy, mother of President John F. Kennedy

▨ Markets can remain irrational longer than you can remain solvent.

John Maynard Keynes, economist

▨ Never be frightened to take a profit. Better in your pocket than theirs.

Michael Levy, American author

▨ Business, more than any other occupation, is a continual dealing with the future; it is a continual calculation, an instinctive exercise in foresight.

Henry Luce, American publisher

▦ There are four things that hold back human progress: ignorance, stupidity, committees and accountants.

Sir Charles Lyall, British Orientalist and civil servant

▦ If you know why you bought a stock in the first place, you'll automatically have a better idea of when to say goodbye to it.

Peter Lynch, American investor

▦ Business is a combination of war and sport.

Andre Maurois, French author

▦ The buck stops with the guy who signs the cheques.

Rupert Murdoch, Australian-born media magnate

▦ The world is changing very fast. Big will not beat small anymore. It will be the fast beating the slow.

Rupert Murdoch

▦ Management cannot be expected to recognise a good idea unless it is presented to them by a good salesman.

David Ogilvy, advertising executive

▦ The secret of business is to know something that nobody else knows.

Aristotle Onassis, Greek shipping tycoon

▦ We don't have as many managers as we should but we would rather have too few than too many.

Larry Page, co-founder of Google

▦ I am grateful for all my problems. I became stronger and more able to meet those that were still to come.

J.C. Penney, American retail pioneer

▦ An economist is an expert who will know tomorrow why the things he predicted yesterday didn't happen today.

Laurence Peter, Canadian academic and humourist

▦ Almost all quality improvement comes via simplification of design, manufacturing, layout, processes, and procedures.

Tom Peters, management guru

quotable quotations *continued*

There is no such thing as a minor lapse of integrity.

Tom Peters

The beginning is the most important part of the work.

Plato, Greek philosopher

A friendship founded on business is a good deal better than a business founded on friendship.

John D. Rockefeller, American oilman

Good management consists in showing average people how to do the work of superior people.

John D. Rockefeller

The secret of success is to get up early, work late and strike oil.

John D. Rockefeller

If advertisers spent the same amount of money on improving their products as they do on advertising then they wouldn't have to advertise them.

Will Rogers, American humourist

The best executive is the one who has sense enough to pick good men to do what he wants done, and self-restraint to keep from meddling with them while they do it.

Theodore Roosevelt, president of the United States, 1901–09

It's a very sobering feeling to be up in space and realise that one's safety factor was determined by the lowest bidder on a government contract.

Alan Shepherd, American astronaut

The work of the individual still remains the spark that moves mankind ahead even more than teamwork.

Igor Sikorsky, Russian-born aviation pioneer

If you don't do it excellently, don't do it at all. Because

if it's not excellent, it won't be profitable or fun, and if you're not in business for fun or profit, what the hell are you doing there?

Robert Townsend, American businessman

Sometimes your best investments are the ones you don't make.

Donald Trump, American businessman

My son is now an "entrepreneur". That's what you're called when you don't have a job.

Ted Turner, founder of CNN

Do something. Either lead, follow or get out of the way.

Ted Turner

There is only one boss. The customer. And he can fire everybody in the company from the chairman on down, simply by spending his money somewhere else.

Sam Walton, founder of Wal-Mart

High expectations are the key to everything.

Sam Walton

Making money is art and working is art and good business is the best art.

Andy Warhol, artist

An organisation's ability to learn, and translate that learning into action rapidly, is the ultimate competitive advantage.

Jack Welch, former CEO of GE

My main job was developing talent. I was a gardener providing water and other nourishment to our top 750 people. Of course, I had to pull out some weeds, too.

Jack Welch

In modern business it is not the crook who is to be feared most, it is the honest man who doesn't know what he is doing.

William Wordsworth, English poet

Bad boys

Conrad Black was expelled from school in Canada in the late 1950s for selling exam papers to his fellow students. Ten years later he bought his first newspaper with his business partner, David Radler, and by the mid-1980s Hollinger, his publishing business, owned over 100 newspapers around the world including Britain's *Daily Telegraph*, the *Chicago Sun-Times* and the *Jerusalem Post*. By the end of the 1990s Mr Black's business sense convinced him that the arrival of the internet meant that newspapers faced a bleak future and he began to sell off the local newspaper groups that were the backbone of Hollinger's business. But during these deals Black (who became Lord Black in 2001, after renouncing his Canadian citizenship) siphoned millions from the company with a scheme in which payments were disguised as "non-competition fees". In 2003 investors started asking questions and subsequent investigations led to criminal charges in America. During his trial it emerged that he and his wife lived the high life, partly at shareholders' expense, in several homes dotted around the world and enjoyed the company of billionaires, celebrities and leading politicians. In December 2007 Lord Black was convicted of fraud and sentenced to six-and-a-half years in prison, from where he continues to protest his innocence.

Ivan Boesky, an American arbitrageur, coined the phrase "greed is good" that symbolised the ethos of many of those working in the financial markets during the 1980s. Mr Boesky made his cash betting on corporate takeovers but he did not rely on luck and judgment alone. He was convicted of insider dealing, a crime often overlooked in those freewheeling days on Wall Street, yet the blatancy of his actions earned him three-and-a-half years in prison and a fine of $100m even after plea bargaining and informing on many of his sources.

Alan Bond emigrated to Australia from Britain in 1950 beginning his career as a signwriter. He built up the Perth-based Bond Corporation making a fortune in property development before branching out into brewing, gold mining and television. In 1983 he made himself a national hero by financing Australia's successful attempt to wrest the America's Cup yachting trophy from America, which had held it since 1851. Mr Bond used his considerable fortune to buy significant artworks but in 1987, after buying Van Gogh's "Irises" for $54 million, using a loan from Sotheby's, an auctioneer, things began to go wrong. He refused to repay the loan and a stockmarket crash exposed the weakness of his businesses and led to bankruptcy and disgrace. In 1996 he was sentenced to three years for fraud for selling a Manet painting owned by the Bond Corporation to a family firm for well below market value. In 1997 he got seven years for diverting cash from a public company he ran to prop up another family business. In prison he took up art.

Bernie Cornfeld, a social worker turned mutual-fund salesman, decided to start his own operation in the 1960s. Investors Overseas Services (IOS) was based in Geneva to escape regulation and targeted ex-pat Americans seeking to avoid income tax, although about half of his investors were German, also lured by his pitch – "Do you seriously want to be rich?". After ten years, IOS had raised $2.5 billion and had 1m shareholders. IOS, in effect a glorified Ponzi scheme (see Charles Ponzi below), collapsed in 1970. Cornfeld spent 11 months in a Swiss jail before fraud charges were finally dropped.

Bernie Ebbers, a cowboy-hat and boot wearing businessman and former night-club bouncer, built WorldCom from modest beginnings into a telecoms firm worth over $175 billion at the height of the stockmarket boom by relentlessly acquiring assets. In 1998, he masterminded a $37 billion merger with MCI, one of America's leading long-distance phone companies. But as the dotcom boom ran out of steam, WorldCom resorted to

bad boys _continued_

accounting tricks to maintain the appearance of ever-growing profitability. The fraud failed to keep the company afloat. In April 2002, Mr Ebbers was forced to step down as chief executive and later the firm admitted an $11 billion accounting fraud, resulting in America's biggest-ever bankruptcy. In 2004, Mr Ebbers was found guilty of fraud, conspiracy and filing false documents with regulators, and was sentenced in July 2005 to 25 years in jail.

Enron became one of the world's largest energy firms by trading electricity and natural gas. It had stakes in nearly 30,000 miles of gas pipeline and a 15,000-mile fibre-optic cable network. In 1999, it launched a plan to buy and sell access to high-speed internet bandwidth as well as EnronOnline, a web-based commodity-trading site, making it an e-commerce company. The company reported revenues of $101 billion in 2000 and its stock hit a record high of $90. But in October 2001 Enron reported a $638m third-quarter loss and admitted that the Securities and Exchange Commission had launched a formal investigation into a possible conflict of interest related to the company's dealings with its partners. The next month Enron revised its financial statements for the past five years to account for further losses. Enron shares plunged below $1 and in December it filed for bankruptcy protection. A congressional investigation later concluded that Enron had set up an array of dizzyingly complex schemes to hoodwink the Internal Revenue Service and enrich its executives through tricky accounting off-balance-sheet deals and tax avoidance scams. Enron management created a virtual company with virtual profits. Sixteen former Enron executives have pleaded guilty to various crimes. Andrew Fastow pleaded guilty to fraud and agreed to co-operate with prosecutors in return for a ten-year sentence. In December 2005, Richard

Causey, the firm's former chief accounting officer, pleaded guilty to securities fraud. But for prosecutors the greatest prize was the conviction of Jeffey Skilling and Kenneth Lay, the firm's two top bosses, in May 2006 after a 16-week trial. Mr Lay was found guilty of six counts of conspiracy and fraud, and Mr Skilling was found guilty on 18 counts but was acquitted on all but one charge of insider trading. In a separate trial in front of the judge, Mr Lay was also found guilty of bank fraud. Both faced very long sentences but Mr Lay died in July 2006 before sentence had been passed.

Martin Frankel, an American money manager, was arrested in Germany in 1999 after an international manhunt. He was reportedly in possession of nine fake passports, 547 diamonds, an astrological chart drawn up to answer the question "Will I go to prison?" and a to-do list that included "launder money". In 2002, Mr Frankel pleaded guilty to 24 federal corruption charges for defrauding more than $200m from insurance companies in the southern United States. His technique was to buy small insurance firms and help himself to their assets in order to fund his lavish lifestyle. He was sentenced to 17 years in prison in 2004.

Yasuo Hanamaka became known as "Mr Five Percent" for the slice of the copper market he was said to control. But in 1996 the firm he worked for, Japan's Sumitomo Corporation, caused the copper market to tumble by revealing that Mr Hanamaka had lost $2.6 billion in his attempt to manipulate the copper price in order to reap big profits. Mr Hanamaka insisted that his activities were intended to recover losses for the bank rather than for personal gain. Nevertheless, Mr Hanamaka admitted forgery and fraud and was sentenced to eight years in prison.

Kim Woo Choong, founder of South Korea's Daewoo, was held in high esteem for building his small textile-trading house into one of the country's largest industrial

bad boys *continued*

conglomerates. The business reached from automobiles and electronics to financial services and construction. After the Asian financial crisis of 1997, the firm struggled to repay huge sums borrowed to finance expansion and the group collapsed in 1999 with debts of some $70 billion. After seven of Mr Kim's top aides were arrested on charges of fraud and embezzlement, Mr Kim went on the run. He is thought to have nipped between Europe and Africa to avoid prosecution on similar charges of running a massive accounting fraud to prop up his ailing business. Mr Kim returned to South Korea in 2005 to face justice. The 69-year-old was found guilty of embezzlement and accounting fraud. He was ordered to hand back around $22 billion and sentenced to ten years in prison.

Toshihide Iguchi, a senior employee at Daiwa Bank's New York office, sent the bank's president a 30-page letter which he received on July 13th 1995. It took the form of a confession that Mr Iguchi had lost $1.1 billion of the bank's money over an 11-year period while trading American Treasury bonds. Mr Iguchi admitted forging over 30,000 trades and covering up his losses by selling securities belonging to the banks and its customers. Daiwa in turn covered up Mr Iguchi's dealings for several months, only alerting American regulators in September. Mr Iguchi was sentenced to four years in prison and fined $2.6m. Daiwa's reputation was badly damaged, it was fined $340m and booted out of America for its role in covering up Mr Iguchi's losses. And in September 2000 a Japanese court ruled that 11 board members and executives should pay the bank $775m in damages over the affair.

Jérôme Kerviel, a junior trader at Société Générale, turned out to be the "financial terrorist" responsible for a large loss at the French bank. In January 2008 the bank said it had fallen victim to unauthorised trading that had led to losses of €4.9 billion. Mr Kerviel had started his career in the "back-room", where trades are processed, and used his knowledge of the bank's computer system to bypass internal controls and set up an elaborate web of risky and fictitious trades. At one point his total exposure is said to have topped €50 billion, far more than the bank's market value. He claimed that he was just trying to make money for his employer. The ungrateful bank, characterising Mr Kerviel as an IT genius, brought charges of forgery and breaking into computer systems. Mr Kerviel, while awaiting trial, took a job with an IT firm specialising in network security.

Dennis Kozlowski built Tyco, an obscure New England electronics-maker, into one of America's biggest conglomerates through an audacious series of mergers and acquisitions after assuming the role of chief executive in 1992. Mr Kozlowski led an extravagant life but the cash that paid for it was ill-gotten. Mr Kozlowski and Mark Swartz, Tyco's former finance chief, were accused of looting $600m from the firm through fraudulent share sales and unauthorised compensation. Their first court appearance ended in a mistrial after the only juror pressing for acquittal complained that she felt threatened. However, many examples of the misuse of Tyco's money emerged: $2m birthday party for Mr Kozlowski's wife in Sardinia featuring an ice sculpture of Michelangelo's David dispensing vodka; a lavish $18m Manhattan apartment; a $6,000 shower curtain and jewellery, flowers, clothing and wine. After a second trial in June 2005 both men were found guilty and were sentenced to up to 25 years in jail.

Ivar Kreuger, "the Swedish match king", gained monopolies for match production in many countries after the first world war. He then set up the International Match Corporation in America, which went on to control two-thirds of world match production. But his business began to fail after the Wall Street crash of 1929 and he hit a

bad boys *continued*

liquidity crisis. He was found dead in a hotel room in Paris in 1932 having seemingly shot himself. After his death, it was discovered that, through false accounting, American investors had been fleeced of millions of dollars.

Nick Leeson worked for Barings, a respectable and long-established bank based in the City of London. His work, trading futures on the Singapore Monetary Exchange, led to big losses when bets on the future direction of the Japanese stockmarket went spectacularly wrong after the Kobe earthquake of 1995 sent Asian markets plummeting. He kept the losses hidden from his superiors and made a series of increasingly risky investments in an effort to recoup the cash. These failed, and when his losses hit $1.4 billion Mr Leeson went on the run. He was apprehended in Germany and sent back to Singapore where he was sentenced to six-and-a-half years in prison. Barings collapsed and was bought by ING, a Dutch insurance giant, for the nominal sum of £1.

Liu Qibing, a Chinese metal trader thought to be working for the Chinese State Reserve Bureau, disappeared in 2005 after making large bets that copper prices were going to fall just before they rose steeply. He is reckoned to have amassed losses of anything between $200m and $1 billion. However, his Chinese employer denied Mr Liu's existence even though traders on the London Metals Exchange knew him well as an important player in the copper market. His current whereabouts are unknown.

Bernard Madoff, a pillar of the New York investment community, was finally undone by the financial crisis that led from the credit crunch that began in 2007. This distinguished, kindly looking old gent ran an investment business that, in retrospect, offered oddly stable, though hardly spectacular, returns. The business turned out to be a giant Ponzi scheme that paid out long-standing clients with money provided by new investors. Mr Madoff was arrested in December 2008 after admitting to his two sons that his empire was a sham. He is reckoned to have swindled investors, many of them wealthy socialites and Jewish charities, out of $65 billion in an operation that a judge described as "extraordinarily evil" before handing down a prison sentence of 150 years. For years some analysts had questioned Mr Madoff's ability to generate such dependable returns. But he had cleverly convinced investors that they belonged to an exclusive club while employing a tiny audit firm which prosecutors say "rubber stamped" the accounts.

Robert Maxwell was born Jan Ludwik Hoch in Czechoslovakia in 1923. He fled the Nazis in 1939 and fought with the British during the second world war, calling himself du Maurier, after a brand of classy cigarettes. After the war he came to Britain and changed his name to Maxwell. In 1951 he purchased Pergamon Press, publisher of textbooks and scientific journals, and published a lot of material from communist eastern Europe, where he developed good connections. In 1964 he became a Labour member of parliament, but a financial scandal put an end to his political career five years later. However, in 1974 the "bouncing Czech" repurchased Pergamon, over which he had lost control, and during the 1980s he built up a substantial publishing empire, which included Macmillan, a big US publisher, and Britain's Mirror Group Newspapers. As the 1980s progressed, Maxwell's financial machinations began to catch up with him. In 1991 it was reported that Maxwell had disappeared from his luxury motor yacht off the Canary Islands and not long after his body was found floating some distance away. After he was buried on the Mount of Olives overlooking Jerusalem, it emerged that he had looted £400m from the Mirror Group's pension fund to prop up his other business interests. Did he jump or was he pushed? Some claim that Mossad agents were

bad boys *continued*

behind his death. It is more likely, however, that he knew the game was finally up and couldn't face the consequences.

Michael Milken, the "junk bond king" of Wall Street, financed a slew of corporate takeovers in the 1980s through the pioneering use of high-yield high-risk bonds, making vast sums for himself and his employer, Drexel Burnham Lambert, in the process. He and co-conspirators constructed a web of deceitful transactions that led to 98 charges of racketeering, insider trading and securities fraud, and in 1989 he was sentenced to ten years in prison for securities fraud – "the greatest criminal conspiracy the financial world has ever known". In 1991 his sentence was reduced to two years in prison and three years' probation. In 1998 he settled with the government, paying $42m plus interest. Since then Mr Milken has devoted much of his time and money to charity work.

Asil Nadir, the former boss of Polly Peck International, a British-based conglomerate that included an electronics business and the Del Monte fruit business acquired through a series of audacious acquisitions, fled to northern Cyprus to take advantage of its lack of an extradition treaty with Britain (which does not recognise the territory) after the firm collapsed with previously concealed debts of over £1 billion. The businessman, who had made generous donations to Britain's Conservative Party (to its subsequent embarrassment), was facing 66 charges of theft amounting to £34m but fled by private jet in 1993, shortly before he was due to stand trial. He still lives in northern Cyprus with the hope that one day he will be able to cut a deal that will allow him to return to Britain.

Charles Ponzi was born in Italy and moved to America in 1903, taking a series of menial jobs before launching a scheme in 1919 that promised to double investors' money in 90 days. By 1920 he had taken millions of dollars by paying former investors with later deposits, thus requiring ever greater numbers of dupes to join the scam. The business collapsed only after 40,000 people had handed over some $15m. Despite a wrangle over jurisdiction, Ponzi got five years in federal prison for mail fraud and was later sentenced to seven to nine years in Massachusetts. He jumped bail and started up a new scheme in Florida based on selling land. This collapsed and he received another year in jail, and was sent back to Boston to serve his former sentence. Ponzi died in poverty in Rio de Janeiro in 1949 but his legacy is the pyramid-selling schemes that still bear his name.

John Rusnak seemed an unlikely "rogue trader". Employed as a lowly foreign-exchange dealer in 1993 by Allfirst, a Baltimore-based subsidiary of Allied Irish Bank, he was the epitome of church-going middle-American solidity. But in 2002 routine checks by the bank uncovered losses of $691m run up by Mr Rusnak over several years as a result of betting that the yen would rise against the dollar. At one time he is reckoned to have made gambles worth $7.5 billion without hedging the trades (customary in these sort of transactions) and despite a trading limit of $2.5m. But a swift 10% appreciation by the dollar uncovered his deception. After plea bargaining he got a seven-and-a-half-year prison sentence and was ordered to pay back all the losses (though how much of his debt he has repaid so far is unclear).

Eliot Spitzer made his name as attorney-general of New York state by relentlessly pursuing Wall Street's wrong-doers. He battled against New York's powerful financiers, holding them to the highest of ethical standards and earned a reputation for zealously unearthing wrong-doers. *Time* even anointed him "Crusader of the Year" in 2002, after his landmark settlement with securities firms accused of misleading investors. It was this image that

bad boys *continued*

convinced voters to elect Mr Spitzer as governor of New York in 2006 with a sweeping mandate to clean up state affairs. But in March 2008, in investigations of a high-class prostitution ring, it emerged that Mr Spitzer was caught arranging a rendezvous at a swanky hotel in Washington, DC, with a prostitute from Emperors Club VIP, and this was not the first time he had used the club's services. He had little option but to stand down, since when he has been a model of contrition.

Allen Stanford's financial empire had its roots in a Houston property business in the 1980s, but for the 15 years until his arrest in 2009 he lived in the Caribbean and even received a knighthood from the government of Antigua, where Stanford International Bank was based. This brash Texan financier's flamboyance knew no bounds – stretching to millions of dollars spent in promoting the traditional sport of cricket. In early 2009 Mr Stanford came under investigation for fraud and in February was charged by America's Securities and Exchange Commission of fraud of "shocking magnitude". He was accused of running a $7 billion Ponzi scheme using investors' funds from certificates of deposit issued by his bank. In June criminal charges followed.

Yoshiaki Tsutsumi was briefly adjudged the world's richest man at the height of Japan's property boom in the late 1980s, having inherited a real estate business from his father who was once said to have owned a sixth of all the land in Japan. But in 2005 Mr Tsutsumi, one of Japan's best-known businessmen, was arrested on suspicion of falsifying shareholder information and selling shares based on the false data. He pleaded guilty and was given a suspended jail sentence and a fine of 5m yen (about $42,000).

Robert Vesco got involved with Bernie Cornfeld's IOS (see above) as a "white knight" to save the foundering fund. He was later accused of looting the company of $224m and fled to Costa Rica after making large illegal contributions to Richard Nixon's re-election campaign. He was charged *in absentia* with theft (and drug smuggling, for good measure). In 1996, Mr Vesco was sentenced to 13 years in prison in Cuba on charges of producing and marketing a miracle cancer cure to overseas investors without the communist government's knowledge.

David Wittig made his fortune on Wall Street before returning to the state of his birth, Kansas, in 1995 as an executive of Westar Energy. He swiftly rose to become chief executive of the utility company and set about establishing himself as a leading member of Topeka's social elite by organising lavish charity events and even buying and renovating at great expense the former governor's mansion. However, in 2002 Mr Wittig and Douglas Lake, a senior executive at Westar, resigned amid accusations that they had systematically looted the company for personal gain and used the corporate jet for personal trips. The case, known as the "Enron of Kansas", came to court at the end of 2003 but ended in a mistrial. After another trial in 2004 the two men were found guilty of conspiracy, wire fraud and money laundering. Mr Wittig was sentenced to 18 years in jail; Mr Lake to 15 years. Each was ordered to pay $5m in fines plus over $53m to Westar.

Leading management thinkers

Warren Bennis

A laid-back, silver-haired professor at the University of Southern California who has been a hugely influential authority on leadership for decades, consulted by many of the world's most famous leaders, including at least four American presidents. Bennis's fundamental tenet is that leaders are made, not born. In organisations, he believes they should not merely be the best manager around. Being a manager is very different from being a leader. "Managers do things right. Leaders do the right thing," is probably Bennis's most famous quotation.

Managers, however, can learn to be leaders. "I believe in 'possible selves'," Bennis has written, "the capacity to adapt and change." To become good leaders, people first have to develop as individuals. Among other things, that involves learning not to be afraid of being seen to be vulnerable. Leadership qualities, he maintains, can only emerge from an "integrated self".

Bennis was greatly influenced by Douglas McGregor (see below) and Theory X and Y. In the late 1960s he tried to run the college where he was provost along the lines of Theory Y. But he found in practice that leaving staff to be entirely self-motivated did not work very well. Many people need more structure and direction than McGregor's scheme allowed.

Howard Schultz, the founder and chairman of Starbucks, says that Bennis once told him that in order to become a great leader you have to develop "your ability to leave your own ego at the door, and to recognise the skills and traits that you need in order to build a world-class organisation".

Marvin Bower

For many years the management-consulting business was dominated by one firm. It advised the world's biggest corporations, and indeed the world's biggest countries, about high-level strategy. So outstanding was the firm that it became known simply as "The Firm".

That firm, McKinsey, was the creation of one man. Not James McKinsey, the man whose name hangs over its front door (and who died young of pneumonia in 1937), but Marvin Bower, the most powerful influence on the firm in the 65 years from McKinsey's death to Bower's own, at the age of 99, in 2003.

Bower modelled the consultancy along the lines of a professional law firm. It was driven by a set of values – for example, its clients' interests came before growth in revenue. "If you looked after the client, the profits would look after themselves," Bower wrote in his 1966 book *The Will to Manage*. But he was not afraid to confront clients. One colleague has recalled an occasion when Bower "bellowed out, 'The problem with this company, Mr Little, is you.' And there was a deathly silence. It happened to be totally accurate. That was the end of our work with that client, but it didn't bother Marvin."

Nowadays The Firm's consultants advise top-flight managers, and are sometimes criticised for not being around to follow through the consequences of their advice. They have a reputation for arrogance. *The Economist* once wrote of one of them: "He suffers the lack of self-doubt common in former McKinsey consultants." Some of them, such as Tom Peters and Kenichi Ohmae, have gone on to become gurus in their own right.

The Firm relies heavily on fresh graduates with MBAs or good degrees from top universities to churn numbers and do the analysis of its clients' problems. These are fed into the "teams" that are put together for each project. The graduates stay only for as long as they continue to progress

leading management thinkers *continued*

up the hierarchy. If they stick for too long at one level they are asked to leave. The Firm's policy is "up or out".

Jim Collins

A former professor at Stanford Business School who found himself with a publishing sensation when he expanded his Stanford research about what it takes to make companies endure into a book. *Built to Last*, published in 1994, allowed Collins to retire from teaching.

Collins excels at the American method of empirical business research. He gathers masses of data about a group that he wishes to study (in this case, enduringly excellent companies); then he compares it with a "carefully selected" control group that is not enduringly excellent, and sees what are the statistically significant differences. It is a method that takes time to bear fruit, and Collins says that *Built to Last* took six years of research.

His second book, *Good to Great* (2001), has become the best-selling business book of all time, overtaking the long-standing holder of that title, *In Search of Excellence*. Written after Collins had left Stanford, it took five years of research by 21 assistants at his own "management laboratory" in Boulder, Colorado, near the mountains that he loves to climb. Although Collins can command the highest fees on the business lecture circuit, he prefers to stay close to Boulder.

In one sense, Collins took Tom Peters and Robert Waterman's concept of excellence, and what it is to be an excellent company, and stretched it over time. What does it take to be an excellent company decade after decade?

On his website Collins talks of a professor he knew who walked into his first class and wrote on the board: "The best students are those who never quite believe their professors." What then are we to make of Professor Collins's findings?

W. Edwards Deming

Deming was a statistician who applied the ideas about variance of a little-known American mathematician, Walter Shewhart, to business processes – and with dramatic effect in terms of quality and productivity. The surprising thing was that he did it not in his native America, but in Japan. To this day Japanese industry awards a prestigious annual prize (called the Deming Prize) to companies that have demonstrated exceptional improvements in quality.

After the second world war Deming was sent to Japan to advise on a census taking place there. He ended up advising Japanese businessmen how to inject quality into their manufacturing industry, which at the time had a reputation around the world for producing shoddy goods. His secret was to demonstrate that all business processes are vulnerable to a loss of quality through variation. Reduce the variation; increase the quality. Deming once said: "If I had to reduce my message for management to a few words, I'd say it all had to do with reducing variation."

Deming's method of bringing this about was built on what became known as the quality circle (or, in Japan, the Deming circle). This is a group of workers who seek to improve the processes they are responsible for in four stages – through planning how to do it; implementing the plan; checking the variance from anticipated outcomes; and taking action to correct it. Spreading this system throughout an organisation has come to be known as TQM (Total Quality Management), and has been adopted in America as widely as in Japan.

leading management thinkers *continued*

Peter Drucker

The most enduring and one of the most endearing gurus of them all. From his 1946 book, *The Concept of the Corporation*, based on his wartime experience as a consultant with General Motors, to his 2004 article ("What Makes an Effective Executive?") – which won the McKinsey prize for the best article to appear in the *Harvard Business Review* that year – Peter Drucker never failed to throw light on the tasks and difficulties of management.

Born in Austria before the first world war, Drucker moved to England in the late 1920s and thence to America in 1937, where he died in 2005. His academic career did not begin until after the second world war. His interests subsequently were eclectic, and he invented a quiver of management theories – "management by objectives"; decentralisation; and "structure follows strategy". He coined the phrase "knowledge worker" in 1969. But his focus was always on the practical – how to make businesses and their managers perform more effectively.

However, Drucker always set this pragmatic task in a much broader context, and therein lay his enduring appeal. Rosabeth Moss Kanter, a Harvard academic, once wrote: "In the Drucker perspective ... quality of life, technological progress and world peace are all the products of good management ... at root, Drucker is a management Utopian, descended as much from Robert Owen as Max Weber."

Drucker thought of himself as a loner, as someone outside the mainstream of management education. "I work best outside," he once said. "That's where I'm most effective. I would be a very poor manager. Hopeless. And a company job would bore me to death."

Henri Fayol

While American manufacturing processes were being revolutionised by Taylorism (see below), France's were being overturned by Fayolism. This was a method devised by an engineer, Henri Fayol, who rescued a troubled mining company at the end of the 19th century and turned it into one of France's most successful businesses. Fayol's theory was in stark contrast to Frederick Taylor's. He looked for general management principles that could be applied to a wide range of organisations – business, financial or even government – and he separated the tasks of management into four categories – planning, organisation, co-ordination, command and control. His method became known particularly for the last two, "command and control".

He was a great believer in the value of specialisation and of the unity of command: that each employee should be answerable to only one person.

Fayol remained virtually unknown outside his native France until a quarter of a century after his death (in 1949) when his most important work *General and Industrial Management* – first published in French in 1916 – was finally translated into English. He then became extraordinarily influential as the founding father of what became known as the Administration School of Management. As recently as 1993 he was listed in one poll as the most popular management writer of all time.

Sumantra Ghoshal

A soft-spoken physicist from Calcutta, Ghoshal began his career at Indian Oil and came to management studies with a solid grounding in corporate life. After doctorates at Harvard and MIT, he worked at INSEAD and the London Business School before dying at the age of 55 in 2004.

Ghoshal's influence far exceeded his written output. He

leading management thinkers *continued*

first made his mark in a seminal critique of the widely used matrix form of organisational structure in which managers report in two directions – along both functional and geographic lines. Written in 1990 with his closest collaborator, Christopher Bartlett, the article argued that this dual reporting leads to "conflict and confusion". In large multinationals, "separated by barriers of distance, language, time and culture, managers found it virtually impossible to clarify the confusion and resolve the conflicts".

Bartlett and Ghoshal argued that companies need to alter their organisational psychology (the shared norms and beliefs) and their physiology (the systems that allow information to flow around the organisation) before they start to redesign their anatomy (the reporting lines). Their work set off a search for new metaphors for organisational structures – borrowing in particular from psychology and biology (eg, corporate DNA; the left brain of the organisation).

Shortly before he died, Ghoshal wrote one of his most contentious papers in which he suggested that much of the blame for corporate corruption in the early 2000s could be laid at the feet of business schools and the way they try to teach management as a science. Their method, he argued, leaves no room for morality – a point of view shared by Henry Mintzberg and Warren Bennis, among others.

Gary Hamel

Hamel is perhaps best known for the idea of core competence, a phrase that has spread far beyond the management lexicon. He propounded the idea in a 1990 paper written with an Indian academic, C.K. Prahalad. "Core competencies," they wrote, "are the collective learning in the organisation, especially how to coordinate diverse production skills and integrate multiple streams of technologies" – in short, they are the things an organisation does particularly well. The idea dovetailed with the phenomenon of outsourcing, whereby companies handed over to others the processes and operations (such as IT or book-keeping) that were not "core" to their business, thus freeing them to concentrate on those things that they did best.

Hamel took corporate strategy away from the precision of traditional planning, which he saw as a calendar-driven ritual that had little to do with real strategy. He recommended that companies identify their core competencies and then reinvent themselves around that base of knowledge and skill. He saw strategy as a matter of revolution, of dramatic change. Strategic innovation, he said, will be the source of competitive advantage in the future.

The brightness of Hamel's star dimmed somewhat in the wake of the Enron collapse. Enron was a company that he had held up as an exemplar of his style of strategic innovation. He had also lauded a number of large Japanese companies whose business model stalled badly at the end of the 20th century.

Michael Hammer

Hammer was a professor of computer science at MIT who came up with the biggest business idea of the 1990s, re-engineering, which he defined as "the fundamental rethinking and radical redesign of business processes to achieve dramatic improvements in critical measures of performance".

The idea was first propounded in a 1990 *Harvard Business Review* article entitled "Re-engineering Work: Don't Automate, Obliterate". This was followed by a book, *Re-engineering the Corporation*, written with James Champy, the founder of the CSC Index consulting firm. The book sold several million copies.

leading management thinkers *continued*

Hammer marked a symbolic shift from a time when traditional mechanical engineers dominated management thinking to an era in which electronic engineers with computer skills began to play a part. Re-engineering was a sort of Taylorism updated to take account of information technology.

So popular was re-engineering that one survey in the 1990s showed it to have been adopted by almost 80% of *Fortune* 500 companies. It was often blamed for the widespread lay-offs that became a part of almost every company's radical redesign of its processes at that time.

Hammer never managed to repeat his success. He opened his own consultancy business and worked on the idea of "the process enterprise". If you really want to make re-engineering successful, he tried to argue, you need a whole new type of organisation.

Charles Handy

An Irish protestant whose broad interests spread from religion and philosophy to the organisation of the workplace. His vivid use of metaphor and accessible writing style have made his books extremely popular – with titles like *The Empty Raincoat* and *The Gods of Management* (in which he identified four different management cultures, which he likened to four Greek Gods: Apollo, Athena, Dionysus and Zeus).

Handy began his career as an employee of the Shell oil company, and was sent to work with a drilling operation in the jungles of Borneo. He later vividly described how little relation his life on the job had to the goal he had been given at headquarters: to maximise the company's return on equity. Handy's written work has almost always been a search for ways in which companies can go beyond the pure pursuit of profit. How can they be transformed into communities and soar above being mere properties to be bought and sold?

Handy's academic career began when he went to MIT's Sloan School of Management where, among others, he met Warren Bennis (see above) who, he says, has been his "godfather". On his return to the UK he helped set up London Business School in a country that then had no management education as such. The school's teaching was based around the MBA course that Handy had seen in the United States, a development that he later seemed to come to regret.

Robert Kaplan

A Harvard professor credited with coming up with two of the most influential management ideas of the late 20th century: activity-based costing (ABC) and the balanced scorecard. Both are concerned with measurement, with finding better measures of corporate performance. The first is an alternative to traditional accounting where overheads (indirect costs) are allocated in proportion to an activity's direct costs. For businesses whose goods are customised, this is not a very accurate method. ABC attempts to improve on it by allocating indirect costs more accurately. Popular for a while, ABC fell into disrepute when it became clear that it was much simpler in theory than it was in practice. It was far from being as easy as ABC.

The concept of the balanced scorecard was developed with David Norton, a consultant. It starts with the idea that existing business systems invariably mean that what you measure is what you get. If you measure only financial performance, then financial performance is the target people aim for. In the balanced scorecard things are measured from a number of different perspectives, not just the financial one, but also, for example, from the customer's perspective, from the company's own internal

leading management thinkers *continued*

perspective, and from the perspective of innovation and improvement. How can a company continue to create value in the future? The idea appealed to managers who found traditional measures of performance unduly focused on shareholders' interests.

Niccolo Machiavelli

The author of one of the most famous books on management ever written, Niccolo Machiavelli remains famous five centuries after the publication of *The Prince*, the short volume in which he outlined what a prince must do to survive and prosper, surrounded as he inevitably is by general human malevolence. Dedicated to Lorenzo de Medici – the greatest patron of Renaissance art – the book draws on examples such as Alexander the Great and the German city states, to teach its readers eternal lessons about how to stay in power. To this day, there are corporate leaders who keep a copy of *The Prince* by their bedside.

Machiavelli's tripartite division of leaders' tactics – "Some princes, in order to hold on to their states securely, have disarmed their subjects; some have kept their subject towns divided; and some have fostered animosity against themselves" – first expounded in Florence in the 1520s, has been developed in recent years into a modern theory about corporate structure.

For a long time Machiavelli's advice was considered amoral and dishonourably scheming. But in the 1860s Victor Hugo reinstated him. "Machiavelli," he wrote, "is not an evil genius, nor a cowardly writer. He is nothing but the fact … not merely the Italian fact, he is the European fact." Now we can add with some confidence: he is the global fact.

Abraham Maslow

Maslow is the most influential anthropologist ever to have worked in industry. He lived among the Blackfoot Indians of Alberta, Canada (where he "found almost the same range of personalities as I find in our society"), before becoming a professor of psychology at Brandeis University near Boston, Massachusetts.

Maslow is best known for developing the popular concept of the hierarchy of needs, a framework for thinking about human motivation. We have five different levels of need, he suggested – physiological ones (hunger, thirst and so on); safety needs (job security, risk avoidance, etc); social needs (parties, meetings, family); esteem needs (also called ego needs) such as self-respect, esteem and sense of achievement; and self-actualisation, described by Maslow as: "A musician must make music, an artist must paint, a poet must write, if he is to be ultimately happy. What a man can be, he must be. This need we may call self-actualisation."

Needs in the earlier categories have to be satisfied before needs in the higher ones can act as motivators. (Although the image of the starving poet is a recurring one, and not only in fiction.) Any single act may satisfy more than one need. We have a drink at a bar because we're thirsty and also because we want to meet friends. It was not Maslow's intention that his theory be applied to the workplace, but managers soon saw its relevance for compensation packages.

Douglas McGregor

A social psychologist by training, McGregor spent most of his relatively short life (he died in 1964 at the age of 58) as an academic at Harvard and MIT. Yet in 1993 he was listed one of the most popular management writers ever, alongside the Frenchman Henri Fayol. He had an engaging teaching style which endeared him to his students.

leading management thinkers continued

McGregor was the first effective counterweight to the mechanistic thinking of Frederick Taylor's scientific management. His most influential idea was expounded in his book *The Human Side of Enterprise*, published in 1960. In it he argued that there are two fundamentally different styles of management. One he called Theory X, an authoritarian style which maintains that management "must counteract an inherent human tendency to avoid work". The other, Theory Y, "assumes that people will exercise self-direction and self-control in the achievement of organisational objectives to the degree that they are committed to those objectives". Management's job is to maximise their commitment.

McGregor urged companies to adopt Theory Y. Only it, he believed, could motivate human beings to the highest levels of achievement. His thinking resounds in today's team-based management styles. But McGregor's bifurcated theory has been criticised (by Abraham Maslow, among others) as being tough on the weaker members of society, those who need guidance. Not everyone is sufficiently self-controlled and self-motivated to thrive in a Theory Y environment.

Shortly before he died, McGregor was developing something which he called Theory Z, where he developed answers to many of the criticisms of Theories X and Y.

Henry Mintzberg

A consistently contrary Canadian academic who sometimes seems to be undermining the very industry in which he works, Mintzberg first came to fame with a brilliant article in the *Harvard Business Review* in 1975 entitled "The Manager's Job: Folklore and Fact". He studied what a number of managers in different industrial sectors actually did, day in, day out. And he found that

"Jumping from topic to topic, he (the manager) thrives on interruptions and more often than not disposes of items in ten minutes or less. Though he may have 50 projects going, all are delegated." A sample of British managers were found to work for more than half an hour without interruption "about once every two days". They spent most of their time in oral communication. To be a good manager, Mintzberg concluded, you need to be a good listener.

In *Managers not MBAs*, published in 2004, Mintzberg argued that the MBA, the bread-and-butter course of many business schools, and the *sine qua non* of fast-track management careers, "prepares people to manage nothing". Synthesis, not analysis, he says, "is the very essence of management", and MBA courses teach only analysis. Failed leaders such as Ford's Robert McNamara and Enron's Jeffrey Skilling, who came near the top of their class at Harvard Business School, were star MBA students and brilliant analysts. That was not enough, however, to turn them into great managers or leaders. It did not help make them good listeners.

Kenichi Ohmae

The only management guru of any stature to have emerged from Japan. Trained as a nuclear physicist at MIT, Ohmae was head of McKinsey's Tokyo office when he published his most famous book, *Triad Power*, in 1985. At a time when multinational firms were busily spreading their operations around the world, he argued that they needed to be strong in all three major economic blocs – Europe, North America and the Pacific Rim, "the Triad" – if they were to compete successfully against others who were strong in those places.

Ohmae was also influential in spreading the idea that the major difference between Japanese firms and their western counterparts is their time frame. Japanese firms look to the longer-term, while western firms, driven by

leading management thinkers *continued*

the demands of their stockmarkets, are more focused on short-term profits. He argued that this short-term focus led western companies to pay too little attention to their customers.

Ohmae's interests are broad. He is an accomplished clarinettist and once stood for election as governor of the city of Tokyo. He says his main interest is "society, social systems and large corporate activities on a global scale."

Ohmae's books are full of Japanese examples and they helped familiarise western audiences with Japan's management breakthroughs – for example, the introduction of the just-in-time (JIT) system at Toyota. Ohmae tells how it came about because one worker, Taiichi Ohno, continually asked why the company needed to (expensively) stockpile vast quantities of components for its production line.

Tom Peters

Tom Peters was the co-author of what was, for over 20 years, the best-selling business book of all time. *In Search of Excellence*, written with his fellow McKinsey consultant, Robert Waterman, was first published in the United States in 1982 and sold millions of copies. Part of its success lay in capturing the zeitgeist of the times. Corporate America was feeling overwhelmed by Japan's evident superiority in manufacturing. It needed a reminder that there were still excellent businesses to be found back home.

Peters and Waterman identified 43 American companies out of the *Fortune* 500 that had consistently outperformed the average over a 20-year period. They then identified a number of features these companies had in common – including a bias for action, sticking to their knitting and staying close to their customers.

After the book was published, the two authors went their separate ways. Peters became an energetic and entertaining speaker on the business circuit, earnings tens of thousands of dollars per performance. The more retiring Waterman set up his own consultancy. They never wrote another book together although each separately wrote several. Peters's 1987 book *Thriving on Chaos* begins with the memorable line: "There are no excellent companies."

The focus of Peters's later work is the management of continuous change in a chaotic world. His books moved ever more downmarket. *Re-imagine*, published in 2003 by Dorling Kindersley, a publisher famous for its artwork, contains lots of sidebars, exclamation marks and pictures of things like frogs leaping.

Michael Porter

Michael Porter redefined the way that businessmen think about competition. He began by simplifying the notion of competitive advantage and then created a new framework for companies to think about how to achieve it.

Competitive advantage, he wrote, is "a function of either providing comparable buyer value more efficiently than competitors (low cost) or performing activities at comparable cost, but in unique ways that create more buyer value than competitors and, hence, command a premium price (differentiation)".

Porter maintained that there are five forces driving competition in business:

- existing rivalry between firms;
- the threat of a new entrant to a market;
- the threat of substitute products and services;
- the bargaining power of suppliers;
- the bargaining power of buyers.

Like many leading management thinkers, from Frederick

leading management thinkers *continued*

Taylor on, Porter trained first as an engineer. But after a doctorate in economics he became a professor at Harvard Business School – where his very own Institute for Strategy and Competitiveness is now based on the campus.

In his book *Competitive Advantage* (1985), Porter introduced the idea of the value chain, which has been highly influential in subsequent strategic thinking. He created a model in which the firm is structured as a chain of value-creating activities. The chain is divided into five main links – inbound logistics, operations, outbound logistics, marketing and sales, and services.

In his more recent work Porter has begun to apply his thinking about competition to social issues, writing about health care and corporate social responsibility, among other things. To reflect his broadening interests, he was in 2000 made a professor of Harvard University, only the fourth HBS faculty member to be so honoured.

Frederick Winslow Taylor

A true pioneer, Taylor was, in Peter Drucker's words, "the first man in history who did not take work for granted, but looked at it and studied it. His approach to work is still the basic foundation." Taylor trained as an engineer but then worked in the late 19th century as a manager at the Midvale Steel Works in Philadelphia. There he took to walking around with a stop-watch and a notepad breaking down manual tasks into a series of components and thereby measuring the workers' productivity. Out of this grew the idea of piece work.

Taylor's first book, *A Piece-Rate System*, was published in 1895. A later publication made him the author of the very first business bestseller, *The Principles of Scientific Management*, published in 1911. Its influence spread to unlikely places. Lenin at one time exhorted Soviet workers to "try out every scientific and progressive suggestion of the Taylor system". Subsequent failure to achieve Taylor-like production targets led many Soviet workers to the gulag.

Today, scientific management – sometimes called "Taylorism" – is often seen as representing the dehumanising aspect of industrialisation, a system that has no room for the nuances of human nature as it surges on to find the one best way.

Sun Tzu

The ultimate military strategist, Sun Tzu was a general who lived in China over 2,400 years ago whose victories would be no more recalled than those of many other military leaders had he not put down his thoughts in a slim tome (of a mere 25 pages of text). Called in the original Chinese, *The Military Method of Mr Sun*, today the book is better known as *The Art of War*.

The Art of War contains much wisdom of relevance today. For example, Sun Tzu asks: "Why destroy when you can win by stealth and cunning?" His fundamental strategy is a bit like that of judo: undermine your enemy by using the power of his own momentum against him.

Gary Hamel (see above) put Sun Tzu in his proper place when he wrote: "Strategy didn't start with Igor Ansoff, neither did it start with Machiavelli. It probably did not even start with Sun Tzu. Strategy is as old as human conflict." Nevertheless, *The Art of War* is still almost compulsory reading for businessmen in the east. Sun Tzu's advice to businessmen in the west would probably be: "To beat your enemies, first know their strategy – or at least where they are likely to be getting that strategy from."

Some management styles

Management by exception – the policy of only looking closely at events that deviate significantly from an expected norm; for example, a drop in more than a certain percentage in sales revenue or a payment that is more than a specified number of days overdue.

Management by objectives – used to describe a management system whereby employees agree with their managers what their objectives are to be and then track progress in moving towards those objectives with their managers.

Management by walking about – most famously demonstrated by Hewlett-Packard, a computer firm, management by walking about is a style of management that emphasises the importance of face-to-face contact.

Managerial grid – a way to classify managerial styles by plotting "concern for results" against "concern for people", each on a scale of 1–9. For example:

1,1 the impoverished style – only concerned to get the necessary work done with the minimum effort

9,1 the scientific management style – where there is a concentration on maximising efficiency

5,5 the middle of the road style – where the aim is to get reasonable results and keep people reasonably happy

9,9 the team management style – where everyone works together to get the best out of themselves and others.

The oldest stock exchanges

Exchange	City	Founding year
Amsterdam Stock Exchange	Amsterdam	1602
Paris Bourse	Paris	1724
Philadelphia Stock Exchange	Philadelphia	1790
London Stock Exchange	London	1801*
Milan Stock Exchange	Milan	1808
New York Stock Exchange	New York	1817†
Frankfurt Stock Exchange	Frankfurt	1820‡
Bolsa de Madrid	Madrid	1831
Toronto Stock Exchange	Toronto	1861
Australian Stock Exchange	Sydney	1872
Bombay Stock Exchange	Mumbai	1875
Zurich Stock Exchange	Zurich	1877
Tokyo Stock Exchange	Tokyo	1878
Chicago Stock Exchange	Chicago	1882
Pacific Stock Exchange	San Francisco	1882
Johannesburg Stock Exchange	Johannesburg	1887
Bovespa	São Paulo	1890
Hong Kong Stock Exchange	Hong Kong	1891
Cairo Stock Exchange	Cairo	1903
Istanbul Stock Exchange	Istanbul	1929**
Mercado de Valores (Merval)	Buenos Aires	1929
NASDAQ	United States	1971
Stock Exchange of Singapore	Singapore	1973

*Preceded by Jonathan's Coffee House, records beginning 1698.

†Preceded by the Buttonwood Agreement, signed 1792.

‡First share issue traded; had existed as bond exchange since late 18th century.

**Originally Istanbul Securities and Foreign Exchange Bourse.

Note: Amsterdam is not the only exchange claiming to be the oldest but it does seem to have been the first established stock exchange.

Sources: stock exchanges; www.interactivebrokers.com

Leading stockmarkets

Total market capitalisation, 2008, $bn		Total value traded, 2008, $bn	
US	11,738	US	36,467
Japan	3,220	UK	6,587
China	2,794	Japan	5,879
UK	1,852	China	5,471
France	1,492	France	3,265
Hong Kong	1,329	Germany	3,105
Russia	1,322	Spain	2,440
Germany	1,108	Canada	1,771
Canada	1,002	Hong Kong	1,626
Spain	946	Switzerland	1,505
Switzerland	863	South Korea	1,466
Australia	676	Netherlands	1,143
India	645	India	1,050
Brazil	589	Australia	1,018
Italy	521	Taiwan	944
South Korea	495	Brazil	728
South Africa	491	Italy	669
Netherlands	388	Sweden	642
Taiwan	381	Russia	562
Sweden	253	Saudi Arabia	525
Saudi Arabia	246	South Africa	401
Mexico	233	Finland	390
Malaysia	187	Norway	368
Singapore	180	Singapore	271
Belgium	167	Turkey	240
Finland	154	Denmark	213
Israel	134	Belgium	212
Chile	132	UAE	145
Denmark	132	Kuwait	123
Norway	126	Thailand	117
Turkey	118	Indonesia	111
Kuwait	107	Israel	109
Thailand	103	Mexico	108
Indonesia	99	Austria	105
UAE	98	Malaysia	85
Greece	90	Portugal	83
Poland	90	Egypt	70
Colombia	87	Poland	68
Egypt	86	Pakistan	54
Qatar	76	Qatar	48

Source: Standard & Poor's

Number of listed domestic companies

2008

US	5,603	South Africa	425
India	4,921	Mongolia	420
Canada	3,755	Indonesia	396
Spain	3,536	Croatia	376
Japan	3,299	Egypt	373
UK	2,415	Iran	356
Australia	1,924	Poland	349
Romania	1,824	Sweden	341
South Korea	1,798	Bulgaria	334
China	1,604	Russia	314
Taiwan	1,260	Italy	294
Hong Kong	1,251	Bangladesh	290
Malaysia	977	Turkey	284
France	966	Greece	280
Pakistan	653	Jordan	262
Germany	638	Switzerland	253
Israel	630	Ukraine	251
Thailand	476	Philippines	244
Singapore	455	Chile	235
Brazil	432	Sri Lanka	234

Source: Standard & Poor's

Total market capitalisation by region, $trn

	1990	1995	2000	2005	2006	2007	2008
Americas	3.4	7.6	16.5	19.5	22.7	24.3	13.9
Europe, Africa & Middle East	2.0	4.4	9.6	12.1	16.2	18.6	9.4
Asia-Pacific	3.5	5.1	4.9	9.3	11.8	17.9	9.2
World total	8.9	17.1	31.0	40.9	50.7	60.9	32.6

Source: World Federation of Exchanges

Some stockmarket indices explained

Australia All Ordinaries Index

Australia's All Ordinaries Index comprises nearly 500 companies, representing 95% of Australia's market capitalisation. Constituents are reviewed on an annual basis. Its base value is 500 as of December 31st 1979.

Bombay Stock Exchange Sensex Index

Shares have been traded in Bombay (Mumbai) since 1875, but the Sensex index wasn't created until 1986. The index comprises 30 shares representing large, established companies in 12 sectors. It has a base date of the average for 1978–79 with a value of 100.

CAC 40 Index

The CAC 40 is France's benchmark index for the Paris Bourse. CAC stands for "*Cotation Assistée en Continu*", or "continuous-time computer-assisted quotation". The index comprises the 40 biggest companies on the Paris Bourse. It has a base value of 1,000 starting on December 31st 1987. The index is reviewed quarterly.

DAX 30 Index

The DAX (*Deutsche Aktienindex*) 30 is composed of Germany's 30 largest and most liquid listed companies. Its base value is 1,000 starting on December 31st 1987. Unlike most stock indices, the DAX includes dividend calculations and thus is a measure of total returns, not just price performance.

Dow Jones EURO STOXX 50 Index

The EURO STOXX 50 Index includes 50 of the biggest blue-chip companies from 12 euro area countries, representing nearly 60% of the euro area's free-float market capitalisation. The component companies are reviewed once a year in September, but the individual weightings are recalculated on a quarterly basis. The base value is 1,000 as of December 31st 1991.

Dow Jones Industrial Average Index

The Dow Jones Company started tracking an index of 12 industrial companies' stock prices on May 26th 1896. It now comprises 30 stocks which are no longer necessarily in the industrial sector. The index is price-weighted, rather than market-capitalisation weighted, unlike most major stock indices. Also unlike most other indices, its component companies change irregularly and rarely, and changes are based not on specific criteria but on the judgment of editors of the *Wall Street Journal*. It is the most quoted stockmarket index in print, television and internet media.

FTSE Actuaries All-Share Index and FTSE 100 Index

The FTSE ("Footsie") indices derive their name from the acronym for the "Financial Times Stock Exchange" index. The All-Share index was first calculated in 1962. The more closely followed FTSE 100 index began on January 3rd 1984, with a value of 1,000. It includes the top 100 listed firms by market capitalisation on the London Stock Exchange and is reviewed quarterly. The FTSE 250, created in 1985, represents mid-capitalisation companies in Britain not covered by the FTSE 100 and has become increasingly popular in recent years.

Hang Seng Index

The Hang Seng Index derives its name from Hong Kong's Hang Seng Bank, which created the index in 1969. Optimistically, "Hang Seng" means "ever-growing" in Chinese. It comprises the 42 largest companies drawn from four industry groups, and accounts for about 70% of the Hong Kong stockmarket's value. The index's base value is 100, corresponding to August 1964.

some stockmarket indices *continued*

IGBM – Madrid General Index

The IGBM (*Índice General de la Bolsa de Madrid*) is the principal index in Spain. It includes almost 125 companies which are reviewed on an annual basis. It has a base date of December 31st 1985 with a value of 100.

MSCI Emerging Markets Free Index

The MSCI Emerging Markets Index measures the stockmarket performance of the most popular emerging markets. It currently tracks the markets of 22 emerging-market countries, including: Brazil, Chile, China, Colombia, Czech Republic, Egypt, Hungary, India, Indonesia, Israel, Malaysia, Mexico, Morocco, Peru, Philippines, Poland, Russia, South Africa, South Korea, Taiwan, Thailand and Turkey. It is commonly quoted in US dollar terms.

NASDAQ 100

NASDAQ is the acronym for the "National Association of Securities Dealers Automated Quotations" system. The NASDAQ 100 tracks the performance of the top 100 companies traded on the NASDAQ exchange system. The NASDAQ is dominated by technology firms, so the performance of the NASDAQ 100 is closely watched as a barometer for the information-technology industry.

Nikkei 225 Index

The Nikkei 225 is Japan's most closely watched stock index, published by the business daily *Neihon Keizai Shimbun (Nikkei)*. It measures the performance of 225 of the top stocks on the Tokyo Stock Exchange. Established on September 7th 1950, but with a base value of 100 starting on May 16th 1949, it is a price-based index like the Dow Jones Industrial Average. It is reviewed at least once a year but only a maximum of six stocks can be replaced each year.

Shanghai Stock Exchange A-Share Index

Although shares were traded in Shanghai as far back as the 1860s, the current stock exchange wasn't opened until 1990. A-shares are available for purchase only to Chinese investors, thus the performance of this index reflects local investment conditions. More than 850 companies are listed on the Shanghai bourse. The index has a base date of December 19th 1990 with a value of 100.

Standard & Poor's 500 Index

Standard & Poor's, a credit-rating agency and provider of securities research, created the S&P 500 index in 1957. However, its base value of 10 represents the average value of its components from 1941 to 1943. The index is designed to reflect the performance of the largest US companies by market capitalisation, but by virtue of the number of constituents, to a significant degree it reflects the market as a whole. It is reviewed at least once a month.

S&P/TSX Composite Index

The Standard & Poor's/Toronto Stock Exchange Composite Index is Canada's benchmark index. It includes over 200 of the largest companies listed on the Toronto exchange, accounting for around 95% of its market capitalisation. The index was launched on January 1st 1977 with a base value of 1,000 for 1975. Its constituents are reviewed on a quarterly basis.

Topix Index

Japan's Topix index is a broader stock index than the Nikkei 225 and includes the stocks of all large companies (currently about 1,700) on the Tokyo exchange. It is weighted by market capitalisation and constituents are reviewed once a year. Its base value of 100 corresponds to January 8th 1964.

Stockmarket performance

Year end	FTSE All-Share Index	FTSE All-Share % change	FTSE 100 Index	FTSE 100 % change	US S&P 500 Index
1980	292	27	647	27	135.8
1981	313	7	684	6	122.6
1982	382	22	834	22	140.6
1983	471	23	1,000	20	164.9
1984	593	26	1,232	23	167.2
1985	683	15	1,413	15	211.3
1986	836	22	1,679	19	242.2
1987	870	4	1,713	2	247.1
1988	927	6	1,793	5	277.7
1989	1,205	30	2,423	35	353.4
1990	1,032	-14	2,144	-12	330.2
1991	1,188	15	2,493	16	417.1
1992	1,364	15	2,847	14	435.7
1993	1,682	23	3,418	20	466.5
1994	1,521	-10	3,066	-10	459.3
1995	1,803	19	3,689	20	615.9
1996	2,014	12	4,119	12	740.7
1997	2,411	20	5,136	25	970.4
1998	2,674	11	5,883	15	1,229.2
1999	3,242	21	6,930	18	1,469.3
2000	2,984	-8	6,223	-10	1,320.3
2001	2,524	-15	5,217	-16	1,148.1
2002	1,894	-25	3,940	-24	879.8
2003	2,207	17	4,477	14	1,111.9
2004	2,411	9	4,814	8	1,211.9
2005	2,847	18	5,619	17	1,248.3
2006	3,221	13	6,221	11	1,418.3
2007	3,287	2	6,457	4	1,468.4
2008	2,209	-33	4,434	-31	903.3
Compound growth:		7		7	
Average change:		9		9	
Standard deviation:		16		16	

| | | US | | | Japan | |
S&P 500 % change	Dow Jones Index	Dow Jones % change	NASDAQ 100 Index	NASDAQ 100 % change	Nikkei 225 Index	Nikkei 225 % change
26	964	15			7,063	8
-10	875	-9			7,682	9
15	1,047	20			8,017	4
17	1,259	20	133.1		9,894	23
1	1,212	-4	108.6	-18	11,543	17
26	1,547	28	132.3	22	13,083	13
15	1,896	23	141.4	7	18,821	44
2	1,939	2	156.3	11	21,564	15
12	2,169	12	177.4	13	30,159	40
27	2,753	27	223.8	26	38,916	29
-7	2,634	-4	199.4	-11	23,849	-39
26	3,169	20	326.7	64	22,984	-4
4	3,301	4	360.2	10	16,925	-26
7	3,754	14	398.3	11	17,417	3
-2	3,834	2	404.3	2	19,723	13
34	5,117	33	576.2	43	19,868	1
20	6,448	26	821.4	43	19,361	-3
31	7,908	23	990.8	21	15,259	-21
27	9,181	16	1,836.0	85	13,842	-9
20	11,497	25	3,707.8	102	18,934	37
-10	10,787	-6	2,341.7	-37	13,786	-27
-13	10,022	-7	1,577.1	-33	10,543	-24
-23	8,342	-17	984.4	-38	8,579	-19
26	10,454	25	1,467.9	49	10,677	24
9	10,783	3	1,621.1	10	11,489	8
3	10,718	-1	1,645.2	1	16,111	40
14	12,463	16	1,756.9	7	17,226	7
4	13,265	6	2,084.9	19	15,308	-11
-38	8,776	-34	1,211.7	-42	8,860	-42
7		8		9		1
9		10		15		4
17		16		16		23

stockmarket performance *continued*

Year end	Hong Kong Hang Seng		Canada S&P/TSX 60		Germany DAX 30	
	Index	% change	Index	% change	Index	% change
1980	1,474	68	113.9	25	481	-3
1981	1,406	-5	98.1	-14	490	2
1982	784	-44	99.7	2	553	13
1983	875	12	127.2	28	774	40
1984	1,200	37	120.4	-5	821	6
1985	1,726	44	143.8	19	1,366	66
1986	2,568	49	147.0	2	1,432	5
1987	2,303	-10	156.9	7	1,000	-30
1988	2,687	17	167.5	7	1,328	33
1989	2,837	6	198.0	18	1,790	35
1990	3,025	7	168.4	-15	1,398	-22
1991	4,297	42	184.4	9	1,578	13
1992	5,512	28	175.1	-5	1,545	-2
1993	11,888	116	221.5	27	2,267	47
1994	8,191	-31	221.8	0	2,107	-7
1995	10,073	23	250.5	13	2,254	7
1996	13,451	34	321.6	28	2,889	28
1997	10,723	-20	378.1	18	4,250	47
1998	10,049	-6	376.0	-1	5,002	18
1999	16,692	66	495.9	32	6,958	39
2000	15,096	-10	528.7	7	6,434	-8
2001	11,397	-25	442.6	-16	5,160	-20
2002	9,321	-18	373.2	-16	2,893	-44
2003	12,576	35	458.7	23	3,965	37
2004	14,230	13	511.9	12	4,256	7
2005	14,876	5	634.7	24	5,408	27
2006	19,965	34	742.8	17	6,597	22
2007	27,813	39	808.5	9	8,067	22
2008	14,387	-48	541.8	-33	4,810	-40
Compound growth:		8		6		9
Average change:		16		8		12
Standard deviation:		36		16		27

Source: Thomson Reuters

France CAC40		Emerging markets MSCI Emg Mkts		The World FTSE World	
Index	% change	Index	% change	Index	% change
				100.0	
1,000		100.0		99.1	-1
1,580	58	134.9	35	123.2	24
2,001	27	214.7	59	151.3	23
1,518	-24	185.2	-14	115.6	-24
1,766	16	288.8	56	132.3	14
1,858	5	314.9	9	127.4	-4
2,268	22	539.3	71	149.9	18
1,881	-17	492.6	-9	146.7	-2
1,872	0	458.4	-7	170.1	16
2,316	24	476.3	4	194.2	14
2,999	30	412.5	-13	231.6	19
3,943	31	299.0	-28	272.7	18
5,958	51	489.4	64	344.7	26
5,926	-1	333.8	-32	314.0	-9
4,625	-22	317.4	-5	267.2	-15
3,064	-34	292.1	-8	201.6	-25
3,558	16	442.8	52	247.9	23
3,821	7	542.2	22	272.7	10
4,715	23	706.5	30	312.8	15
5,542	18	912.7	29	357.9	14
5,614	1	1,245.6	36	374.4	5
3,218	-43	567.0	-54	224.6	-40
	6		9		4
	9		14		5
	26		35		18

Stockmarkets: the best and worst of times

MSCI World Index

Best days				Worst days			
Date	Close	Change, points	Change, %	Date	Close	Change, points	Change, %
13/10/2008	997.02	86.69	9.52	19/10/1987	421.28	-46.00	-9.84
21/10/1987	418.89	32.47	8.40	20/10/1987	386.42	-34.87	-8.28
28/10/2008	892.19	58.15	6.97	15/10/2008	950.36	-72.23	-7.06
24/11/2008	849.29	54.45	6.85	01/12/2008	830.33	-62.60	-7.01
19/09/2008	1,286.44	69.67	5.73	29/09/2008	1,163.53	-86.84	-6.94
08/12/2008	894.89	46.49	5.48	22/10/2008	909.84	-62.28	-6.41
10/03/2009	725.26	36.62	5.32	20/11/2008	771.52	-50.11	-6.10
23/03/2009	830.16	40.22	5.09	26/10/1987	378.35	-24.05	-5.98
29/07/2002	821.13	39.08	5.00	06/11/2008	925.09	-57.89	-5.89
17/01/1991	460.54	21.45	4.88	06/10/2008	1,072.99	-65.68	-5.77

MSCI World Index

Best years				Worst years			
Date	Close	Change, points	Change, %	Date	Close	Change, points	Change, %
1933	22.29	9.02	68.02	2008	920.23	-668.58	-42.08
1986	356.83	100.31	39.11	1931	13.48	-9.40	-41.08
1954	38.25	10.60	38.33	1920	14.98	-6.51	-30.28
1985	256.51	69.31	37.02	1974	78.24	-30.17	-27.83
2003	1,036.32	244.10	30.81	1930	22.89	-7.63	-25.00
1958	52.34	12.06	29.95	1946	22.73	-6.22	-21.47
1975	100.86	22.63	28.92	2002	792.22	-211.30	-21.06
1959	66.73	14.39	27.49	1990	461.53	-105.81	-18.65
1999	1,420.88	270.93	23.56	2001	1,003.52	-217.73	-17.83
1998	1,149.95	213.36	22.78	1937	24.81	-5.13	-17.13

US S&P 500 Index

Best days				Worst days			
Date	Close	Change, points	Change, %	Date	Close	Change, points	Change, %
15/03/1933	6.81	0.97	16.60	19/10/1987	224.84	-57.86	-20.47
30/10/1929	22.99	2.56	12.53	28/10/1929	22.74	-3.20	-12.34
06/10/1931	9.91	1.10	12.43	29/10/1929	20.43	-2.31	-10.16
21/09/1932	8.51	0.89	11.74	06/11/1929	20.61	-2.19	-9.61
13/10/2008	1,003.35	104.13	11.58	18/10/1937	10.76	-1.11	-9.34
28/10/2008	940.51	91.59	10.79	15/10/2008	907.84	-90.17	-9.03
05/09/1939	12.64	1.11	9.61	20/07/1933	10.57	-1.03	-8.90
20/04/1933	7.82	0.68	9.52	01/12/2008	816.21	-80.03	-8.93
21/10/1987	258.38	21.55	9.10	29/09/2008	1,106.39	-106.62	-8.79
14/11/1929	19.24	1.58	8.95	21/07/1933	9.65	-0.92	-8.70

US S&P 500 Index

Best years				Worst years			
Date	Close	Change, points	Change, %	Date	Close	Change, points	Change, %
1862	2.63	0.94	55.36	1931	8.12	-7.22	-47.04
1933	10.10	3.21	46.62	1937	10.54	-6.64	-38.64
1954	35.99	11.17	45.03	2008	903.25	-565.10	-38.49
1843	2.33	0.72	45.02	1907	6.57	-3.27	-33.23
1879	4.92	1.48	42.96	1857	1.48	-0.67	-30.99
1935	13.44	3.94	41.51	1917	6.80	-3.00	-30.61
1958	55.21	15.22	38.06	1854	2.03	-0.88	-30.21
1863	3.63	1.00	38.01	1974	68.56	-28.99	-29.72
1928	24.35	6.69	37.88	1930	15.34	-6.11	-28.48
1908	9.03	2.46	37.44	1920	6.81	-2.21	-24.51

Note: These calculations are based on monthly data 1800–1917; weekly data 1918–27; daily data from 1928.

stockmarkets: best and worst *continued*

Financial Times 30 Industrials

Best days				Worst days			
Date	Close	Change, points	Change, %	Date	Close	Change, points	Change, %
23/09/1931	56.89	6.46	12.81	20/10/1987	951.95	-120.45	-11.23
24/11/2008	4,152.96	372.00	8.26	19/10/1987	1,072.40	-117.52	-9.88
24/01/1975	91.29	7.81	9.36	10/10/2008	3,932.06	-381.74	-7.16
19/09/2008	5,311.33	431.34	1.92	06/10/2008	4,589.19	-391.06	-5.19
10/02/1975	117.53	9.31	8.60	01/03/1974	138.40	-10.87	-7.28
29/09/1938	79.90	6.20	8.41	15/10/2008	4,079.59	-314.62	-5.30
13/10/2008	4,256.90	324.84	9.84	26/10/1987	863.73	-66.60	-7.16
29/10/2008	4,242.54	316.16	8.84	29/05/1962	261.30	-18.00	-6.44
30/01/1975	106.22	7.13	7.20	02/01/1975	62.60	-4.29	-6.41
07/02/1975	108.22	6.36	6.24	31/01/1975	236.90	-15.40	-6.10

Financial Times All-Share Index

Best years				Worst years			
Date	Close	Change, points	Change, %	Date	Close	Change, points	Change, %
1975	158.08	91.19	136.33	1974	66.89	-82.87	-55.34
1824	45.53	21.65	90.67	1721	20.42	-10.11	-33.12
1959	106.93	32.36	43.39	2008	903.25	-565.10	-32.78
1971	193.39	57.13	41.93	1973	149.76	-68.42	-31.36
1977	214.53	62.57	41.18	2002	1,893.73	-630.15	-24.97
1968	168.60	46.42	37.99	1705	13.51	-4.20	-23.72
1954	62.66	16.07	34.48	1931	21.83	-6.69	-23.46
1958	74.57	18.59	33.20	1825	35.17	-10.35	-22.74
1817	19.13	4.71	32.62	1866	20.89	-6.04	-22.42
1967	122.18	29.70	32.12	1803	16.60	-4.66	-21.92

Japan Topix Price Index

Best days				Worst days			
Date	Close	Change, points	Change, %	Date	Close	Change, points	Change, %
14/10/2008	956.30	115.44	13.73	20/10/1987	1,793.90	-307.27	-14.62
02/10/1990	1,668.83	145.40	9.54	16/10/2008	864.52	-90.99	-9.52
21/10/1987	1,962.41	168.51	9.39	05/03/1953	32.32	-3.10	-8.75
30/10/2008	899.37	69.05	8.32	08/10/2008	899.01	-78.60	-8.04
21/08/1992	1,251.70	87.93	7.56	24/10/2008	806.11	-65.59	-7.52
10/04/1992	1,282.56	86.37	7.22	30/04/1970	159.33	-12.86	-7.47
17/11/1997	1,257.85	80.33	6.82	27/10/2008	746.46	-59.65	-7.40
31/01/1994	1,629.22	101.40	6.64	02/04/1990	2,069.33	-158.15	-7.10
06/01/1988	1,820.03	112.14	6.57	10/10/2008	840.86	-64.25	-7.10
16/04/1953	32.79	1.97	6.39	22/10/2008	889.23	-67.41	-7.05

Japan Topix Price Index

Best years				Worst years			
Date	Close	Change, points	Change, %	Date	Close	Change, points	Change, %
1952	32.20	17.46	118.38	1920	2.44	-2.33	-48.83
1972	401.70	202.25	101.40	2008	859.24	-616.44	-41.77
1932	2.69	1.25	86.31	1990	1,733.83	-1,147.54	-39.83
1948	6.47	2.98	85.28	1946	2.55	-1.05	-29.13
1951	14.75	5.70	62.95	2000	1,283.67	-438.53	-25.46
1999	1,722.20	635.21	58.44	1992	1,307.66	-407.02	-23.74
1915	2.85	0.98	52.01	1973	306.44	-95.26	-23.71
1949	9.76	3.29	50.89	1930	1.49	-0.40	-21.09
1986	1,556.37	506.97	48.31	1997	1,175.03	-295.91	-20.12
2005	1,649.76	500.13	43.50	2001	1,032.14	-251.53	-19.59

Sources: Global Financial Data (www.globalfinancialdata.com); *The Economist*

Stock exchange trading activity

Domestic turnover velocity as % of market capitalisation, 2008

Exchange	%	Exchange	%
NASDAQ	1,026	NASDAQ OMX Nordic	
Deutsche Börse	264	Exchange	138
NYSE Euronext (US)	240	Istanbul SE	135
Shenzhen SE	236	Osaka SE	134
Korea Exchange	196	SIX Swiss Exchange	122
Borsa Italiana	182	Shanghai SE	118
BME Spanish Exchanges	171	Australian SE	113
London SE	153	TSX Group	104
Tokyo SE Group	151	Budapest SE	95
Taiwan SE Corp.	146	Hong Kong Exchanges	86
Oslo Børs	143	Irish SE	81
NYSE Euronext (Europe)	142	National Stock Exchange India	76

Source: World Federation of Exchanges

Clocking the stockmarkets

DST factor: January GMT	+/−−5		−2	+0	+1
When the			the time in		
market	Local	New	São	London	Frankfurt
opens in:	opening	York	Paulo		
	times		is		
New York	9:30	9:30	12:30	14:30	15:30
São Paulo	11:00	8:00	11:00	13:00	14:00
London	8:00	3:00	6:00	8:00	9:00
Frankfurt	9:00	8:00	6:00	8:00	9:00
Bombay	10:00	14:30	2:30	4:30	5:30
Singapore	9:00	18:00	21:00	1:00	2:00
Hong Kong	10:00	17:00	20:00	2:00	3:00
Tokyo	9:00	19:00	22:00	0:00	1:00
Sydney	10:00	18:00	21:00	23:00	0:00

Sources: Stock exchanges; *The Economist* diary

Exchange	%	Exchange	%
Thailand SE	75	Jasdaq	44
BM&FBOVESPA	67	Bursa Malaysia	36
Egyptian Exchange	66	Mexican Exchange	30
Indonesia SE	66	Bombay SE	29
Wiener Börse	66	Tehran SE	26
Singapore Exchange	64	Philippine SE	24
Johannesburg SE	63	Santiago SE	20
Athens Exchange	61	Colombia SE	19
Amman SE	59	Colombo SE	14
Tel Aviv SE	55	Cyprus SE	14
New Zealand Exchange	46	Ljubljana SE	12
Warsaw SE	44	Lima SE	9

+5.5	+8	+8	+9	+11
		the time in		
Bombay	Singapore	Hong Kong	Tokyo	Sydney
		is		
20:00	22:30	22:30	23:30	1:30
18:30	21:00	21:00	22:00	0:00
13:30	16:00	16:00	17:00	19:00
13:30	16:00	16:00	17:00	19:00
10:00	12:30	12:30	13:30	15:30
6:30	9:00	9:00	10:00	12:00
7:30	10:00	10:00	11:00	13:00
5:30	8:00	8:00	9:00	11:00
4:30	7:00	7:00	8:00	10:00

Investment formulas

Black-Scholes model

A pricing model for options that ranks among the most influential. It was devised by Fischer Black and Myron Scholes, two Chicago academics, in 1973, the year that formalised options trading began on the Chicago Board of Trade. Behind the model is the assumption that asset prices must adjust to prevent arbitrage between various combinations of options and cash on the one hand and the actual asset on the other.

Call price = $S\,[N(d_1)] - E/e^{rt}[N(d_2)]$
Where:
S = current stock price
$N(d_1)$ = normal distribution function of d_1
E = exercise price of option
e = the base of natural logarithms (= 2.718)
r = risk-free interest at an annual rate
t = time to expiry of option (as a fraction of a year)
$N(d_2)$ = normal distribution function of d_2

To solve for d_1:
$d_1 = [\ln(S/E) + (r + 0.5sd^2)t] / [sd(t)^{1/2}]$
Where:
$\ln(S/E)$ = the natural log of S/E
sd = the standard deviation of annual returns on the share price (where the share price is squared, it is the variance)

To solve for d_2:
$d_2 = d_1 - [sd(t)^{1/2}]$

Capital asset pricing model

Because of its comparative simplicity, the capital asset pricing model (CAP-M) is a much-used formula for modelling the theoretically correct price of assets and portfolios.

$E(R_s) = RF + \beta_s[E(R_m) - RF]$

Where:

$E(R_s)$ = the expected return on security s
RF = the risk-free rate of return
β_s = the beta of security s
$E(R_m)$ = the expected return on the market

Capital fulcrum point

An important formula for valuing a warrant, which measures the minimum annual percentage increase required from the value of the underlying ordinary shares for investors to hold warrants in a company's shares in preference to the shares themselves.

$CFP = [(e/(s-w))^{1/y}] \times 100\%$
Where:
e = exercise price   s = share price
w = warrant price   y = years to expiry of warrant

Capital market line

The graphical depiction of the trade-off between risk and return for an efficient portfolio. In other words, it is a chart line which shows how much extra return investors would expect for taking on extra risk.

$[E(R_m) - RF]/[sd(R_m)]$
defines the slope of the market line, where:
$E(R_m)$ = the expected return from the market
RF = the risk-free rate of return
$sd(R_m)$ = the standard deviation of returns from the market

Thus the expected return from any portfolio on the capital market line is:

$E(R_p) = RF + \{[E(R_m) - RF]/[sd(R_m)]\}sd(R_p)$

Where:
$E(R_p)$ = the expected return on portfolio p
$sd(R_p)$ = the standard deviation of returns on portfolio p

Dividend discount model

A tool for valuing a stock or share which says that the value of the share equals the present value of all its future dividends. It provides a basis for comparing the price of

investment formulas *continued*

shares in the market with their theoretical value and thus judging whether the shares are cheap or expensive.

Where the growth rate in dividends is assumed to be constant, the fair price of a common stock can be stated as follows:

$P = D/(k - g)$
Where:
P = the price of the stock
D = expected dividend
k = the required rate of return
g = the expected growth rate in dividends

From this, the required rate of return can stated as:
$k = (D/P) + g$

and the stock's price/earnings ratio as:

$P/E = (D/E) / (k - g)$
Where:
E = the expected level of earnings

Single index model

Shows a security's return as a function of the market's return.

$R_{st} = a_s + b_s(R_{mt}) + e_{st}$
Where:
R_{st} = the return on security $_s$ over period $_t$
a_s = the constant return on security $_s$
b_s = the sensitivity of the security's return to the market's return (ie, its beta)
R_{mt} = the market's return over period $_t$
e_{st} = the difference between the actual return on security $_s$ during a given period $_t$ and its expected return

Source: *Investment: An A–Z Guide*, Philip Ryland, The Economist/Profile Books

Private equity

United States

The United States accounted for nearly 60% of the private-equity funds raised throughout the world in 2008. Over $265 billion in new private-equity funds were raised (over 10% of which was for venture capital), and almost $206 billion in investments were made. US long-term returns to private equity neared 13% at the end of 2008.

Europe

In 2008, €79 billion in private-equity funds were raised throughout Europe, down from the peak of €112 billion in 2006. Around 25% of these funds are expected to be used for venture-capital investments, with most of the rest going towards buy-outs. Over €54 billion was invested in private-equity in 2008, down from the 2007 peak of almost €74 billion. Since inception (1980) to end-2004, European private equity has earned an average 9.5% return on investment.

Britain

Britain accounts for nearly a quarter of the European private-equity market and as a country its market is second only to the United States. In 2008, £23.1 billion in funds were raised by British private-equity firms, with £20 billion in made in investments. Since 1980, British private-equity funds have averaged a 16.4% return on investment.

Sources: National Venture Capital Association; European Private Equity & Venture Capital Association; British Venture Capital Association; Thomson Venture Economics

Hedge funds

	Hedge-fund assets, $bn	Number of hedge funds
1990	38.91	610
1991	58.37	821
1992	95.72	1,105
1993	167.79	1,514
1994	167.36	1,945
1995	185.75	2,383
1996	256.72	2,781
1997	367.56	2,990
1998	374.77	3,325
1999	456.43	3,617
2000	490.58	3,873
2001	539.06	4,454
2002	625.55	5,379
2003	820.01	6,297
2004	972.61	7,436
2005	1,105.39	8,661
2006	1,464.50	9,462
2007	1,868.40	10,096
2008	1,407.10	9,284
2009*	1,430.00	8,900

*Q2
Source: Hedge Fund Research

Hedge-fund strategies

Distressed securities: funds that invest in, or sell short, the debt or equity of companies experiencing financial distress, such as bankruptcy or corporate restructuring.

Emerging markets: funds that invest in companies or the sovereign debt of developing countries. Many funds have a regional focus.

Equity hedge: funds that use a mixture of long and short positions. Some try to hedge market risks by limiting market exposure, while more aggressive funds use leverage to magnify potential rewards.

Event-driven: funds that invest in opportunities created by corporate events, such as spin-offs, mergers, bankruptcy, recapitalisation and share buybacks.

Fixed-income: funds that invest in fixed-income instruments. Strategies vary and these funds can specialise in fixed-income arbitrage, convertible bonds, high-yield bonds or mortgage-backed securities.

Macro: funds that make leveraged bets on anticipated price movements of stockmarkets, interest rates, currencies and commodities.

Relative value: funds that attempt to profit from pricing inefficiencies of the market. This can be done using convertible bonds, fixed-income securities, the shares of companies involved in a merger or acquisition, or any financial instrument where relative values can be exploited by arbitrage. Quantitative funds use sophisticated mathematical models to spot price discrepancies.

Sector: funds that focus on a particular sector for investment. Popular sectors include energy, financial firms, health care and biotechnology, metals and mining, real estate and technology.

Hedge-fund assets under management by strategy

Q1 2009, %	
Equity hedge	31.4
Relative value	24.8
Event-driven	23.8
Macro	20.0

Sources: Hedge Fund Research; *The Economist*

Bonds

Credit ratings

	Moody's	Standard & Poor's
Highest credit quality; issuer has strong ability to meet obligations	Aaa	AAA
Very high credit quality; low risk of default	Aa1, Aa2, Aa3	AA+, AA, AA-
High credit quality, but more vulnerable to changes in economy or business	A1, A2, A3	A+, A, A-
Adequate credit quality for now but more likely to be impaired if conditions worsen	Baa1, Baa2, Baa3	BBB+, BBB, BBB-
Below investment grade, but good chance that issuer can meet commitments	Ba1, Ba2, Ba3	BB+, BB, BB-
Significant credit risk, but issuer is currently able to meet obligations	B1, B2, B3	B+, B, B-
High default risk	Caa1, Caa2, Caa3	CCC+, CCC, CCC-
Issuer failed to meet scheduled interest or principal payments	C	D

Source: *Guide to Financial Markets*, Marc Levinson, The Economist/Profile Books

US corporate bonds issued

The US corporate bond market contracted sharply in the financial crisis. But business started to boom at the beginning of 2009, up 65% in the first five months compared with a year earlier, to more than all of 2008.

	High yield, $bn	Investment grade, $bn	Total, $bn
2001	77.8	698.3	776.1
2002	57.2	579.5	636.7
2003	131.1	644.7	775.8
2004	137.9	642.8	780.7
2005	96.3	656.5	752.8
2006	146.6	912.3	1058.9
2007	136.0	991.5	1127.5
2008	44.5	661.7	706.2
2009 to May	42.6	764.3	806.9

Note: Excludes all issues with maturities of a year or less and certificates of deposit. High-yield bonds are below investment grade so likely to be more speculative and volatile.

Source: Securities Industry and Financial Markets Association/Thomson Financial

International bond and note issues

International bonds are issued or traded in a foreign country – eg, eurobonds. Around 90% are held by institutional investors such as insurance companies, pension funds and mutual funds. Almost a third of the net total in 2008 was issued in the UK, followed by the US with almost a quarter of the market.

	2008, $bn	Amounts outstanding, end March 2009
Floating rate issues	1,206	7,769
Straight fixed-rate issues	1,141	14,714
Equity-related issues	8	387
Euro	954	10,684
US dollar	690	8,570
Sterling	564	1,773
Yen	21	683
Other currencies	126	1,159
Developed countries	2,293	19,868
UK	710	3,097
US	575	5,454
Euro area*	851	9,703
Offshore centres	1	1,442
Emerging markets	5	897
Financial institutions	1,990	17,873
Corporate issuers	280	2,497
Governments	29	1,836
International organisations	55	663
Total issues, net	2,355	22,869

*14 members (excludes Malta and Slovenia).

Source: Bank for International Settlements

Bubbles that burst

Tulipmania

Tulips were introduced into western Europe from Turkey in the 16th century. In the 17th century they gave rise to one of the most curious episodes in Holland's history. In the early 1600s single-colour tulips were being sold at relatively modest prices in Dutch markets, but as new varieties were created the fashion for tulips intensified and prices soared. By 1623 a particularly admired and rare variety, *Semper Augustus*, was selling for 1,000 florins for a single bulb, more than six times the average annual wage. Ten years later the price had increased more than fivefold, and then reached a peak at the height of the tulip craze of some 10,000 florins, roughly the same as it cost to buy a fine canalside house in the centre of Amsterdam.

As the mania took hold more and more people sought to cash in on the boom, and the tulip business developed from dealing in actual bulbs to dealing in what were in effect tulip futures.

It couldn't last, and it didn't. In 1637 the bulb bubble burst when it became clear that at the end of the long chain of those speculating in bulb futures there was no one who actually wanted to buy the bulbs at such high prices. Within a period of a few months the market had crashed leaving thousands of people ruined.

The Mississippi Bubble

In 1716 John Law, a Scottish businessman who had come to France two years earlier, persuaded the French government, which was in financial distress, to let him set up a bank that could issue bank notes, which he believed would provide a spur to commerce and help get the government out of its financial difficulties. At the time France controlled the Louisiana colony, which covered an area larger than France itself. In August 1717 Law bought a controlling interest in the then derelict Mississippi Company and was granted a 25-year monopoly by the French government on trade with the West Indies and North America. The company acquired other French trading companies and was renamed the Compagnie des Indes, in effect controlling all French trade outside Europe. Law had raised money to fund the Mississippi Company's activities by issuing shares that could be purchased using notes issued by Law's Banque Générale or government bonds.

As Law's business empire grew and there was more and more excitement about the riches that were to be exploited across the Atlantic, the share price rose dramatically. People from outside France as well as within couldn't get enough of the shares and Law issued more and more banknotes to enable people to buy them. By the end of 1719, the year of initial issue, the share price had increased twentyfold.

The crunch came at the beginning of 1720 when investors started to sell shares and realise their gains in gold. Law stepped in to prevent people being paid more than a certain amount in gold for their shares, with the rest being payable in notes. Within a year the share price had fallen to a tenth of its value at the peak and Banque Générale notes were worth only half their face value. A year later the shares were back to their issue price, and Law subsequently took his leave of France. Opinion is divided as to whether Law was in fact a rogue or simply an honest man undone by a misguided scheme.

The South Sea Bubble

In 1711 the South Sea Company was given a monopoly of all trade to the South Seas in return for assuming a portion of the national debt that England had accumulated during the War of the Spanish Succession, which had started in 1703 and was still continuing. It was

bubbles that burst *continued*

anticipated that when the war ended, which it did in 1713, there would be rich trade pickings to be had among the Spanish colonies in South America. But the South Sea Company did little trading, preferring to accumulate money from investors attracted by its future prospects.

War between Spain and England broke out again in 1718 and the following year the South Sea Company made a proposal to assume the whole of England's national debt. Inducements were offered to influential people and the proposal was accepted. New shares were issued in the company and the stock price was talked up and up.

Speculation fever took hold; a large number of companies that were to trade in the "New World" or which had other supposedly promising futures were set up, many of which were plain and simple scams to separate investors from their money. Confidence in the market was dented and in an effort encouraged by the managers of the South Sea Company to restore it, the "Bubble Act" was passed in 1720 requiring all joint stock companies to have a royal charter. It did the trick: the South Sea Company's share price increased more than fivefold in four months to reach over £1,000. And then the bubble burst – or rather started to deflate. A gradual slide in the share price accelerated and within three months the company was worthless. Many people were ruined and a committee set up in 1721 to investigate the affair discovered widespread corruption involving businessmen and politicians.

Railway mania

The British "railway mania" of the 1840s and the American railway boom up to 1873 shared many similarities. Entrepreneurs used the stockmarket to raise huge sums to build proposed lines. Overinvestment led to excess capacity, failing revenues and defaults on loans; so much capital was diverted to railway projects that other businesses suffered and interest rates spiralled. In America, as a result of generous land grants, around 170m acres was given to some 80 rail companies, though half the projected tracks were never built. The railway bubble burst in the "Panic of 1873", the same year as America's first successful train robbery.

The Wall Street crash

In 1929 stock prices were 400% higher than they had been in 1924, pushed up way beyond any relationship with the actual worth of their companies, as investors, lured by the prospect of easy riches, piled into the market, accumulating some $6 billion of debt in the process. In early September 1929 prices fell sharply but recovered before falling again. In late October panic selling gave rise to the Wall Street crash, which ushered in a worldwide economic crisis, the Great Depression. Many shareholders were ruined, banks and businesses failed, and unemployment subsequently rose to around 17m.

Japan's monetary mistake

When through the Plaza Accord in 1985 Japan agreed to loosen its monetary policy to boost the value of the yen and trim its exports, things did not turn out quite as expected. Rather than restraining Japanese companies, the sudden doubling of the value of the yen against other currencies allowed big multinational firms to go on a buying spree of American and European assets, using bank loans and the rising value of their property portfolios as collateral. Bank lending on property ballooned as the initial loans drove up land prices and the higher land prices made those loans look like good business. At the height of the boom, property around the imperial palace in Tokyo was worth more than California, and Australia paid off its national debt by selling a small parcel of land around its embassy. When the bubble burst after rises in interest rates in the early 1990s, property values slumped. Japan's economic problems since are partly attributable to the bubble and its bursting.

bubbles that burst *continued*

The dotcom boom and bust

The late 1990s saw a speculative frenzy of investment in internet-related shares as investors took the view that anything that took advantage of the burgeoning popularity of the new technology was certain to make buckets of money. Venture capitalists threw money at any half-baked scheme as long as the entrepreneurs projected vast profits in a short space of time. Huge sums were spent on notional projects to build market share and vast increases in share price accompanied initial public offerings of the firms that were taken to market, making shareholders dotcom millionaires overnight (on paper at least). The dotcom boom rubbed off on other shares, especially technology stocks of any kind, and money poured into the stockmarket.

In 1999 stockmarkets around the world hit record peaks. The January 2000 Super Bowl featured 17 dotcom companies which had each paid over $2m for a 30-second spot. But not long after, share prices for e-businesses started to fall as it finally struck home that firms were burning through cash with no prospect of ever making a profit. Eventually, all but the most robust dotcoms went to the wall and stockmarkets plunged, with Nasdaq falling by over 70% between 1999 and 2002.

The credit crunch

The credit crunch that struck the world's biggest banks and threatened the global financial system had its origins in the American housing market. Years of lax lending were encouraged by rock-bottom interest rates. But between 2004 and 2006 the Federal Reserve raised interest rates from 1% to over 5% to control inflation. By 2006 a growing trend towards deregulation had pushed three-quarters of all lending outside the oversight of regulators.

And securitisation, in the form of collateralised debt obligations (CDOs), created a serious problem. Loan originators, who were paid up-front, had no incentive to avoid bad credit risks. As interest rates rose default on subprime mortgages to high-risk borrowers with bad or no credit histories rose to record levels. The impact reverberated across the financial system as many of the mortgages had been bundled up and sold on to banks and investors as CDOs.

In April 2007 New Century Financial, which specialised in subprime mortgages, filed for bankruptcy and in July Bear Stearns, an investment bank, said that investors would get almost nothing from two hedge funds it ran after rival banks refused to step in with a bail-out. Banks, fearful of the liabilities on rivals' balance sheets and wary of letting go of cash, began to stop lending short-term funds to each other causing paralysis in credit markets. By August the world's leading central banks were forced to pump liquidity into the financial system as LIBOR, the interest rate on interbank lending, soared to its highest level for years.

In the following months some of the world's biggest banks began to reveal huge subprime-related losses and central banks continued to pump money into the banking system to keep it operating. In February 2008 Northern Rock, a struggling British mortgage lender that relied on the money markets for funding, was taken into government control and a month later Bear Stearns was acquired by JPMorgan Chase for a paltry $236m (backed by guarantees of some $30 billion from the Fed).

In April the IMF warned that the total cost of bailing out the financial system could top $1 trillion and fears mounted over the effects of the credit crunch on a teetering world economy. The crisis intensified in July when the American government stepped in to prop up Freddie Mac and Fannie Mae, huge mortgage lenders that were close to collapse. By September the government was forced to rescue the pair with a vast bail-out.

A few days later Lehman Brothers, a long-standing Wall Street investment bank, collapsed under the weight of subprime losses, and Merrill Lynch, another American bank with huge subprime exposure, was taken over by Bank of America for $50 billion. The Fed then announced an $85 billion rescue package for AIG, the country's biggest insurer and another subprime victim and in Britain Lloyds TSB took over the country's biggest mortgage lender, HBOS, in a deal worth $12 billion. A week afterwards Washington Mutual, a huge American mortgage lender, was closed by regulators and sold to JPMorgan Chase. In Europe Fortis and Dexia were partially nationalised as was Bradford & Bingley in Britain.

After the peak of the crisis in September governments began to take startling measures to rescue the world's financial system and stimulate flagging economies. In October Congress finally passed a $700 billion government bail-out plan. Germany stumped up €50 billion to save Hypo Real Estate, a big bank, and Britain's government announced a £50 billion rescue package. The G7 group of rich countries hatched a plan to unfreeze credit markets and make the financial system function again. And central banks continued to cut interest rates to encourage interbank lending to start again and boost economies. In November China unveiled a huge $586 billion stimulus package to kick-start its economy, and America was forced to rescue Citigroup, the country's biggest bank, and also announced that it would inject another $800 billion into the financial system. The EU announced a €200 billion injection. But as the threat from the financial crisis started to recede the problems for the world economy mounted as Europe, America and other big economies slipped into recession. Meanwhile, governments around the world began to propose new measures to regulate banks to ensure that a similar crisis would be avoided in future.

Oil reserves and price

Proven reserves, barrels, bn

	North America	South & Central America	Europe & Eurasia	Middle East	Africa	Asia Pacific
end 1985	101.5	62.9	78.6	431.3	57.0	39.1
end 1995	89.0	83.8	81.5	661.5	72.0	39.2
end 2005	59.5	103.5	140.5	742.7	114.3	40.2
end 2008	70.9	123.2	142.2	754.1	125.6	42.0

Source: BP

Average oil price*

	$ per barrel		$ per barrel
1946	1.4	1989	19.6
1950	2.6	1990	24.5
1960	3.0	1991	21.6
1970	3.4	1992	20.6
1971	3.6	1993	18.4
1972	3.6	1994	17.2
1973	3.9	1995	18.4
1974	10.4	1996	22.0
1975	11.2	1997	20.6
1976	12.6	1998	14.4
1977	14.3	1999	19.3
1978	14.9	2000	30.3
1979	22.4	2001	25.9
1980	37.4	2002	26.1
1981	36.7	2003	31.0
1982	33.6	2004	41.4
1983	30.4	2005	56.8
1984	29.4	2006	66.1
1985	28.0	2007	72.3
1986	15.1	2008	99.6
1987	19.2	2009†	51.3
1988	16.0		

* West Texas Intermediate (WTI).
†Jan–Jun average.
Sources: Dow Jones Energy Service; Thomson Reuters

Gold reserves and price

	m ounces, year-end	Gold bullion av. price per troy oz, $
1975	1028.740	161.98
1976	1023.550	125.09
1977	1030.350	148.00
1978	1037.980	193.46
1979	946.890	307.37
1980	955.560	612.24
1981	955.190	459.79
1982	951.280	376.19
1983	950.150	423.45
1984	949.030	360.57
1985	951.520	317.64
1986	951.490	367.82
1987	945.990	446.75
1988	946.690	437.03
1989	941.040	381.52
1990	939.390	383.70
1991	939.440	362.39
1992	928.895	343.83
1993	923.322	360.11
1994	919.273	384.27
1995	910.943	384.29
1996	909.103	387.77
1997	892.242	331.19
1998	968.359	294.23
1999	967.980	278.85
2000	953.063	279.15
2001	944.157	271.16
2002	932.333	310.37
2003	914.609	364.00
2004	897.552	409.79
2005	878.980	445.31
2006	867.738	604.40
2007	852.612	696.80
2008	848.290	871.80
2009	847.120*	916.20†

*Jan–Apr average.   †Jan–Jun average.

Note: It was in 1971 that the dollar was finally cut loose from the gold standard, signalling the end of the Bretton Woods arrangements.

Sources: IMF: International Financial Statistics; Thomson Reuters

Gold facts

Gold is a yellow metal. Its chemical symbol is Au from the Latin word *aurum*, which means "glowing dawn".

Gold's atomic number is 79. Its specific gravity, a measure of density, is 19.3-times that of water and it is rated at about 2.5 on Moh's scale of hardness, placing it between gypsum and calcite.

Gold's proportion in an alloy is measured in karats. Pure gold is 24 karats, or 99.999% pure. 100% pure gold is almost impossible to refine.

Gold is the most non-reactive of all metals. It does not react with oxygen and does not rust or tarnish.

Gold will only dissolve in acids such as aqua regia (a mixture of hydrochloric and nitric acids) and some others.

Gold is among the most electrically conductive of all metals. It can convey a tiny electrical current in temperatures between –55°C and 200°C.

Gold is the most ductile of all metals, allowing it to be drawn out into tiny wires or threads without breaking. A single ounce of gold can be drawn into a wire 5 miles long.

Gold's malleability is also unequalled. It can be shaped or extended into very thin sheets. One ounce of gold can be hammered into a 100-sq. ft (9.3 sq. m) sheet.

Total world production of gold down the ages is estimated at 3 billion ounces (85,000 tonnes). This would fit into a cube with sides measuring 55 feet (16.8m).

Source: The Gold Institute

Rich producers

Silver, 2008, m ounces

Peru	118.3
Mexico	104.2
China	82.8
Australia	61.9
Chile	44.9
Poland	38.9
Russia	36.1
US	36.0
Bolivia	35.8
Canada	21.5

Gold, 2008, tonnes

China	275.9
US	237.3
Australia	222.6
South Africa	219.3
Peru	179.9
Russia	176.0
Canada	94.1
Uzbekistan	88.4
Indonesia	76.9
Ghana	72.2

Platinum, 2008, tonnes

South Africa	153.0
Russia	25.0
Canada	7.2
Zimbabwe	5.6
US	3.7

Palladium, 2008, tonnes

Russia	88.0
South Africa	80.0
Canada	12.5
US	12.4
Zimbabwe	4.4

Diamonds, 2008, m carats

	Gemstones		Industrial*
Botswana	25.0	Congo-Kinshasa	23
Russia	23.3	Australia	18
Canada	18.0	Russia	15
Angola	10.0	South Africa	9
South Africa	6.1	Botswana	8

*World production of manufactured industrial diamonds was 570m carats in 2008.

Producers include United States, Russia, South Africa, Ireland and Japan.

Sources: The Silver Institute; Fortis Bank/VM Group; US Geological Survey; Geology.com

Diamond and platinum facts

Diamonds Unlike precious metals, top diamond producers by volume are not the same countries as top diamond producers by value, as shown in the table. Size and quality vary greatly. One carat = 0.2 grams.

The largest cut diamond is the Golden Jubilee, a yellow diamond weighing 545 carats now part of Thailand's crown jewels. The largest rough diamond is the Cullinan, weighing 3,107 carats and cut into two polished stones, the Great Star of Africa at 530 carats (the second largest polished diamond, now in the Tower of London) and the Lesser Star of Africa at 317 carats, and a further 104 stones.

The highest price paid at auction is the 100-carat Star of the Season bought in 1995 for $16.5m. The diamond bought by Richard Burton for Elizabeth Taylor was 69 carats.

In 2003 thieves broke into the Diamond Centre in Antwerp and stole $100m worth of diamonds from safe-deposit boxes belonging to dealers and cutters.

A diamond was found in 2004 floating in space, the core of a dead star, weighing 10 billion trillion trillion carats, 2,500 miles across, bigger than the moon. It is 50 light years away.

Blood, or conflict, diamonds are those that originate from areas controlled by illegal forces and are then used to fund military action, as happened in Angola and Sierra Leone.

Platinum Platinum is generally 95% pure so does not tarnish or fade, and it is hypoallergenic. As well as being used for jewellery it has industrial and medical uses – catalytic converters and pacemakers.

Behind the currency name

Baht Until the 1940s the Thai currency was known as the tical. A *baht* was a unit of weight of around 15g, the equivalent in silver of one tical.

Bolivar Venezuela's currency takes its name from Simon Bolivar, a Venezuelan known as "El Libertador" who led the defeat of Spanish colonialism in the 19th century, gaining independence for his own country as well as Bolivia, Colombia, Ecuador, Panama and Peru. Ecuador's sucre is named after Antonio José de Sucre, also an independence leader and one of Bolivar's closest friends.

Crown The French gold *denier à la couronne* was issued by Philip of Valois in about 1339 and featured a large embossed crown. The name was adopted by a slew of countries including the Czech Republic (koruna), Denmark (krone), Estonia (kroon), Iceland (króna), Norway (krone), Sweden (krona).

Dinar Its origin dates back to the most widely used Roman coin, the denarius. The silver coin's name means "containing ten" as it originally equalled ten copper *as*. It survives as the denar in Macedonia and dinar in Algeria, Bahrain, Iraq, Jordan, Kuwait, Tunisia and Serbia.

Dollar The name is derived from that of the historic currencies of Bohemia, the tolar, and Germany's thaler. The name *thaler* (from the German *thal*, meaning "valley") itself derives from the *guldengroschen* or "great gulden", a silver coin equal in value to a gold gulden and minted from the silver mined at Joachimsthal in Bohemia. The word "dollar" was in use in English for the thaler for about 200 years before America adopted the term. Spanish dollars, or "pieces of eight", were in circulation in Spain's colonies in the Americas in the 18th century. This and the Maria Theresa Thaler were both in wide use before the American revolution and lent their name to the country's new currency.

Drachma The Greek currency (now superseded by the euro) took its name from the verb "to grasp". The Arabic dirham's name is also derived from the ancient drachma.

Dram The Armenian word for "money".

Escudo Taken from the Portuguese (and Spanish) for "shield" and originally Spanish coins decorated with the coat of arms of the king of Spain – the great shield of the house of Hapsburg. The doubloon was a coin originally worth two escudos.

Franc The name is said to derive from the Latin inscription *francorum rex* ("King of the Franks") inscribed on gold coins first made during the reign of Jean le Bon (1350–64).

Guilder The name is taken from coins struck in Florence in the 13th century decorated with a lily, the *florensus*, derived from *fiorino*, Old Italian for flower. The Netherlands adopted the name *gulden*, short for *gulden florijn* (or golden florenus), of which guilder is a corruption. The abbreviation fl or f remained in use. The currency survives in Aruba and the Netherlands Antilles.

Kina Papua New Guinea's money takes its name from the kina shell, which was traditionally used as currency on the island.

Kuna The word means "marten" in Croatian, and is etymologically unrelated to the various currency names derived from the crown. It comes from the use of marten pelts as a trading commodity by medieval merchants.

Kwacha Zambia's currency is taken from the county's main language, Bemba. It means "dawn" and is taken from the country's nationalist slogan "new dawn of freedom".

Kwanza The official currency of Angola is named either after the Kwanza River or the Bantu word for "first".

behind the currency name *continued*

Leu Dutch thalers circulating in Romania and Moldova in the 17th century bearing the impression of a lion were widely known as *lei* (lions). A form of the name was kept as a generic term for money (though becoming the lev in Bulgaria).

Lira The Vatican City and Malta retain a currency with a name originating from the value of a troy pound (Latin *libra*) of high purity silver. Turkey's lira shares the same root.

Manat In Azerbaijan and Turkmenistan the currency derives its name from Manah, a goddess of fate and destiny in pre-Islamic Arabia.

Mark An archaic unit of weight for precious metal in Europe equal to eight troy ounces. Germany's mark has been replaced by the euro but Bosnia has its marka and Finland its markka.

Pataca Macau's currency takes its name from a silver coin once popular in Asia, the Mexican eight *reales* or "pieces of eight", known in Portuguese as the Pataca Mexicana.

Peseta Spain's former currency takes its name from the Catalan word *peceta*, meaning "little piece".

Peso The Spanish word for "weight". The main colonial-era coin was worth eight *reales* (the "piece of eight") and was later called the *peso in* Argentina, Chile, Colombia, Cuba, Dominican Republic, Mexico, the Philippines and Uruguay.

Pound The term originates from the value of a troy pound weight of high purity silver. The symbol is based on a traditional capital "L" with a horizontal line through it, derived from the Latin word *libra*, meaning pound. Sterling dates back to the reign of Henry II in the 12th century and is probably derived from Easterling silver, mined in the area of Germany of the same name. It was famed for the high quality of its silver, which was imported to Britain to form the basis of coinage at the time. Another explanation is that sterling silver's hallmark featured a starling.

Pula In the Setswana language pula means "rain", a scarce and valuable resource in Botswana.

Quetzal Named after the national bird of Guatemala.

Rand South Africa's rand is named after a gold-mining area in Transvaal, short for Witwatersrand.

Real Brazil's money takes its name from the Portuguese and means "Royal currency". The basic silver unit of Spanish America was the real until about 1860.

Ringgit Malaysia's currency means "jagged" in Malay in reference to the serrated edges of Spanish silver dollars that circulated in the area.

Rouble The name is derived from the Russian word meaning "to chop". Historically, a ruble was a piece of silver chopped off an ingot.

Rupee India's currency takes its name from a Sanskrit word, *rupyah*, meaning "wrought silver".

Yen See Yuan.

Yuan China's currency is taken from the word meaning "round object" in Chinese. Japan's yen is taken from the same source.

Zloty Poland's currency means "golden" in Polish.

Notes and coins in circulation

US dollar

	Notes value, $bn	Coins value, $bn	
2000	563.9	29.9	
2001	612.3	31.1	
2002	654.8	32.8	
2003	690.2	33.9	
2004	719.9	34.9	
2005	758.3	35.2	
2006	783.5	36.6	
2007	792.2	36.7	
2008	853.6	36.2	
2009*	864.1	39.6	

Pound†

	Notes value, £bn	New notes issued, bn	
2005	35.4	0.74	
2006	36.9	0.64	
2007	38.4	0.77	
2008	45.0	1.23	
2009	48.6	1.09	

Euro

	Notes value, €bn	Coins value, €bn	
2005	565.2	16.7	
2006	628.2	17.9	
2007	676.6	19.3	
2008	762.8	20.4	
2009‡	761.3	20.7	

*End March.   †End February.   ‡End May.

Sources: Financial Management Service, US Treasury; Bank of England; European Central Bank

Euros printed

Banknotes produced

	Quantity, bn	Value, €bn
2002	4.78	115.0
2003	3.09	103.6
2004	1.58	108.0
2005	3.63	185.9
2006	7.00	186.0
2007	6.30	260.0
2008	6.45	129.3
2009	10.94	476.0

Banknotes produced since January 1st 2002

Denomination	Quantity, m
5	6,319
10	9,985
20	13,430
50	10,850
100	2,327
200	133
500	724
Total	43,768

Source: European Central Bank

The life of $ and £ notes

$	Months, av.	£	Months, av.
1	21.6	5	12–24
5	15.6	10	24–36
10	18.0	20	24–36
20	24.0	50	60+
50	55.2		
100	88.8		

Sources: Federal Reserve; Bank of England

Exchange rates

Period average	$1 = €	$1 = £	$1 = ¥
1950	...	0.36	361.10
1960	0.63	0.36	360.00
1970	0.66	0.42	360.00
1980	0.65	0.43	226.74
1990	0.77	0.56	144.79
1995	0.75	0.63	94.06
2000	1.09	0.66	107.77
2001	1.18	0.69	121.53
2002	1.06	0.67	125.39
2003	0.89	0.61	115.93
2004	0.81	0.55	108.19
2005	0.80	0.55	110.22
2006	0.80	0.54	116.30
2007	0.73	0.50	117.75
2008	0.68	0.54	103.36

Period average	$ = €1	$ = £1	$ = ¥1
1950	...	2.80	0.0028
1960	1.59	2.80	0.0028
1970	1.52	2.40	0.0028
1980	1.54	2.33	0.0044
1990	1.30	1.78	0.0069
1995	1.33	1.58	0.0106
2000	0.92	1.52	0.0093
2001	0.85	1.44	0.0082
2002	0.94	1.50	0.0080
2003	1.12	1.63	0.0086
2004	1.23	1.83	0.0092
2005	1.24	1.82	0.0091
2006	1.25	1.84	0.0086
2007	1.37	2.00	0.0086
2008	1.46	1.85	0.0097

Note: Synthetic $/€ rate until 1999.

Sources: IMF: International Financial Statistics; Thomson Reuters

Exchange rate pegs

Exchange rates can be tied to a particular currency as a currency union (eg, the countries in the euro area) or individually (eg, fixed to the US$). A peg reduces volatility, but it also reduces flexibility in monetary policy.

Euro currency members

Austria	France	Italy	Portugal
Belgium	Germany	Luxembourg	Slovenia
Cyprus	Greece	Malta	Spain
Finland	Ireland	Netherlands	

Slovakia joined on January 1 2009. Non-members using or pegged to the euro: Bosnia, Bulgaria, Croatia, Denmark, Estonia, Kosovo, Latvia, Lithuania, Macedonia, Montenegro and members of the CFA franc zone:

CFA franc zone, pegged to the euro

Benin	Chad	Gabon	Senegal
Burkina Faso	Congo-Brazzaville	Guinea-Bissau	Togo
Cameroon	Côte d'Ivoire	Mali	
Cen Afr Rep.	Equatorial Guinea	Niger	

Countries using the US$

Ecuador	Marshall Is	Palau	Timor-Leste
El Salvador	Micronesia	Panama	

Countries with currencies pegged to US$

Angola	Eritrea	Neth Ant	Tajikistan
Argentina	Guyana	Oman	Trinidad & Tob
Aruba	Honduras	Qatar	Turkmenistan
Bahamas	Hong Kong	Rwanda	UAE
Bahrain	Jordan	Saudi Arabia	Vietnam
Bangladesh	Kazakhstan	Seychelles	Yemen
Barbados	Lebanon	Sierra Leone	Zimbabwe
Belarus	Malawi	Solomon Is	
Belize	Maldives	Sri Lanka	
Djibouti	Mongolia	Suriname	

and members of the Eastern Caribbean Currency Union*

*Antigua & Barbuda, Dominica, Grenada, St Kitts & Nevis, St Lucia, St Vincent & the Grenadines. Anguilla and Montserrat (British overseas territories) also use the EC$.
Sources: IMF as at April 2008; currency boards

The world economy

Biggest economies

GDP, 2007

	$bn	PPP		$bn	PPP
US	13,751	13,751	Saudi Arabia	383	554
Japan	4,384	4,297	Taiwan	383	784
Germany	3,317	2,830	Austria	373	311
China	3,206	7,097	Greece	313	319
UK	2,772	2,143	Denmark	312	197
France*	2,590	2,078	Iran	286	778
Italy	2,102	1,802	South Africa	283	467
Spain	1,436	1,416	Argentina	262	523
Canada	1,330	1,181	Ireland	259	195
Brazil	1,313	1,833	Finland	245	183
Russia	1,290	2,087	Thailand	245	519
India	1,177	3,097	Venezuela	228	334
Mexico	1,023	1,485	Portugal	223	241
South Korea	970	1,202	Colombia	208	378
Australia	821	734	Hong Kong	207	293
Netherlands	766	634	UAE	199	226
Turkey	656	957	Malaysia	187	359
Sweden	464	336	Czech Republic	175	250
Belgium	453	371	Romania	166	267
Indonesia	433	838	Nigeria	165	291
Switzerland	424	307	Chile	164	230
Poland	422	609	Israel	164	189
Norway	388	252	Singapore	161	228

*Includes overseas departments.

Regional GDP

$bn, 2008		% annual growth 2003–08	
World	60,690	World	4.6
Advanced economies	42,100	Advanced economies	2.5
G7	32,221	G7	2.1
Euro area (16)	13,633	Euro area (16)	2.1
Asia*	7,239	Asia*	9.1
Latin America	4,210	Latin America	5.3
Eastern Europe[†]	4,049	Eastern Europe[†]	6.7
Middle East	1,814	Middle East	5.9
Africa	1,278	Africa	6.0

Regional purchasing power

GDP, % of total, 2008		$ per head, 2008	
World	100.0	World	10,220
Advanced economies	55.3	Advanced economies	36,900
G7	42.1	G7	38,720
Euro area (16)	15.7	Euro area (16)	32,110
Asia[a]	21.0	Asia[a]	4,070
Latin America	8.6	Latin America	10,430
Eastern Europe[†]	8.1	Eastern Europe[†]	12,090
Middle East	3.9	Middle East	10,760
Africa	3.1	Africa	2,460

Regional international trade

Exports of goods & services, % of total, 2008			
Advanced economies	65.1	Latin America	5.1
G7	36.5	Eastern Europe[†]	7.6
Euro area (16)	28.6	Middle East	5.6
Asia[a]	13.8	Africa	2.7

*Excludes Hong Kong, Japan, Singapore, South Korea and Taiwan.
[†]Includes Russia, other CIS and Turkey.

Leading traders

Biggest exporters

% of total world exports (goods, services and income), 2007

Euro area (13)	16.36	Belgium	2.34
US	11.49	South Korea	2.15
China	10.42	Spain	2.14
Germany	8.81	Russia	2.05
UK	6.10	Switzerland	1.83
Japan	4.69	Ireland	1.44
France	4.40	Taiwan	1.41
Netherlands	3.35	Mexico	1.39
Italy	3.28	Sweden	1.38
Canada	2.62	Singapore	1.25

Biggest traders of goods

% of world, 2007	Exports		Imports
Euro area (13)	15.49	Euro area (13)	14.99
Germany	10.12	US	14.83
China	9.11	Germany	8.10
US	8.61	China	6.82
Japan	5.07	UK	4.68
France	4.08	France	4.53
Italy	3.75	Japan	4.32
Netherlands	3.45	Italy	3.75
UK	3.30	Netherlands	3.07
Canada	3.23	Canada	2.92

Biggest earners from services and income

% of world exports of services and income, 2007

Euro area (13)	17.80	France	4.95
US	16.27	Japan	4.08
China	12.60	Netherlands	3.18
UK	10.76	Luxembourg	2.82
Germany	6.64	Spain	2.51

How the world economy has changed

Shares of world GDP at purchasing-power parity exchange rates, %

	1820	1870	1913	1950	1973	2001	2008*
Western Europe	23.0	33.0	33.0	26.2	25.6	20.3	16.0
US, Canada, Australia, New Zealand	1.9	10.0	21.3	30.7	25.3	24.6	24.0
Japan	3.0	2.3	2.6	3.0	7.8	7.1	6.0
China	32.9	17.1	8.8	4.5	4.6	12.3	16.0
Other Asia	23.5	19.0	13.5	11.0	11.8	18.6	21.0
Latin America	2.2	2.5	4.4	7.8	8.7	8.3	8.0
Eastern and Central Europe	9.0	12.0	13.4	13.1	12.8	5.6	6.0
Africa	4.5	4.1	2.9	3.8	3.4	3.3	3.0
World	100.0	100.0	100.0	100.0	100.0	100.0	100.0

* Estimated.

Sources: *The World Economy* by Angus Maddison; IMF

GDP per person, PPP$, 1990 prices

	1820	1870	1913	1950	1973	2001	2008*
US	1,257	2,445	5,301	9,561	16,689	27,948	30,800
UK	1,706	3,190	4,921	6,939	12,025	20,127	22,900
Japan	669	737	1,387	1,921	11,434	20,683	22,800
France	1,135	1,876	3,485	5,271	13,114	21,092	22,500
Germany	1,077	1,839	3,648	3,881	11,966	18,677	20,400
Italy	1,117	1,499	2,564	3,502	10,634	19,040	19,200
Spain	1,008	1,207	2,056	2,189	7,661	15,659	17,100
China	600	530	552	439	839	3,583	6,800
India	533	533	673	619	853	1,957	3,000
World	667	875	1,525	2,111	4,091	6,049	7,300

* Estimated.

Note: GDP is the sum of all output produced by economic activity. PPP statistics adjust for cost of living differences by replacing normal exchange rates with rates designed to equalise the prices of a standard "basket" of goods and services.

Sources: *The World Economy* by Angus Maddison; IMF; World Bank

Sovereign wealth funds

"A SWF is a government investment vehicle which is funded by foreign exchange assets and which manages these assets separately from official reserves" – Clay Lowery, Acting Under-Secretary for International Affairs, 2007

SWFs have been going since the 1950s, unless you include the Dutch Stichting Pensioenfonds (1922) and the California Public Employees' Retirement System (1932). The early ones were largely used as a way of recycling petrodollars (Saudi Arabia 1952, Kuwait 1953). Singapore's Temasek also has a long history (1974). More recently, emerging economies with large current-account surpluses, such as China and Russia, have used SWFs to invest around the world.

Big SWF deals

Fund	Target	$bn	Date announced
Government of Singapore Investment Corporation	UBS	9.8	Dec 08
Abu Dhabi Investment Authority	Citigroup	7.5	Nov 08
Government of Singapore Investment Corporation	Citigroup	6.9	Jan 08
Korea Investment Corporation/ Kuwait Investment Authority	Merrill Lynch	5.4	Jan 08
China Investment Corporation	Morgan Stanley	5.0	Dec 08
Temasek	Merrill Lynch	5.0	Apr 08/Dec 08
Korea Investment Corporation	Citigroup	3.0	Jan 08
Kuwait Investment Authority/ Qatar Investment Authority/ others	General Motors building, NY	2.8	Jun 08
Korea Investment Corporation	Merrill Lynch	2.0	Jan 08
Dubai International Capital	The Tussauds Group	1.5	Mar 05
Dubai International Capital	Travelodge Hotels	1.3	Aug 06

Sources: UNCTAD; Deloitte; press reports

Major sovereign wealth funds

Fund name	Country	Assets* $bn
Abu Dhabi Investment Authority	UAE	650
SAMA Foreign Holdings	Saudi Arabia	433
Government of Singapore Investment Corporation	Singapore	330
SAFE Investment Company	China	312
The Government Pension Fund - Global	Norway	301
Kuwait Investment Authority	Kuwait	264
China Investment Corporation	China	200
Hong Kong Monetary Authority Investment Portfolio	Hong Kong	180
Temasek Holdings	Singapore	85
Investment Corporation of Dubai	UAE	82
National Wealth Fund	Russia	76
National Social Security Fund	China	74
Qatar Investment Authority	Qatar	60
Libyan Investment Authority	Libya	51
Revenue Regulation Fund	Algeria	47
Australian Future Fund	Australia	44
Alaska Permanent Fund	US	40
Kazakhstan National Fund	Kazakhstan	38
National Pensions Reserve Fund	Ireland	31
Korea Investment Corporation	South Korea	30
Brunei Investment Agency	Brunei	30
Strategic Investment Fund	France	29
Khazanah Nasional	Malaysia	26
Social and Economic Stabilisation Fund	Chile	21
Alberta Heritage Savings Trust Fund	Canada	17

* Information available as at July 2009.

Sources: www.sovereignwealthfundsnews.com; UNCTAD

Foreign direct investment

Inflows, $bn

	1995–99 ave.	2000	2002	2004	2006	2007	Stocks, % of GDP, end 2007
Euro area (15)	146	500	244	120	327	488	37.8
EU27	238	698	309	214	562	804	40.9
Other western Europe	11	27	7	4	37	44	46.1
North America	157	381	97	136	300	342	17.1
Other developed countries	15	29	30	49	42	58	10.3
Africa	9	10	15	18	46	53	31.0
Latin America & the Caribbean	68	98	58	94	93	126	32.4
Other Asia	97	148	99	170	273	319	28.6
South-east Europe & CIS	7	7	11	30	57	86	28.0
Total	602	1,398	625	718	1,411	1,833	27.9

Developing economies with the biggest inflows in 2007, $bn

	1995–99 ave.	2000	2002	2004	2006	2007	Stocks, % of GDP, end 2007
China	42.1	40.7	52.7	60.6	72.7	83.5	10.1
Hong Kong	13.5	61.9	9.7	34.0	45.1	59.9	573.0
Russia	3.1	2.7	3.5	15.4	32.4	52.5	25.1
Brazil	18.3	32.8	16.6	18.1	18.8	34.6	25.0
Mexico	11.6	18.0	23.0	22.9	19.3	24.7	29.7
Saudi Arabia	0.2	0.2	0.5	1.9	18.3	24.3	20.2
Singapore	11.8	16.5	7.2	19.8	24.7	24.1	154.7
India	2.6	3.6	5.6	5.8	19.7	23.0	6.7
Turkey	0.8	1.0	1.1	2.8	20.0	22.0	22.2

Note: Foreign direct investment (FDI) is long-term investment in companies in a foreign country, implying a certain degree of control of those companies. Stocks indicate the value of those investments.
Source: United Nations Conference on Trade and Development

Sending money home

Workers overseas send about $100 billion back to their
home country each year, and it is growing at double-digit
rates. India received over $20 billion from overseas in
2003, nearly double the 2000 amount. The Philippines
received $9 billion in 2004, compared with only $125m
in 2000. Mexico has more than doubled its inflow, to over
$16 billion. Other rapidly growing recipients are China
(eight times the 2000 amount) and Guatemala (more
than four times).

Countries' receipts, $bn	2000	2002	2004	2006	2008*
India	12.9	15.7	18.8	25.4	52.0
China	6.2	13.0	19.0	23.3	40.6
Mexico	7.5	11.0	19.9	26.9	26.3
Philippines	6.2	9.7	11.5	15.3	18.6
France	8.6	10.4	12.3	12.3	15.1
Spain	4.5	5.2	7.5	8.9	11.8
Germany	3.6	4.7	6.6	7.6	11.1
Poland	1.7	2.0	4.7	8.5	10.7
Nigeria	1.4	1.2	2.3	5.4	10.0
Egypt	2.9	2.9	3.3	5.3	9.5
Romania	0.1	0.1	0.1	6.7	9.4
Belgium	4.0	4.7	6.9	7.5	9.3
Bangladesh	2.0	2.9	3.6	5.4	9.0
UK	3.6	4.5	6.4	7.0	8.2
Vietnam	...	2.7	3.2	4.8	7.2
Pakistan	1.1	3.6	3.9	5.1	7.0
Indonesia	1.2	1.3	1.9	5.7	6.8
Morocco	2.2	2.9	4.2	5.5	6.7
Lebanon	1.6	2.5	5.6	5.2	6.0
Russia	1.3	1.4	2.5	3.3	6.0

*Estimates.
Source: World Bank

Interest rates

Short-term rates

London interbank offered rates, %

	US	UK	Japan	Euro area
1979	12.09	13.88	6.08	...
1980	14.19	16.35	11.30	...
1981	16.87	14.32	7.73	...
1982	13.29	12.58	6.99	...
1983	9.72	10.18	6.57	...
1984	10.94	10.02	6.43	...
1985	8.38	12.25	6.68	...
1986	6.84	10.97	5.12	...
1987	7.19	9.80	4.26	...
1988	7.97	10.36	4.51	...
1989	9.28	13.94	5.46	...
1990	8.28	14.79	7.76	...
1991	5.98	11.67	7.38	...
1992	3.83	9.70	4.46	...
1993	3.30	6.06	3.00	...
1994	4.74	5.54	2.31	...
1995	6.04	6.73	1.27	...
1996	5.51	6.09	0.63	...
1997	5.74	6.90	0.63	...
1998	5.56	7.39	0.72	...
1999	5.41	5.54	0.22	2.96
2000	6.53	6.19	0.28	4.41
2001	3.78	5.04	0.15	4.26
2002	1.79	4.06	0.08	3.32
2003	1.22	3.73	0.06	2.33
2004	1.62	4.64	0.05	2.11
2005	3.56	4.76	0.06	2.18
2006	5.19	4.85	0.30	3.08
2007	5.30	6.01	0.79	4.28
2008	2.91	5.51	0.93	4.63
2009 March	1.27	1.83	0.62	1.63

Source: Thomson Reuters

Some notable highs Money-market interest rates in Argentina averaged nearly 1.4m% in 1989 and over 9m% in 1990. Russian rates averaged 190% in 1995. Zimbabwe's rates averaged over 100% in 2003 and 2004. Turkey's interbank money-market rate came down from an average of 92% in 2001 to 13.25% in early 2006.

Central bank rates

America The US federal funds rate went from 4.75% in 1977 to 19% in 1981. Its next low point was 3% in 1993 before going up to 6.5% in 2000. The 45-year low point of 1% ran from June 2003 to June 2004, then rising in 17 quarter-point moves to 5.25% by June 2006, where it stayed until September 2008 when the cuts started, going right down to a target range of 0 to 0.25% in December 2008, the lowest recorded rate.

Britain The UK's minimum lending rate went to 15% in 1976, down to 5% in 1977 then up to 17% in 1979. On Black Wednesday (September 16th 1992) the rate went briefly up to 15%. The repo rate, which became the new official rate in May 1997, went to a low of 3.5% in July 2003 but by July 2007 it was 5.75%. Then, as the financial crisis became more acute, it was brought down to a record low of 0.5% in March 2009. When the Bank of England started business in 1694, the bank rate was 6%.

Japan The Bank of Japan's official discount rate was set at a high of 9% in 1973 and again in 1980. It has been 0.1% since September 2001. After six years of a zero-rate policy, the bank raised the key overnight call rate to 0.25% in July 2006. Following America's cut at the end of 2008, the Bank cut back again to around 0.1%.

Sources: IMF; Federal Reserve; Bank of England; Bank of Japan

The tax take

Total tax revenue as % of GDP

	1970	1980	1990	2000	2007
Australia	21.5	26.7	28.5	31.1	30.6*
Canada	30.9	31.0	35.9	35.6	33.3
France	34.1	40.1	42.0	44.4	43.6
Germany	31.5	36.4	34.8	37.2	36.2
Ireland	28.4	31.0	33.1	31.7	32.2
Italy	25.7	29.7	37.8	42.3	43.3
Japan	19.6	25.4	29.1	27.0	27.9*
South Korea	...	17.2	18.9	23.6	28.7
Spain	15.9	22.6	32.5	34.2	37.2
Sweden	37.8	46.4	52.2	51.8	48.2
Switzerland	19.3	24.7	25.8	30.0	29.7
UK	37.0	35.1	36.1	37.1	36.6
US	27.0	26.4	27.3	29.9	28.3

*2006.

Total tax revenue per head of population, $

	1970	1980	1990	2000	2006
Australia	752	3,067	5,296	6,458	11,586
Canada	1,261	3,524	7,555	8,562	13,213
France	965	5,030	8,983	9,695	15,847
Germany	782	3,947	6,936	8,598	12,585
Ireland	411	1,925	4,517	8,049	16,428
Italy	522	2,421	7,554	8,149	13,276
Japan	397	2,358	7,317	9,958	9,619
South Korea	...	289	1,164	2,565	4,923
Spain	186	1,355	4,337	4,931	10,230
Sweden	1,665	7,375	14,922	14,335	21,241
Switzerland	704	4,335	9,030	10,408	15,190
UK	823	3,348	6,284	9,129	14,700
US	1,349	3,209	6,286	10,334	12,265

Taxes on company income, % of GDP

	1970	1980	1990	2000	2006
Australia	3.6	3.2	4.0	6.3	6.6
Canada	3.5	3.6	2.5	4.4	3.7
France	2.1	2.1	2.2	3.1	3.0
Germany	1.8	2.0	1.7	1.8	2.1
Ireland	2.5	1.4	1.6	3.7	3.8
Italy	1.7	2.3	3.8	2.9	3.4
Japan	5.2	5.5	6.5	3.7	4.7
South Korea	...	1.9	2.5	3.3	3.8
Spain	1.3	1.1	2.9	3.1	4.2
Sweden	1.7	1.1	1.6	3.9	3.7
Switzerland	1.6	1.6	2.0	2.7	3.0
UK	3.2	2.9	3.6	3.6	4.0
US	3.6	2.8	2.4	2.6	3.3

Taxes on personal income, % of GDP

	1970	1980	1990	2000	2006
Australia	8.0	11.7	12.2	11.8	11.4
Canada	10.0	10.6	14.7	13.1	12.1
France	3.7	4.7	4.5	8.0	7.7
Germany	8.4	10.8	9.6	9.4	8.7
Ireland	5.2	9.9	10.6	9.5	8.9
Italy	2.8	6.9	9.9	10.5	10.8
Japan	4.2	6.2	8.1	5.7	5.1
South Korea	...	2.0	4.0	3.4	4.1
Spain	1.8	4.6	7.1	6.5	6.9
Sweden	18.8	19.0	20.1	17.2	15.7
Switzerland	6.9	9.6	10.0	10.5	10.5
UK	11.7	10.3	10.6	10.9	10.8
US	9.9	10.3	10.1	12.5	10.2

Source: OECD

Corporate tax rates

Average, %

	1998	2008	% change, 1998–2008
Argentina	33.00	35.00	6.06
Australia	36.00	30.00	-16.67
Austria	34.00	25.00	-26.47
Bangladesh	40.00	30.00	-25.00
Belgium	40.17	33.99	-15.38
Bolivia	25.00	25.00	0.00
Brazil	25.00	34.00*	36.00
Canada	44.60	33.50	-24.89
Chile	15.00	17.00	13.33
China	33.00	25.00	-24.24
Colombia	35.00	33.00	-5.71
Costa Rica	30.00	30.00	0.00
Czech Republic	35.00	21.00	-40.00
Denmark	34.00	25.00	-26.47
Dominican Republic	25.00	25.00	0.00
Ecuador†	36.25	25.00	-31.03
Finland	28.00	26.00	-7.14
France	41.66	33.33	-20.00
Germany	50.13	29.51	-41.13
Greece†	37.50	25.00	-33.33
Hong Kong	16.50	16.50	0.00
Hungary	18.00	16.00	-11.11
Iceland‡	33.00	15.00	-54.55
India	35.00	33.99	-2.89
Indonesia	30.00	30.00	0.00
Ireland	32.00	12.50†	-60.94
Italy	41.25	31.40	-23.88
Japan	51.60	40.69	-21.14
Luxembourg	37.45	29.63	-20.88
Malaysia	28.00	26.00	-7.14
Mexico	34.00	28.00	-17.65
Mozambique	35.00	32.00	-8.57
Netherlands†	33.00	25.50	-22.73

New Zealand	28.00	30.00	7.14
Norway	30.00	28.00	-6.67
Pakistan	37.00	35.00	-5.41
Panama	25.00	30.00	20.00
Papua New Guinea	30.00	30.00	0.00
Peru	30.00	30.00	0.00
Philippines	34.00	35.00	2.94
Poland	36.00	19.00	-47.22
Portugal	37.40	25.00	-33.16
Russia	…	24.00	…
Singapore	26.00	18.00	-30.77
South Africa	…	34.55	…
South Korea	30.80	27.50	-10.71
Spain	35.00	30.00	-14.29
Sri Lanka	35.00	35.00	0.00
Sweden	28.00	28.00	0.00
Switzerland	27.80	21.17	-23.85
Taiwan	…	25.00	…
Thailand	30.00	30.00	0.00
Turkey	44.00	20.00	-54.55
UK	31.00	28.00	-9.68
Ukraine	…	25.00	…
Uruguay	30.00	25.00	-16.67
US	40.00	40.00	0.00
Venezuela	34.00	34.00	0.00
Vietnam	32.50	28.00	-13.85

*Includes social contribution tax on profits.   †Average rate from a tax band.
‡Applies to limited liability companies only.
Source: KPMG

Average corporate tax rates by region, %

	OECD	EU	Latin America	Asia-Pacific
2000	34.1	33.9	28.7	31.9
2002	31.4	30.9	28.4	31.5
2004	29.8	28.3	28.0	30.0
2006	28.2	25.8	28.1	30.0
2008	26.7	23.2	26.6	28.4

Source: KPMG

How taxing for top earners?

Top personal income tax rate, %

	1975	1980	1985	1995	2000	2005	2008
Australia	65.0	...	60.0	47.0	47.0	47.0	45.0
Austria	62.0	62.0	62.0	50.0	50.0	50.0	50.0
Belgium	60.0	76.3	71.6	55.0	55.0	50.0	50.0
Canada	47.0	...	34.0	29.0	29.0	29.0	29.0
Denmark	...	...	39.6	34.5	28.0	26.5	26.5
Finland	...	...	...	39.0	37.5	33.5	31.5
France	60.0	60.0	65.0	...	53.0	48.0	40.0
Germany	56.0	56.0	56.0	53.0	51.0	42.0	45.0
Greece	63.0	60.0	63.0	45.0	45.0	40.0	40.0
Hungary	...	...	...	44.0	40.0	38.0	36.0
Ireland	77.0	60.0	65.0	48.0	44.0	42.0	41.0
Italy	72.0	72.0	65.0	51.0	45.0	43.0	43.0
Japan	75.0	93.0	70.0	50.0	37.0	37.0	40.0
South Korea	...	...	55.0	45.0	40.0	35.0	35.0
Luxembourg	57.0	58.4	57.0	50.0	46.0	38.0	38.0
Mexico	...	55.0	55.0	35.0	40.0	30.0	28.0
Netherlands	71.0	72.0	72.0	60.0	60.0	52.0	52.0
New Zealand	60.0	60.0	66.0	33.0	39.0	39.0	39.0
Norway	73.0	...	40.0	13.7	29.0	27.0	25.3
Poland	...	...	...	40.0	40.0	40.0	40.0
Portugal	...	...	60.0	40.0	40.0	40.0	42.0
Spain	62.0	65.5	66.0	56.0	40.0	29.0	27.1
Sweden	87.0	...	80.0	30.0	25.0	25.0	25.0
Switzerland	44.0	...	11.5	11.5	12.0	12.0	11.5
UK	83.0	...	60.0	40.0	40.0	40.0	40.0
US	70.0	70.0	50.0	39.6	40.0	35.0	35.0

Sources: OECD; The Tax Policy Centre, Urban Institute, Brookings Institution

Wealth and debt

Net wealth as % of disposable income

	1995	1998	2000	2005	2008
UK	555.9	686.4	768.1	824.1	909.4*
Italy	716.6	722.9	762.6	834.5	868.4*
France	462.5	494.9	552.5	748.2	749.2
Japan	735.8	726.9	747.7	740.4	727.8*
Germany	541.0	530.5	540.8	580.8	605.7†
Canada	481.5	498.4	502.2	534.3	544.8
US	511.7	580.7	584.0	640.0	485.8

*2007
†2006
Net wealth is defined as non-financial and financial assets minus liabilities (consumer debt); non-financial assets include stock of durable goods at replacement cost & dwellings at market value; financial assets comprise currency & deposits, securities (except shares), loans, shares and other equity, insurance technical reserves.

Consumer debt as % of disposable income

	1995	1998	2000	2005	2008
UK	106.6	109.4	117.1	161.6	183.3
Canada	103.4	112.0	112.6	129.6	142.6
US	93.5	97.2	102.8	134.4	133.9
Japan	130.2	132.6	134.6	131.9	127.7
France	65.7	72.5	76.8	91.0	100.1
Germany	96.8	109.3	114.5	107.2	98.6*
Italy	32.1	45.5	52.8	65.3	72.5*

*2007
Source: OECD

Great business books

Here is a selection of business books that stand out from the vast crowd published over the years.

Barbarians at the Gate
Bryan Burrough and John Helyar, 1990
The fall of RJR Nabisco

Competitive Strategy
Michael Porter, 1980
How to gain competitive advantage

Corporate Strategy
Igor Ansoff, 1965
The ABC of strategic planning

The Dilbert Principle
Scott Adams, 1996
The foolish ways of managers

Future Shock
Alvin Tofler, 1970
Fast change is traumatic and inevitable

Good to Great
Jim Collins, 2001
What it takes to make the transition

The Human Side of Enterprise
Douglas McGregor, 1960
The origin of Theories X and Y

In Search of Excellence
Tom Peters and Robert Waterman, 1982
Boosting the ego of corporate America

Liar's Poker
Michael Lewis, 1990
Wall Street laid bare

Microserfs
Douglas Coupland, 1995
Get a life in Silicon Valley

My Years with General Motors
Alfred Sloan, 1963
How GM was built – by the man who did it

The Organisation Man
William Whyte, 1956
The anatomy of an enduring type

The Peter Principle
L.J. Peter and R. Hull, 1969
The rise of the incompetent

The Practice of Management
Peter Drucker, 1954
The definitive description

The Principles of Scientific Management
Frederick Winslow Taylor, 1911
The very first business bestseller

Re-engineering the Corporation
Michael Hammer and James Champy, 1993
Revolution through process design

Small is Beautiful
E.F. Schumacher, 1973
The title says it all

The Smartest Guys in the Room
Bethany McLean and Peter Elkind, 2003
The best telling of the scandalous fall of Enron

Strategy and Structure
Alfred Chandler, 1962
Why structure follows strategy

The Tipping Point
Malcolm Gladwell, 2002
How little things make big differences

Up the Organisation
Robert Townsend, 1970
Ex-Avis boss teaches the world how to try harder

Compiled by Tim Hindle

Latin that lawyers like to use

A fortiori	for a compelling reason
Ad valorem	value
Affidavit	he has said it (a sworn statement)
Bona fide	in good faith, honestly, sincerely, without deception (Mala fide in bad faith)
Bona vacantia	vacant goods; goods without an owner
Caveat emptor	buyer beware
De minimis non curat lex	the law is not concerned with trivial matters
De facto	in point of fact
Eiusdem generis	of the same kind
Ex gratia	as a favour; without liability
Ex parte	on behalf of one party
Fieri facias	make it happen
Functus officio	having shot one's bolt; spent
Habeas corpus	let him have his body back
Ignorantia legis non excusat	ignorance of the law is not an excuse
In flagrante delicto	in the act of committing a crime
In personam	in respect of the person; personally
In re	in the matter of
In rem	in respect of the thing; reality
Inter alia	among other things
Inter partes	between the parties
Inter vivos	between living people
Intra vires	within the permitted powers
Ipso facto	by the very fact itself
Lex fori	the law of the place where the case is being heard
Lex loci	the law of the place where the act was done
Locus standi	official standing; recognition

Mala in se	wrongs in themselves
Mala prohibita	forbidden wrongs
Mandamus	we command
Mens rea	guilty mind
Mutatis mutandis	change and change about
Nemine contradicente (nem. con.)	with no one speaking against
Nemo dat quod non habet (nemo dat)	no one can give what he does not have
Nolle prosequi	do not pursue
Non est factum	it is not his act (he didn't mean to do it)
Obiter dicta	incidental comments
Pari passu	of equal power
Prima facie	on the face of it
Per diem	by the day; an allowance paid businessmen to cover daily expenses while travelling
Pro rata	for the rate; divided in proportion
Pro tempore	for the time being; sometimes shortened to pro tem
Quantum meruit	as much as he deserves
Quid pro quo	something for something (you scratch my back, I'll scratch yours)
Ratio decidendi	the reason for deciding
Res ipsa loquitur	it speaks for itself
Sine die	without specifying a day
Sine qua non	without which, not (anything indispensable)
Sub judice	under adjudication
Sui generis	of its own kind
Uberrimae fidei	of the utmost good faith
Ultra vires	outside the permitted powers
Verbatim	word-for-word; a precise rendering of a discussion or text

What's in a word

Many terms and expressions are used in business without people giving a second thought to how they have come about. Here are the origins of some popular ones.

Acid test A term meaning to test the true worth of something is derived from the practice of testing the purity of gold with nitric acid in the days when the metal was used as a currency.

Bear A speculator who sells securities in the expectation that prices will fall. Bears may sell short, ie, sell securities they do not own, leading to suggestions that the expression refers to the phrase "selling the skin before you have caught the bear". Trappers were also in the habit of short selling their wares. Short sellers were called "bearskin jobbers" in 18th century London.

Bellwether The term for a closely watched company that indicates the fortunes of an entire industry takes its name from castrated male sheep that lead flocks. These sheep used to wear bells to help shepherds find them at night or in bad weather.

Benchmark The technique for comparing performance in business and finance refers to a surveyor's mark made on a stationary object for use as a reference point for subsequent observations.

Big cheese Important people may have derived their epithet from colonial India. The Urdu word "*chiz*", which means thing, like so many other phrases was taken up by the British. Its meaning was altered to mean "good".

Bite the bullet Taking a difficult decision is probably less painful than suffering an operation without anaesthetic. Before modern pain-killing drugs were available soldiers were given a bullet to bite to stop cries of agony during surgery.

Blue chip An American term referring to the colour of the highest value poker chip.

Boss The Dutch word *baas*, meaning master, was adopted in America from Dutch colonisers and in South Africa by the British from the Afrikaners.

The buck stops here American poker players in the 19th century would use a bit of buckshot to denote which player was the dealer and so had ultimate responsibility to pass out the cards.

Bull An investor who buys hoping that prices will rise. Probably named just to contrast them with bears. Bull and bear baiting were popular sports in Britain at the time that the forerunner of the modern stockmarket emerged.

Cash cow Came into common usage only recently but the term milch cow was used as early as the 17th century to mean a dependable source of prosperity.

Dead cat bounce A small improvement in a bear market is so called because "even dead cats bounce".

Dead wood Someone or something serving no purpose, taken from a technique in shipbuilding. Timbers were laid on the keel for no other reason than to make it a little more rigid.

Line your pockets It has been suggested that the term originates from the practice by tailors in Regency England of sending garments to George "Beau" Brummell stuffed with banknotes in order to seek the patronage of the famous dandy and fashion leader.

Pac-Man strategy A measure to avoid takeover whereby the intended target counterattacks by making an offer for the firm that is trying to acquire it, named after the 1980s computer game.

Pay through the nose The Danes of the 9th century imposed a "nose" tax on the Irish, so-called because those who avoided paying had their nostrils slit.

what's in a word *continued*

Poison pill An anti-takeover measure that attempts to make the potential acquiree a less attractive target, named after the cyanide pills that enemy agents swallow in the event of capture.

Red tape British lawyers and government officials formerly used to bind documents together with red cloth tape. The term was first used to describe bureaucracy by Charles Dickens.

Smart Alec The term was originally non-pejorative and is thought to derive from an American conman, Alec Hoag. He perfected a method for stealing from the unsuspecting clients of prostitutes by using a sliding panel to hide in the room while a hooker and customer went about their business. He later emerged to remove wallets and watches while the punter slept, supposedly a considerable improvement on the previous preferred method of bursting in while the satisfied client slept.

Stag Someone who applies for an allotment of shares in an initial public offering, with a view to selling them straight away at a healthy premium. It is suggested that the term originates because stag is also a term used for a castrated bull.

Tycoon Wealthy and successful businessmen get their names from the Japanese *taikun*, a powerful military leader. The word became popular in the early part of the 20th century.

White knight A friendly potential buyer of a firm that is threatened by a less welcome suitor. In *Alice through the Looking Glass* the heroine is captured by the red knight but is rescued at once by the white knight.

Brand names that entered the language

Aspirin Bayer still owns the trademark for the acetylated derivative of salicylic acid in many countries.

AstroTurf Commonly applied to any artificial grass surface. AstroTurf, developed by Monsanto industries, was originally called Chemgrass.

Band Aid The original plastic adhesive plaster was developed by Johnson & Johnson.

Biro The original ball-point pen, invented by a Hungarian, Laszlo Biro, in 1938 is the name given to all such writing implements today. The patent was acquired by BIC Crystal.

Bubble Wrap Transparent air-pocket-filled plastic sheeting for wrapping fragile goods is also great fun to pop by hand. The term for the genuine article is a trademark of the Sealed Air Corporation.

Breathalyser The instrument for police checks for alcohol consumed by a suspect driver is a trademark of Draeger Safety.

Coke The common name for any cola-based soft drink is still a trademark of Coca-Cola.

Filofax At the height of their popularity in the 1980s, before electronic devices took over, any leather-bound personal organiser was known as a Filofax. The Filofax company had made the products since1921.

Frisbee Of the many varieties of flying disk available, only Wham-O owns the brand name and registered trademark of Frisbee.

Google The internet search engine has become a verb. To google means to obtain information from the internet by whatever means.

brand names *continued*

Hoover Was once a synonym for vacuum cleaners and even made it as a verb. The Hoover Company has been making the devices since 1907.

Hula-Hoop The twirling hoop around hips or knees is a Hula-Hoop only if made by Wham-O.

Jacuzzi Only the whirlpool baths made by the company founded by Roy Jacuzzi can rightfully bear the name.

Jeep Rugged four-wheel drive vehicles may not bear the name unless they are made by Jeep, which began producing the original vehicles for the American army in the second world war. DaimlerChrysler now owns Jeep.

Jet Ski Small motorised personal watercraft are commonly known as Jet Skis, although the term is a brand name owned by Kawasaki Heavy Industries of Japan.

Kitty Litter Felines in search of relief indoors must thank Edward Lowe, who invented the cat-box filler in 1947.

Kleenex The brand name of Kimberley-Clark's product has become synonymous with paper tissues around the world.

Linoleum Patented in England by Frederick Walton in 1860 and giving its name to almost any man-made flexible floorage material, lino, like escalator and harmonica, had a trademark that has long-since elapsed but the generic term remains.

Muzak Anonymous, bland and faintly irritating background music heard in shops and other public places may genuinely be called Muzak only if produced by the South Carolina-based company of the same name.

Rawlplug In 1919 Rawlings invented a fibre or plastic plug that allows the insertion of a screw into a hole drilled into masonry. The company, which is still in existence, now competes with dozens of competitors to produce the devices to which it has lent its name.

Rollerblade The Rollerblade company that started the craze for in-line rollerskating can claim the trademark.

Scotch Tape Transparent cellophane adhesive tape is widely known as Scotch tape in America though the name is a trademark of the 3M company. In Britain the product is known as Sellotape, another brand name now owned by Henkel Consumer Adhesives.

Styrofoam Expanded polystyrene is often called Styrofoam though the word is a trade name of the Dow Chemical Company.

Teflon The trade name for a solid, chemically inert polymer of tetrafluoroethylene manufactured by Dupont rather than any non-stick coating on cooking utensils.

Thermos The first vacuum flasks were made Germany in 1904 by Thermos GmbH. The tradename for their flasks is still registered.

Tupperware Plastic storage boxes produced by any firm other than the Tupperware Corporation have no right to take that name.

Vaseline Petroleum jelly produced by Unilever is known as Vaseline. Anything else is just plain petroleum jelly.

Walkman Mobile personal stereo systems not produced by Sony cannot properly bear the name.

Xerox Photocopiers of any stripe were routinely known as Xerox machines for many years. The financial plight of the company and its slide out of the world's offices has all but stopped the practice.

Business jargon

Jargon can amuse, irritate and perplex. What it cannot do is clarify. Its whole purpose is to make English less plain. Policemen become law-enforcement officers. Teachers become curriculum deliverers. Cooks become catering operatives.

Business is the area of society where jargon breeds most prolifically. Boardroom presentations groan with words like "optimise", "buy-in" and "hard stops". Everything must be actionable (it is, after all, no use trying to boil the ocean). Executives ask each other what the "upside" is, exhort their baffled colleagues to "shake the trees" and "pick the low-hanging fruit", and plan horizon-scanning exercises in windowless offices.

Business-book titles act as hors d'oeuvres for the feast of babble inside. To create the title of your own jargon-stuffed publication, simply combine an ordinary verb and a meaningless noun: "Drive Change"; "Grow Strategy"; "Lead Execution". If you want to make it to the bestseller lists, add a lot of misplaced aggression: "Voracious Growth"; "Strategy Roadkill"; "Annihilate Change".

The supreme monarchs of jargon are management consultants. They spout so much of the stuff that there is jargon for their jargon: consultese. Some of the worst sentences on the planet come from some of its highest-paid people.

All of which raises an obvious question. Why is business so fond of jargon? The most appealing explanation is that it is all done out of a gigantic sense of irony. Po-faced executives describe themselves as "Six Sigma black belts" in public and then fall about laughing in private. It is a nice idea. But there are two far more compelling explanations for the tortured relationship between business and language: status and subterfuge.

The status explanation reflects a desire to put management on an equal footing with other professions, such as law, medicine and accountancy. One symptom of this desire is the stilted managerial oath sworn by MBA graduates from Harvard Business School for the first time in 2009: "As a manager, my purpose is to serve the greater good by bringing people and resources together to create value that no single individual can create alone. Therefore I will seek a course that enhances the value my enterprise can create for society over the long term."

Another symptom is a scientific-sounding lexicon. A daunting vocabulary helps to confer a bit more status on the people who run businesses. Anyone can have a go at improving the way things work. But the idea of "optimising processes" and "enhancing value" is much more impressive, the preserve of people with deep pools of knowledge.

That may explain why the need to create jargon seems to run deepest in the area where knowledge counts least: the job of managing people themselves. The challenges of running teams, enthusing colleagues and handling disputes are immense. Few people do it well, and those that do tend to have judgment, empathy, charisma and other characteristics that are difficult to teach and even harder to codify.

But rather than admitting that good managers are born, not made, executives use jargon to pretend the opposite. People are turned into "human resources", a kind of raw material to be extracted and hammered into shape. They are given "360-degree" feedback, a dizzying process of appraisals from colleagues both senior and junior to them. The lucky ones are placed in succession pools.

They are subjected to psychometric tests, and are categorised by their Myers-Briggs indicators. Creative types are sometimes known as right-brain executives, logical ones are called left-brainers. If you hear someone

business jargon *continued*

babbling about a both-brain leader, they are not talking about a medical disorder. People can also be divided into colour categories. Blue thinkers are analytical problem-solvers; yellow thinkers are more likely to overlook important details. If you mix blue and yellow thinkers together in a team, you presumably get a lot of green thinkers. And so on.

If jargon plays a role in increasing managers' self-regard, it also serves a much simpler commercial purpose. Here, for example, is one way to describe ways that companies ought to respond to a severe recession: "People are poorer. Make decent stuff at an affordable price."

Here is another: "As discretionary spending all but disappears, companies must make adjustments in product mix, pricing, promotions and channel strategy to deliver the innovation today's customers value. By providing offerings with a clear range of desirable benefits and delivering them at the right price point, leading companies will be showing a clear way forward."

The message is the same, but consultants would have less chance of prising open clients' chequebooks, let alone increasing their "share of wallet", with the former as a sales pitch. A thick overlay of jargon obscures the banality of the message; indeed, it creates a sense of deep, almost formidable, expertise.

Most impressive of all is when firms invent entirely new words to describe a concept. These neologisms are usually profoundly ugly. Take "co-opetition", the idea that firms sometimes co-operate and sometimes compete. Or "rightshoring", the concept of striking the right balance between work done locally and work done abroad. Or "trivergence", a word to describe the interaction between devices, their controls and the data they use. But they help their inventors to make money. What greater proof could there be of a company's ability to push the envelope, think outside the box and do all sorts of other strange things with paper-based objects?

The smoke-and-mirrors theory of jargon finds plenty of support in the great boom and bust of recent years. Exhibit A from the bubble is the word "subprime". If you had to pick a word to describe a customer that represented an abnormal credit risk to a lender, subprime is one that applies a particularly pleasant gloss. It has the same obfuscating qualities as "suboptimal", another management favourite.

Other examples abound. Collateralised debt obligations, let alone CDO-squareds and CDO-cubeds, sound like they must have been created by very smart people. Many of the world's biggest banks were undone by their exposure to something called "super senior" debt. How could anyone fail to be reassured by a name like that? In a rare victory for plain speaking, all these bad loans later came to be known as "toxic assets", but by then it was too late.

The capacity of jargon to mask the truth has proven useful in smoothing over the painful realities when times are hard. For firms that are laying people off, managers talk about "downsizing" or, better still, "rightsizing" the business. Some like to use the term "leaning" for the process of trimming costs. Even those firms proposing a better option than redundancy cannot bear to be too honest about it. A scheme to save costs by cutting the working week at one of the Big Four accounting firms was given the disarming name of "Flexible Futures".

Expecting greater candour is naive. And appeals for more clarity in the way that businesses communicate are as likely to provoke more jargon as get rid of it – horrifyingly, the "KISS principle" stands for "Keep It Simple, Stupid". But the next time you hear jargon in the workplace, don't just snigger. Ask yourself what is being obscured.

business jargon *continued*

Advice from *The Economist Style Guide*

Jargon Avoid it. You may have to think harder if you are not to use jargon, but you can still be precise. Technical terms should be used in their proper context; do not use them out of it. In many instances simple words can do the job of *exponential* (try *fast*), *interface* (*frontier* or *border*) and so on. If you find yourself tempted to write about *affirmative action* or *corporate governance*, you will have to explain what it is; with luck, you will then not have to use the actual expression.

Avoid, above all, the kind of jargon that tries to dignify nonsense with seriousness:

The appointee ... should have a proven track record of operating at a senior level within a multi-site international business, preferably within a service- or brand-oriented environment

declared an advertisement for a financial controller for The Economist Group.

At a national level, the department engaged stakeholders positively ... This helped ... to improve stakeholder buy-in to agreed changes

avowed a British civil servant in a report.

The City Safe T3 Resilience Project is a cross-sector initiative bringing together experts ... to enable multi-tier practitioner-oriented collaboration on resilience and counter-terrorism challenges and opportunities

explained Chatham House.

Or to obscure the truth:

These grants will incentivise administrators and educators to apply relevant metrics to assess achievement in the competencies they seek to develop

said a memo cited by Tony Proscio in "Bad Words for

Good" (The Edna McConnell Clark Foundation). What it meant, as Mr Proscio points out, was that the grants would be used to pay teachers who agreed to test their students.

Or simply to obfuscate:

A multi-agency project catering for holistic diversionary provision to young people for positive action linked to the community safety strategy and the pupil referral unit

was how Luton Education Authority described go-karting lessons.

Someone with good *interpersonal skills* probably just *gets on well with others*. Someone with poor *parenting skills* is probably a *bad father* or a *bad mother*. *Negative health outcomes* are probably *illness* or *death*. *Intelligent media brands for the high-end audience that clients value* are presumably *good publications for rich people*.

… and on journalese and slang

Do not be too free with slang like *He really hit the big time in 1994*. Slang, like metaphors, should be used only occasionally if it is to have effect. Avoid expressions used only by journalists, such as giving people *the thumbs up*, *the thumbs down* or *the green light*. Stay clear of *gravy trains* and *salami tactics*. Do not use *the likes of*, or *Big Pharma* (*big drug firms*).

Resist saying *This will be no panacea*. When you find something that is indeed a *panacea* (or a *magic* or *silver bullet*), that will indeed be news. Similarly, hold back from offering the reassurance *There is no need to panic*. Instead, ask yourself exactly when there is a need to panic.

Lazy business journalists always enjoy describing the problems of *troubled* company C, a victim of the *revolution* in the gimbal-pin industry (change is always revolutionary in such industries), which, *well-placed insiders* predict, will be riven by a *make-or-break* strike unless one of the *major players* makes an *11th-hour* (or *last-ditch*) intervention in a *marathon* negotiating session.

Six rules of good writing

Do not be stuffy Use the language of everyday speech, not that of spokesmen, lawyers or bureaucrats (so prefer *let* to *permit*, *people* to *persons*, *buy* to *purchase*, *colleague* to *peer*, *way out* to *exit*, *present* to *gift*, *rich* to *wealthy*, *show* to *demonstrate*, *break* to *violate*). Pomposity and long-windedness tend to obscure meaning, or reveal the lack of it: strip them away in favour of plain words.

Do not be hectoring or arrogant Those who disagree with you are not necessarily *stupid* or *insane*. Nobody needs to be described as silly: let your analysis show that he is. When you express opinions, do not simply make assertions. The aim is not just to tell readers what you think, but to persuade them; if you use arguments, reasoning and evidence, you may succeed.

Do not be too pleased with yourself Don't boast of your own cleverness by telling readers that you correctly predicted something or that you have a scoop. You are more likely to bore or irritate them than to impress them.

Do not be too chatty *Surprise, surprise* is more irritating than informative. So is *Ho, ho* and, in the middle of a sentence, *wait for it*, etc.

Do not be too didactic If too many sentences begin *Compare, Consider, Expect, Imagine, Look at, Note, Prepare for, Remember* or *Take*, readers will think they are reading a textbook (or, indeed, a style book).

Do your best to be lucid ("I see but one rule: to be clear", Stendhal) Simple sentences help. Keep complicated constructions and gimmicks to a minimum, if necessary by remembering the *New Yorker*'s comment: "Backward ran sentences until reeled the mind."

Source: *The Economist Style Guide*

Alpha e-mail

What happens when a rousing wartime speech is updated by a modern manager? An e-mail to engineers working on the Sakhalin II oil and gas project in Russia in 2007 provided the answer. David Greer of the Shell-led consortium headlined the e-mail "Pipeliners all" and exhorted his staff to "lead me, follow me or get out of my way".

The memo was memorable for its weird mixture of modern-day jargon ("lift up your level of personal and team energy") and old-fashioned style. At one point, Mr Greer says he is sure that as children, the engineers all admired "the champion marble player". The dissonance is because Mr Greer owed much of his phrasing, marble players and all, to a blood-and-guts speech given to American troops by General George Patton in 1944.

"All Americans love to fight, traditionally," thundered Patton. "All real Americans love the sting and clash of battle." Mr Greer judiciously tweaked the phrasing. "Pipeliners and engineers love to fight and win, traditionally. All real engineers love the sting and clash of challenge." Patton rallied his troops by appealing to group identity ("Americans despise cowards. Americans play to win all the time"). Mr Greer decided to personalise: "I despise cowards and play to win all the time".

To be fair to Mr Greer, who resigned shortly after the email was leaked, his intentions were doubtless good. But finding his own voice would have been smarter. Patton ended his pep talk in inimitable style: "You may be thankful that twenty years from now when you are sitting … with your grandson on your knee and he asks you what you did in the great World War II, you won't have to cough, shift him to the other knee and say: 'Well, your Granddaddy shovelled shit in Louisiana.'" "Today I established a Pipeline Recovery Plan Support Team" would not have the same ring.

Business laws and principles

■ **BENFORD'S LAW** In lists of numbers from many sources of data the leading digit 1 occurs much more often than the others (about 30% of the time). The law was discovered by Simon Newcomb, an American astronomer, in 1881. He noted that the first pages of books of logarithms were much more thumbed than others. Furthermore, the higher the digit, the less likely it is to occur. This applies to mathematical constants as much as utility bills, addresses, share prices, birth and death statistics, the height of mountains, etc.

■ **BROOKS'S LAW** "Adding manpower to a late software project makes it later," said Fred Brooks, in his book *The Mythical Man-Month*.

■ **GOODHART'S LAW** "Any observed statistical regularity will tend to collapse once pressure is placed upon it for control purposes" was the law stated by Charles Goodhart, a chief adviser to the Bank of England during the 1980s. It has been recast more succinctly as "When a measure becomes a target, it ceases to be a good measure."

■ **GRESHAM'S LAW** "Bad money drives good money out of circulation." If coins of the same legal tender contain metal of different value, the coins composed of the cheaper metal will be used for payment, and those made of more expensive metal will be hoarded and disappear from circulation. Named after Sir Thomas Gresham (1519–79), a British financier and founder of the Royal Exchange.

■ **MOORE'S LAW** "The number of transistors on a chip doubles every 18–24 months." An observation by Gordon Moore, a founder of Intel, regarding the pace of semiconductor technology development in 1961.

■ **MURPHY'S LAW** Anything that can go wrong will go wrong.

■ **PARKINSON'S LAW** "Work expands so as to fill the time available for its completion" was formulated by Cecil Northcote Parkinson in *The Economist* in 1955.

■ **PARKINSON'S LAW OF DATA** Data expand to fill the space available for storage, so acquiring more memory will encourage the adoption of techniques that require more memory.

■ **THE PETER PRINCIPLE** In a hierarchy, every employee tends to rise to his level of incompetence, according to Laurence Peter and Raymond Hull in their book of the same name published in 1969.

■ **REILLY'S LAW** This law of retail gravitation suggests that people are generally attracted to the largest shopping centre in the area. William Reilly, an American academic, proposed the law in a book published in 1931.

■ **PARETO PRINCIPLE** Also known as the 80/20 rule and named after Vilfredo Pareto (1848–1923), an Italian economist, who determined that 80% of activity comes from 20% of the people. The principle was extended (or simply misunderstood) by Joseph Juran, an American management guru, who suggested that for many phenomena 80% of consequences stem from 20% of the causes. That is, in many instances a large number of results stem from a small number of causes, eg, 80% of problems come from 20% of the equipment or workforce.

■ **SAY'S LAW** Aggregate supply creates its own aggregate demand. Attributed to Jean-Baptiste Say (1767–1832), a French economist. If output increases in a free-market economy, the sales would give the producers of the goods the same amount of income which would re-enter the economy and create demand for those goods. Keynes's law, attributed to John Maynard Keynes (1883–1946), a British economist, says that the opposite is true and that "demand creates its own supply" as businesses produce more to satisfy demand up to the limit of full employment.

Top business schools

The Economist ranking, 2009

IESE Business School – University of Navarra	Spain
IMD – International Institute for Management Development	Switzerland
University of California at Berkeley – Haas School of Business	US
University of Chicago – Booth School of Business	US
Harvard Business School	US
Dartmouth College – Tuck School of Business	US
Stanford Graduate School of Business	US
London Business School	UK
University of Pennsylvania – Wharton School	US
Vlerick Leuven Gent Management School	Belgium
University of Cambridge – Judge Business School	UK
York University – Schulich School of Business	Canada
New York University – Leonard N. Stern School of Business	US
HEC School of Management, Paris	France
Northwestern University – Kellogg School of Management	US

Source: *The Economist*

FT ranking, 2009

University of Pennsylvania – Wharton School	US
London Business School	UK
Harvard Business School	US
Columbia Business School	US
INSEAD	France/Singapore
Stanford Graduate School of Business	US
Instituto de Empresa – IE Business School	Spain
China Europe International Business School	China
Massachusetts Institute of Technology – MIT Sloan School of Management	US
New York University – Leonard Stern School of Business	US
University of Chicago – Booth School of Business	US
University of Navarra – IESE Business School	Spain
Dartmouth College – Tuck School of Business	US
IMD – International Institute for Management Development	Switzerland

Source: *Financial Times*

Business school costs and rewards

	Cost*, $'000	Five-year gain†, $'000	Pre-MBA salary, $'000	Post-MBA salary, $'000
US				
Stanford Graduate School of Business	82	85	102	225
Dartmouth College – Tuck School of Business	70	80	94	205
Harvard Business School	82	79	102	215
University of Chicago – Booth School of Business	71	63	97	210
University of Pennsylvania – Wharton School	75	57	100	200
Columbia Business School	70	57	99	182
Cornell University - Johnson Booth School of Management	60	57	92	168
Outside US				
INSEAD	67	192	64	218
IMD – International Institute for Management Development	74	177	77	240
London Business School	73	121	64	209
IE - Instituto de Empresa	69	95	33	150
University of Manchester – Manchester Business School	57	92	41	150
University of Cambridge – Judge Business School	56	91	60	149
University of Oxford – Saïd Business School	56	89	69	167
University of Navarra – IESE Business School	91	83	43	178
Ceibs	36	76	13	67

*Out-of-state tuition for complete MBA.
†Five-year total compensation after graduation minus the sum of tuition and forgone compensation.
Source: *Forbes*

From PCs to PDAs

Worldwide PC unit shipments by region

Region	2004	2005	2008
Asia Pacific excluding Japan	27,914,774	31,380,848	72,877,418
Canada	2,698,500	3,116,000	6,233,887
Central/eastern Europe	8,592,836	9,837,482	21,832,037
Japan	6,402,764	6,848,501	14,246,950
Latin America	9,315,073	11,999,442	26,565,271
Middle East/Africa	5,004,240	6,091,260	14,731,183
US	39,352,166	39,697,902	65,482,674
Western Europe	25,238,776	27,134,701	65,348,730
Worldwide	124,519,128	136,106,136	287,318,151

Worldwide notebook and ultra portable shipments

Region	Form factor	2004	2005	2008
Worldwide	Notebook	43,865,481	59,412,310	136,131,524
Worldwide	Ultra portable	5,059,138	5,888,260	6,291,820

Worldwide and US PDA shipments

Region	2003	2004	2005
Worldwide	10,572,143	9,127,726	7,646,638
US	5,066,184	3,698,966	2,650,007

Source: IDC

Worldwide and US BlackBerry shipments

Region	2003	2004	2005	2008
Worldwide	490,263	2,660,899	4,072,122	23,500,000
US	377,690	1,958,167	2,752,352	

Note: Figures include only Smartphones, not PDA shipments.
Source: IDC

Chip power

	Transistors, m	Processor
1971	0.00225	4004
1972	0.0025	8008
1974	0.005	8080
1978	0.029	8086
1982	0.12	286
1985	0.275	Intel386
1989	1.18	Intel486
1993	3.1	Pentium
1997	7.5	Pentium II
1999	28	Pentium III
2000	42	Pentium 4
2002	220	Itanium
2004	592	Itanium 2
2006	1,720	Dual-core Itanium 2
2010	2,000	Tukwila

Note: Advances in chip processing power have followed a path known as Moore's Law, whereby the number of transistors doubles every 18–24 months.
Source: Intel

Computer processing costs

Year	1944	1970	1984	1997	2008
Cost $	200,000	4,674,160	3,995	999	1,000
MIPS*	0.000003	12.5	8.3	166	76,383
$ per MIPS	65,941,300,000	373,933	479	6	0.01

*Millions of instructions per second.
Sources: Federal Reserve Bank of Dallas; *The Economist*

The impact of software piracy

Losses by region, 2008

	$bn
Worldwide	53.0
Asia-Pacific	15.3
Western Europe	13.0
North America	10.4
Eastern Europe	7.0
Latin America	4.3
Middle East & Africa	3.0

Losses by country, 2008

	$m
US	9,143
China	6,677
Russia	4,215
India	2,768
France	2,760
UK	2,181
Germany	2,152
Italy	1,895
Brazil	1,645
Japan	1,495
Canada	1,222
Spain	1,029
Mexico	823
Poland	648
South Korea	622
Australia	613
Thailand	609
Netherlands	53
Indonesia	544
Ukraine	534
Venezuela	484

Sources: International Data Corporation (IDC); Business Software Alliance (BSA)

Spam and e-mail

Leading spam-producing countries

Q1 2009	% of total	Relaying by region, %	
US	15.8	Asia	34.8
Brazil	10.2	Europe	23.6
China (including Hong Kong)	7.7	North America	19.4
India	5.1	South America	19.0
Turkey	4.1	Africa	2.0
South Korea	3.8	Other	1.2
Russia	3.8		
Spain	3.0		
Argentina	2.8		
Poland	2.6		
Colombia	2.6		
Italy	2.3		
Other	36.2		

Source: Sophos

Spam and e-mail forecasts

Bn except where specified	2008	2009	2010	2011	2012
Worldwide messages sent per day	210	247	294	349	419
Worldwide spam traffic per day	164	199	238	286	347
Spam as % of total messages per day	78	80	81	82	83
Delivered spam messages per day	93	109	128	153	183
Corporate messages per day	77	92	108	129	155
Corporate spam messages per day	48	59	69	84	102
Corporate spam as % of corporate messages per day	62	64	64	65	66
Delivered corporate spam messages per day	30	35	41	48	58
Consumer messages per day	132	156	186	220	264
Consumer spam messages per day	116	140	169	202	244
Consumer spam as % of consumer messages per day	88	90	91	92	93

Source: The Radicati Group

Pod facts

iPod sales,* m

2006	39,409	2008	54,828
2007	51,630	2009	33,737†

*Fiscal years ending September. †First half.
Source: Apple

Legal music downloads by single tracks downloaded, m

	2007	2008	Growth, %
France	11	15	27
Germany	31	37	22
UK	78	110	42
US	844	1,072	27
World	1,129	1,400	24

Source: IFPI

Worldwide portable digital music player shipments, m

	2002	2003	2004	2005	2006	2008
Flash	2.8	12.5	26.4	101.5	149.8	188.2
Hard-drive	0.9	2.7	12.5	20.5	21.5	12.3
Total	3.7	15.1	38.9	122.0	171.4	200.5

Source: IDC

Podcast growth

	2008	2009	2010	2011	2012	2013
US podcast audience, m	17.4	21.9	26.7	30.6	34.6	37.6
% of US internet users	9.0	11.0	13.0	14.5	16.0	17.0

Note: Users who download at least one podcast each month.
Source: eMarketer Inc

Internet users who download podcasts, 2008

	Users, m	% of pop.		Users, m	% of pop.
China	45.4	5.4	Philippines	2.3	4.5
US	29.5	16.2	Australia	2.1	16.7
South Korea	13.7	21.3	Canada	2.1	10.4
India	10.3	1.6	Poland	1.7	6.9
Brazil	9.5	8.2	Netherlands	1.6	15.8
Japan	9.0	11.8	Romania	1.4	10.3
UK	7.5	20.6	Pakistan	1.2	1.4
Germany	6.6	13.3	Hong Kong	0.8	16.7
Spain	5.6	22.5	Switzerland	0.8	17.5
Russia	5.0	5.5	Austria	0.5	9.4
Mexico	4.8	7.9	Denmark	0.5	15.5
France	4.4	11.7	Czech Republic	0.4	6.4
Taiwan	3.5	24.0	Greece	0.4	6.4
Italy	2.6	7.4	Hungary	0.3	6.5
Turkey	2.6	6.0			

Note: Selected countries only and for daily internet users aged 15-64.
Source: eMarketer Inc

Internet users who download podcasts, % of respondents

	2006	2007	2008
China	24.3	51.8	74.3
Philippines	8.3	26.4	61.3
Russia	13.8	12.6	57.9
Spain	20.8	16.6	51.0
South Korea	17.9	23.8	49.2
UK	14.3	22.2	42.2
Australia	14.4	21.7	40.2
Germany	12.5	8.9	34.8
France	25.2	20.9	34.2
United States	12.7	14.3	29.5
Italy	16.2	14.7	25.1
Worldwide	18.4	21.8	48.8

Note: Selected countries only and for daily internet users aged 15-64.
Source: eMarketer Inc

Internet suffixes

Afghanistan	.af	Bulgaria	.bg
Aland Islands	.ax	Burkina Faso	.bf
Albania	.al	Burundi	.bi
Algeria	.dz	Cambodia	.kh
American Samoa	.as	Cameroon	.cm
Andorra	.ad	Canada	.ca
Angola	.ao	Cape Verde	.cv
Anguilla	.ai	Cayman Islands	.ky
Antarctica	.aq	Central African Rep	.cf
Antigua and Barbuda	.ag	Chad	.td
Argentina	.ar	Chile	.cl
Armenia	.am	China	.cn
Aruba	.aw	Christmas Island	.cx
Ascension Island	.ac	Cocos (Keeling) Islands	.cc
Australia	.au	Colombia	.co
Austria	.at	Comoros	.km
Azerbaijan	.az	Congo (Democratic	
Bahamas	.bs	Republic of Congo)	.cd
Bahrain	.bh	Congo-Brazzaville	
Bangladesh	.bd	(Republic of Congo)	.cg
Barbados	.bb	Cook Islands	.ck
Belarus	.by	Costa Rica	.cr
Belgium	.be	Côte d'Ivoire	.ci
Belize	.bz	Croatia	.hr
Benin	.bj	Cuba	.cu
Bermuda	.bm	Cyprus	.cy
Bhutan	.bt	Czech Republic	.cz
Bolivia	.bo	Denmark	.dk
Bosnia & Herzegovina	.ba	Djibouti	.dj
Botswana	.bw	Dominica	.dm
Bouvet Island	.bv	Dominican Republic	.do
Brazil	.br	Ecuador	.ec
British Indian Ocean		Egypt	.eg
Territory	.io	El Salvador	.sv
Brunei	.bn	Equatorial Guinea	.gq

Eritrea	.er	Iraq	.iq
Estonia	.ee	Ireland	.ie
Ethiopia	.et	Isle of Man	.im
Falkland Islands	.fk	Israel	.il
Faroe Islands	.fo	Italy	.it
Fiji	.fj	Jamaica	.jm
Finland	.fi	Japan	.jp
France	.fr	Jersey	.je
French Guyana	.gf	Jordan	.jo
French Polynesia	.pf	Kazakhstan	.kz
French Southern		Kenya	.ke
Territories	.tf	Kirgizstan	.kg
Gabon	.ga	Kiribati	.ki
Gambia, The	.gm	Kuwait	.kw
Georgia	.ge	Laos	.la
Germany	.de	Latvia	.lv
Ghana	.gh	Lebanon	.lb
Gibraltar	.gi	Lesotho	.ls
Greece	.gr	Liberia	.lr
Greenland	.gl	Libya	.ly
Grenada	.gd	Liechtenstein	.li
Guadeloupe	.gp	Lithuania	.lt
Guam	.gu	Luxembourg	.lu
Guatemala	.gt	Macau	.mo
Guernsey	.gg	Macedonia	.mk
Guinea	.gn	Madagascar	.mg
Guinea-Bissau	.gw	Malawi	.mw
Guyana	.gy	Malaysia	.my
Haiti	.ht	Maldives	.mv
Heard and McDonald		Mali	.ml
Islands	.hm	Malta	.mt
Honduras	.hn	Marshall Islands	.mh
Hong Kong	.hk	Martinique	.mq
Hungary	.hu	Mauritania	.mr
Iceland	.is	Mauritius	.mu
India	.in	Mayotte	.yt
Indonesia	.id	Mexico	.mx
Iran	.ir	Micronesia	.fm

internet suffixes *continued*

Moldova	.md	Poland	.pl
Monaco	.mc	Portugal	.pt
Mongolia	.mn	Puerto Rico	.pr
Monserrat	.ms	Qatar	.qa
Montenegro	.me	Réunion	.re
Morocco	.ma	Romania	.ro
Mozambique	.mz	Russia	.ru
Myanmar	.mm	Rwanda	.rw
Namibia	.na	St Barthelemy	.bl
Nauru	.nr	St Kitts and Nevis	.kn
Nepal	.np	St Lucia	.lc
Netherlands	.nl	St Martin	.mf
Netherlands Antilles	.an	St Pierre & Miquelon	.pm
New Caledonia	.nc	St Vincent and the	
New Zealand	.nz	Grenadines	.vc
Nicaragua	.ni	Samoa	.ws
Niger	.ne	San Marino	.sm
Nigeria	.ng	Sao Tome and Principe	.st
Niue	.nu	Saudi Arabia	.sa
Norfolk Island	.nf	Senegal	.sn
North Korea		Seychelles	.sc
(Democratic People's		Serbia	.rs
Republic of Korea)	.kp	Sierra Leone	.sl
Northern Mariana		Singapore	.sg
Islands	.mp	Slovakia	.sk
Norway	.no	Slovenia	.si
Oman	.om	Solomon Islands	.sb
Pakistan	.pk	Somalia	.so
Palau	.pw	South Africa	.za
Palestinian Territories	.ps	South Korea	.kr
Panama	.pa	South Georgia and the	
Papua New Guinea	.pg	South Sandwich	
Paraguay	.py	Islands	.gs
Peru	.pe	Spain	.es
Philippines	.ph	Sri Lanka	.lk
Pitcairn	.pn	St. Helena	.sh

St.Pierre & Miquelon	.pm
Sudan	.sd
Suriname	.sr
Svalbard and Jan Mayen Islands	.sj
Swaziland	.sz
Sweden	.se
Switzerland	.ch
Syria	.sy
Taiwan	.tw
Tajikistan	.tj
Tanzania	.tz
Thailand	.th
Timor-Leste	.tl
Togo	.tg
Tokelau	.tk
Tonga	.to
Trinidad & Tobago	.tt
Tunisia	.tn
Turkey	.tr
Turkmenistan	.tm
Turks and Caicos Islands	.tc
Tuvalu	.tv
Uganda	.ug
Ukraine	.ua
UAE	.ae
UK	.gb
US	.us
US Minor Outlying Islands	.um
Uruguay	.uy
Uzbekistan	.uz
Vanuatu	.vu
Vatican	.va
Venezuela	.ve
Vietnam	.vn

Virgin Islands, British	.vg
Virgin Islands, US	.vi
Wallis and Futuna Islands	.wf
Western Sahara	.eh
Yemen	.ye
Zaire	.cd
Zambia	.zm
Zimbabwe	.zw

Aviation	.aero
Pan Asia	.asia
Business	.biz
Catalan community	.cat
Generic	.com
Co-operative organisations	.coop
Educational	.edu
European Union	.eu
US government	.gov
Information	.info
International government organisations	.int
HR managers	.jobs
US department of defence	.mil
Mobile products and services	.mobi
Museums	.museum
Personal	.name
Networks	.net
Organisations	.org
Professionals	.pro
Generic contact data	.tel
Travel industry	.travel

Source: Internet Assigned Numbers Authority

Internet usage

World internet usage, March 2009

Region	Internet users, m	Penetration, %	% of world usage	Usage growth, 2000–08, %
Africa	54.2	5.6	3.4	1,100.0
Asia	657.2	17.4	41.2	474.9
Europe	393.4	48.9	24.6	274.3
Middle East	45.9	23.3	2.9	1,296.2
North America	251.3	74.4	15.7	132.5
Latin America and Caribbean	173.6	29.9	10.9	860.9
Oceania/ Australia	20.8	60.4	1.3	172.7
World total	1,596.3	23.8	100.0	342.2

Source: internetworldstats.com

Top ten languages, March 2009

Language	Internet users, m	% of all users	Speakers, m	Penetration, %	Growth in users, 2000–08, %
English	463.8	29.1	1,247.9	37.2	226.7
Chinese	321.4	20.1	1,365.1	23.5	894.8
Spanish	130.8	8.2	408.8	32.0	619.3
Japanese	94.0	5.9	127.3	73.8	99.7
French	73.6	4.6	414.0	17.8	503.4
Portuguese	72.6	4.5	244.1	29.7	857.7
German	65.2	4.1	96.4	67.7	135.5
Arabic	41.4	2.6	291.1	14.2	1,545.2
Russian	38.0	2.4	140.7	27.0	1,125.8
Korean	36.8	2.3	70.9	51.9	93.3
Top ten languages	1,337.5	83.8	4,406.3	30.4	329.2
Rest of world	258.7	16.2	2,303.7	11.2	424.5
World total	1,596.3	100.0	6,710.0	23.8	342.2

Source: internwetworldstats.com

Global average internet usage, May 2009

Sessions/visits per person per month	37
Domains visited per person per month	70
Web pages per person per month	1,591
Page views per surfing session	42
PC time spent per month	38:00:14
Time spent during surfing session	01:02:11
Duration of a web page viewed	00:00:51
Active digital media universe	381,285,866
Current digital media universe estimate	574,175,185

Source: Nielsen Online

Top internet-search sites, December 2008

	Searches, m	Searches per day, m	Share of searches %
Google	5,421.9	174.9	62.9
Yahoo!	1,448.1	46.7	16.8
Microsoft MSN/Windows Live	851.5	27.5	9.9
AOL	357.0	11.5	4.1
Ask	169.1	5.5	2.0
Others	376.0	12.1	4.4
Total	8,623.7	278.2	100.0

Source: Search Engine Watch

Top ten searches, 2008

The economy	What is
financial crisis	what is love
depression	what is life
bail-out	what is java
mortgage crisis	what is sap
wall street	what is rss
oil	what is scientology
stock market	what is autism
subprime	what is lupus
credit crisis	what is 3g
housing crisis	what is art

Source: Google

Internet growth

End year	Users, m	% of world population
Dec 95	16	0.4
Dec 96	36	0.9
Dec 97	70	1.7
Dec 98	159	2.9
Dec 99	248	4.1
Dec 00	451	7.4
Dec 01	536	8.6
Dec 02	598	9.6
Dec 03	719	11.1
Dec 04	817	12.7
Dec 05	1,018	15.7
Dec 06	1,093	16.7
Dec 07	1,319	20.0
Dec 08	1,574	23.5
Mar 09	1,596	23.8

Source: internetworldstats.com

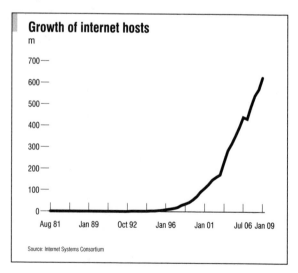

Growth of internet hosts

Source: Internet Systems Consortium

Blogs away

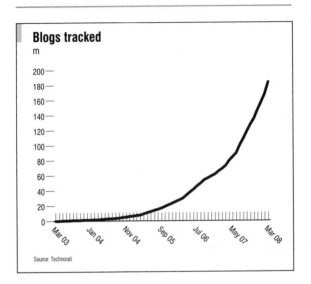

Blogs tracked
m

Source: Technorati

Blog posts by language, June 2009

1 English
2 Japanese
3 Spanish
4 French
5 Portuguese
6 Italian
7 German
8 Chinese
9 Indonesian
10 Dutch

Source: Technorati

Telecommunications

Worldwide telecom services revenue by type, $bn

	1991	1993	1995	2000	2004	2008
Fixed-line	331	359	428	477	552	...
International	37	46	53	60	32	...
Mobile	19	35	78	278	506	...
Other	53	77	89	165	210	...
Total	440	517	648	980	1,300	...
As % of total						
Fixed-line	75.2	69.4	66.0	48.7	42.5	...
International	8.4	8.9	8.2	6.1	2.5	...
Mobile	4.3	6.8	12.0	28.4	38.9	...
Other	12.0	14.9	13.7	16.8	16.2	...
Other telecom statistics						
Fixed-line subscribers, m	546	604	689	975	1,204	1,267
Mobile subscribers, m	16	34	91	738	1,763	4,100
International traffic minutes, bn	38	49	63	114	166	...
Personal computers, m	130	175	235	500	775	...

Source: International Telecommunication Union

Telephone-call prices

Cost of a three-minute call from New York to London, 1990 dollars					
1930	1960	1990	1999	2006	2009
245	47.5	3.00	0.35	0.19	0.05

Fixed-line subscribers by region, m

	2000	2005	2008	2008 penetration, %
Africa	19.7	28.3	31.6	3.4
Americas	290.1	296.8	281.6	30.7
Asia	339.9	596.9	634.0	15.8
Europe	316.9	328.6	318.8	39.4
Oceania	12.6	13.6	11.5	33.8
World total	979.2	1,264.1	1,277.5	19.1

Source: International Telecommunication Union

Mobile phone subscribers by region, m

	2000	2005	2008	2008 penetration, %
Africa	15.6	130.3	364.3	38.5
Americas	182.0	458.8	751.9	81.7
Asia	240.6	849.8	1,910.7	47.6
Europe	291.5	675.6	959.0	118.7
Oceania	10.3	22.5	28.3	82.5
World total	740.0	2,137.0	4,014.2	59.7

Source: International Telecommunication Union

Some first-ever telecommunications messages

- "What hath God wrought?" The first telegraph message sent by Samuel Morse, May 24th 1844.

- "Mr Watson, come here. I want to see you." The first voice telephone call made by Alexander Graham Bell, March 10th 1876.

- "..." Morse code for the letter S, as sent from England to Canada in the first transatlantic wireless message, using equipment invented by Guglielmo Marconi, December 12th 1901.

- "QWERTYUIOP" Believed to be similar to the text of the first electronic-mail message, as tested by Ray Tomlinson in 1971.

The corporate high life

Worldwide business fleets

2008	World total	North America	Europe	Asia & Middle East	Oceania	Other
Jets	16,605	11,824	2,507	853	150	1,271
Turboprops	12,127	8,185	1,102	487	309	2,044

Average age of worldwide business aircraft

2008	Years
Heavy jet	12.5
Medium jet	15.5
Light jet	18.4
Very Light jet	1.6
Heavy turboprop	21.0
Medium turboprop	24.5
Light turboprop	18.2

Summary of fractional fleet

2008	Aircraft	Shareholders*
Jets	956	5,565
Turboprops	122	778
Helicopters	13	57

2008	Years	Aircraft
Major providers	6.1	908
Minor providers	7.8	183

*Shareholder information only available for US operated aircraft.
Source: JETNET LLC Utica, NY 13501

Busiest airports

Passengers

	Total passengers, m, 2008
Atlanta, Hartsfield	89.4
Chicago, O'Hare	68.3
London, Heathrow	66.5
Tokyo, Haneda	65.9
Paris, Charles de Gaulle	60.2
Los Angeles, Intl.	58.6
Beijing, Capital	57.7
Dallas, Ft. Worth	56.3
Frankfurt, Main	52.5
Denver, Intl.	50.8
Madrid, Barajas	49.4
Hong Kong, Intl.	47.4
Amsterdam, Schiphol	46.2
New York, JFK	46.1

Freight

	Total cargo, m tonnes, 2008
Memphis, Intl.	3.65
Hong Kong, Intl.	3.52
Shanghai, Pudong Intl.	2.50
Seoul, Incheon	2.33
Anchorage, Intl.	2.23
Frankfurt, Main	2.03
Paris, Charles de Gaulle	1.99
Tokyo, Narita	1.98
Louisville, Standiford Fd.	1.94
Dubai, Intl.	1.82
Singapore, Changi	1.82
Miami, Intl.	1.73
Los Angeles, Intl.	1.53
Amsterdam, Schiphol	1.49
London, Heathrow	1.43

Source: Airports Council International

Pedal power

- According to the Worldwatch Institute, worldwide bicycle production was 11m in 1950, 20m in 1960, 36m in 1970, 62m in 1980, 92m in 1990, 104m in 2000 and 130m in 2007.

- China remained the largest producer, with two out of every three bikes made worldwide. India, the European Union, Taiwan, Indonesia and Brazil followed, with together around a quarter of the world total.

- While cycling rates are falling in China as more turn to cars, Chinese cities still register some of the highest cycling rates in the world, with bikes accounting for more than half of all journeys in some.

- In the West, Holland, Denmark and Germany have the highest cycling rates, ranging from 10% to 27% of all trips in 2007. In Britain, Australia and America, rates are around 1%.

- Sales of bikes in the 15 member states of the "old" European Union reached 19m in 2007, up 2% on 2006 and 11% higher than 2003. The growth of urban cycling as an alternative to the car is regarded as a factor, and is also thought to be behind the growth in sales of electric bikes, especially in the Netherlands and Germany.

- Continental European countries with high cycling rates achieve them via cycle-friendly policies and infrastructure, such as dedicated cycleways, parking facilities and integration with public transport.

- Cycle safety in these countries tends to be higher: cycling deaths in 2007 were eight times higher in America than in the Netherlands, while injuries per kilometre travelled were 30 times higher.

- European cities have seen a growth in bike-rental schemes. Paris's much-vaunted "Vélib" scheme, launched in 2007, made 20,000 bikes available (although theft and vandalism have posed problems). It followed rental schemes in Copenhagen, Berlin and

Frankfurt, and was followed by Barcelona, Marseilles and Lyon, among others.

- In London, where the mayor, Boris Johnson, is a keen cyclist, moves are afoot for a rental system from 2010. 545,000 bike trips are made daily there, more than 9% more than in 2008 and twice as many as 2000. Bike use along the city's main roads has risen 107% since 2000.
- London's transport authorities are trying to overcome perceptions of danger: in 2008, 6,000 adults and 39,000 children took part in free or subsidised cycle training programmes, and "Cycle Fridays" is an initiative that runs supervised group rides for commuters along six routes once a week.
- In England, of the 8.3m children that travel to school each day, 2% make the journey by cycle, according to 2008 research. Yet one in three children claims they would like to cycle.
- Cycle penetration in Africa remains low, with bikes out of the price range of many, and most cities cycle-unfriendly. However, health-care providers are increasingly using bicycles, especially for delivery of immunisation programmes. One British-based charity, "Re~Cycle", collects and reconditions unwanted bikes and ships them to Africa, where it works with local NGOs, adapts bikes to carry heavy loads (such as water) and teaches cycle maintenance. By mid-2009, it had shipped 31,000 bikes to 14 countries.
- In America, bike sales were projected to reach 18.5m in 2008, up from 18.2m in 2007, and 15.8m in 1998, but down from 20.9m in 2000. 44.7m Americans over seven years old were estimated to have ridden six or more times in 2008, up 11% from 2007 but down from the peak of 56.3m in 1995. In America, bike riding is primarily recreational; riding for transportation is a growing market, but in 2006, only 10% of cyclists surveyed rode for commuting purposes.

Sources: Worldwatch Institute, Bike for All, Bike Europe, *Time Out*, Transport for London, Re~Cycle, National Bicycle Dealers Association, League of American Bicyclists

Ship ahoy

Merchant fleets

2008	By country of domicile, number of vessels		By country of domicile, deadweight tonnage, m
China	3,303	Greece	174.6
Germany	3,208	Japan	161.7
Greece	3,115	Germany	94.2
Japan	3,115	China	84.9
Russia	2,111	Norway	46.9
Norway	1,827	US	39.8
US	1,769	South Korea	37.7
South Korea	1,140	Hong Kong	33.4
Turkey	1,026	Singapore	28.6
UK	876	Denmark	27.4
Singapore	869	Taiwan	26.2
Denmark	861	UK	26.0
Indonesia	850	Canada	18.7
Netherlands	792	Russia	18.0
Italy	773	Italy	17.7
Hong Kong	657	India	16.0
Taiwan	590	Turkey	13.2

Source: Lloyd's Register

Rail popularity

	Passengers, km per person per year, 2007		Freight, million tonnes-km per year, 2007
Switzerland	2,103	US	2,820,061
Japan	1,978	China	2,211,246
France	1,350	Russia	2,090,337
Russia	1,224	India	480,993
Ukraine	1,145	Canada	353,227
Austria	1,104	Ukraine	240,810
Denmark	1,041	Brazil	232,297

Source: International Union of Railways

Business creativity and research

Innovation index

2008

US	5.84	Netherlands	4.82
Finland	5.57	Belgium	4.69
Switzerland	5.54	Austria	4.68
Japan	5.52	France	4.67
Sweden	5.42	UK	4.66
Israel	5.26	Iceland	4.62
Taiwan	5.23	Norway	4.60
Germany	5.22	Australia	4.46
South Korea	5.18	Ireland	4.39
Denmark	5.09	Malaysia	4.28
Singapore	5.08	Luxembourg	4.15
Canada	4.82	Hong Kong	4.11

Technological readiness index

2008

Netherlands	6.01	South Korea	5.51
Sweden	5.99	Finland	5.46
Denmark	5.87	Austria	5.34
Norway	5.81	Taiwan	5.34
Switzerland	5.76	Estonia	5.30
Iceland	5.65	Germany	5.22
Singapore	5.65	Australia	5.21
UK	5.62	France	5.16
Canada	5.61	Japan	5.11
Hong Kong	5.60	New Zealand	5.09
US	5.57	Belgium	5.01
Luxembourg	5.52	Ireland	4.98

The innovation index is a measure of the adoption of new technology, and the interaction between the business and science sectors. It includes measures of the investment into research institutions and protection of intellectual property rights. The technological readiness index measures the ability of the economy to adopt new technologies. It includes measures of Information and communication technology (ICT) usage, the regulatory framework with regard to ICT, and the availability of new technology to business.

business creativity and research *continued*

Total expenditure on R&D

% of GDP, 2006		$bn, 2006	
Israel	4.59	US	343.7
Sweden	3.73	Japan	148.4
Finland	3.45	Germany	73.8
Japan	3.39	France	47.5
South Korea	3.22	UK	42.7
Switzerland*	2.90	China	37.7
US	2.61	South Korea	28.6
Taiwan	2.58	Canada	25.0
Germany	2.53	Italy†	19.4
Austria	2.46	Spain	14.8
Denmark	2.45	Sweden	14.7
Singapore	2.31	Australia*	11.8
France	2.09	Netherlands	11.2
Canada	1.95	Russia	10.6
Australia*	1.84	Switzerland*	10.5
Belgium	1.82	Taiwan	9.4
UK	1.76	Austria	7.9
Netherlands	1.65	Belgium	7.3
Czech Republic	1.55	Brazil†	7.3
Norway	1.52	Finland	7.2
Slovenia	1.50	Denmark	6.7
Luxembourg	1.47	Israel	6.6
China	1.36	Norway	5.1
Ireland	1.30	India	4.8
Spain	1.20	Mexico†	3.9

*2004
†2005
Source: IMD, *World Competitiveness Yearbook*

Inventors and inventions

1450 Leon Battista Alberti, an Italian philosopher, architect, musician, painter and sculptor from Genoa, invented the first mechanical anemometer.

1756 John Smeaton, a British engineer, made concrete by adding aggregate to cement. In 1824, Joseph Aspdin, another Briton, invented Portland cement by burning ground limestone and clay together. In 1867, Joseph Monier, a French gardener, patented the idea of reinforced concrete.

1830 Edwin Beard Budding, an engineer from Stroud in Gloucestershire, was awarded the first patent for a mechanical lawn mower.

1843 Alexander Bain, a Scottish clockmaker, patented the fax machine – 33 years before a patent was granted for the telephone. The first commercial fax service was opened between Paris and Lyon in 1865.

1849 Walter Hunt, a New York inventor, received a patent for the safety pin.

1851 Elias Howe patented an Automatic Continuous Clothing Closure but took the invention no further. In 1896, Whitcomb Judson marketed the Clasp Locker, a hook-and-eye shoe fastener. In 1913, Gideon Sundback, a Swedish-born electrical engineer living in Canada, improved the Judson C-curity Fastener and came up with the modern zip.

1861 Elisha Otis patented the "Improvement in Hoisting Apparatus". Lifts had been in use for some time but Otis invented a safety mechanism that stopped the lift falling if the rope broke, thus opening the way for safe passenger lifts and allowing the development of the high-rise building.

inventors and inventions *continued*

1866 George McGill developed the Patent Single Stroke Staple Press to insert brass fasteners into papers. In 1895 the Jones Manufacturing Company of Norwalk, Connecticut, introduced the first stapler that used steel staples formed into a continuous strip.

1872 Aaron Montgomery Ward sent out the world's first mail-order catalogue for his Chicago-based business.

1873 Joseph Glidden, a farmer from De Kalb, Illinois, applied for a patent on barbed wire.

1873 Levi Strauss, a Bavarian immigrant who had travelled to California during the Gold Rush, and Jacob Davis, a tailor from Reno, Nevada, got a patent for trousers strengthened with rivets to make sturdy workwear. Soon after they began to produce the first blue denim jeans.

1876 Alexander Graham Bell unveiled his "electrical speech machine" in Boston, Massachusetts, later to become known as the telephone, making the first ever phone call to his assistant: "Mr Watson, come here, I want you." He filed for a patent on the invention hours before a competitor, Elisha Grey. Though neither had produced a working telephone at the time, Bell's device controversially incorporated elements of his competitor's phone that had not appeared in his original patent.

1877 Thomas Edison invented the tin-foil phonograph. Alexander Graham Bell's graphophone of 1883 employed a wax cylinder which could be played many times but required separate sound recording for each cylinder. In 1887, Emile Berliner, a German immigrant working in Washington, DC, was granted a patent for the gramophone on which multiple, reproducable, pre-recorded flat-disc records could be played.

1879 Thomas Edison invented the first practical electric light bulb. Though the idea was not new no one had previously managed to produce a bulb that was cheap and robust enough for mass production.

1883 James Ritty and John Birch got a patent for the first mechanical cash register, invented for use in Ritty's saloon in Dayton, Ohio.

1888 Marvin Stone of Washington, DC, patented a spiral-winding process to manufacture the first wax-coated paper drinking straws.

1888 Thomas Edison filed a patent for the Kinetoscope, the forerunner of the modern motion-picture camera.

1891 James Naismith, a Canadian physical-education instructor, invented basketball.

1895 Charles Fey, a San Francisco car mechanic, invented the first mechanical fruit machine, the Liberty Bell.

1895 Guglielmo Marconi sent wireless signals over a mile at his laboratory in Italy. The next year, in Britain, he was granted the world's first patent for a system of wireless telegraphy.

1899 Johan Vaaler, a Norwegian inventor, was granted a patent for the paperclip in Germany. His design never really caught on as the Gem paperclip (the type most common today) was already in production in Britain.

1903 Albert Parkhouse, an employee of Timberlake Wire and Novelty Company in Jackson, Michigan, invented a coat hanger made from a piece of bent wire with the ends twisted together to form a hook. Colleagues had apparently complained that the firm provided insufficient coat storage.

1908 Jacques Brandenberger, a Swiss engineer working for a French textile company, invented Cellophane.

inventors and inventions *continued*

1921 Earle Dickson, a cotton-buyer at Johnson & Johnson, invented the Band-Aid self-adhesive plaster.

1921 John Larson, a medical student at the University of California, invented the polygraph, a lie-detecting machine.

1927 Erik Rotheim, a Norwegian, patented the first aerosol can that dispensed products using a propellant system.

1930 Scotch tape, the world's first transparent cellophane adhesive tape, was introduced. It was invented by Richard Drew, an engineer at 3M, a company located in St Paul, Minnesota. John Borden, another 3M engineer, invented the tape dispenser with a built-in cutter in 1932.

1932 Carlton Cole Magee invented the first parking meter in response to the growing problem of parking congestion in Oklahoma City. Meters were first installed there three years later.

1934 Percy Shaw, a 23-year-old British inventor, patented cats eyes to assist driving in fog or at night.

1938 Laszlo Biro, a Hungarian journalist, invented the ballpoint pen.

1938 Polytetrafluoroethylene (or PTFE) was discovered by Roy Plunkett at DuPont's research facility in New Jersey. PTFE was first marketed as Teflon in 1945.

1940 Norman Breakey of Toronto invented the paint roller.

1942 Cyanoacrylate was invented by Harry Coover at the Kodak Research Laboratories while developing a plastic for gunsights. The product was not considered for commercial application until 1958 and later became known as superglue.

1947 The transistor was invented at Bell Telephone Laboratories by a team led by physicists John Bardeen, Walter Brattain and William Shockley. In 1958, Jack Kilby of Texas Instruments unveiled the integrated circuit, but in 1959 Fairchild Semiconductor filed a patent for a semiconductor integrated circuit invented by Robert Noyce, starting a ten-year legal battle over who had invented the chip. In 1968, Ted Hoff, an employee of Intel, invented the microprocessor. In 1970, Doug Engelbart received a patent for his "X-Y position indicator for a display system", which was developed into the computer mouse. In 1976, Steve Jobs and Steve Wozniak made a microprocessor computer board called Apple I and a year later introduced the Apple II, the first personal computer.

1951 George de Mestral patented Velcro. The Swiss engineer, a keen mountaineer and inventor, noticed how burrs attached themselves to his clothes and his dog's fur and developed the idea for his new fastener.

1952 Joseph Woodland and Bernard Silver, graduate students at the Drexel Institute of Technology in Philadelphia, were issued a patent for the forerunner of the bar code.

1953 Norm Larsen, a chemist, made many attempts to develop an anti-corrosion formula working on the principle of water displacement in his lab in San Diego, California. In 1953, he succeeded and WD-40 (standing for water displacement 40th attempt) was born.

1954 Dee Horton and Lew Hewitt invented the automatic sliding door in Corpus Christi, Texas. The first door that entered service in 1960 was a unit donated to the City of Corpus Christi.

1955 Eugene Polley, an engineer working for America's Zenith Corporation, created the Flash-matic, the first wireless television remote control.

1956 Christopher Cockerell, a British engineer, invented the hovercraft.

inventors and inventions *continued*

1956 Bette Nesmith Graham, a secretary in Dallas, Texas, sold the first batch of Mistake Out, a liquid correcting fluid. Some years later, the product much improved, it was renamed Liquid Paper.

1958 Alfred Neustadter from Brooklyn, New York, first marketed the Rolodex, a rotating index-card holder.

1959 Ernie Fraze invented the easy-open ring-pull can in Kettering, Ohio, reputedly after struggling to open a can of beer at a family picnic.

1965 James Russell was granted 22 patents relating to his compact-disk system. CDs only came into wide use after they were taken up by Philips, a Dutch electronics firm, in 1980.

1965 James Faria and Robert Wright of Monsanto Industries filed a patent for a monofilament ribbon surface that would later become Astro Turf.

1968 Spencer Silver, a researcher at 3M looking into improving adhesives, came up with a new glue that produced a very weak bond. Art Fry, another researcher, who had often become frustrated when bookmarks fell out of his hymnal in church, eventually came up with a use for the product. Post-it notes were introduced in 1980.

1968 Roy Jacuzzi invented the first self-contained whirlpool bath with built-in water jets.

1979 Gordon Matthews's firm VMX (Voice Message Express) in Dallas, Texas, applied for a patent for the first voicemail system, which he then sold to 3M.

1981 IBM launched the first personal computer complete with a new operating system developed by a fledgling software company, the "Microsoft disk operating system" or MS-DOS.

1983 Microsoft announced that its new operating system would be on sale by the next year. Though originally called Interface Manager, the product was soon renamed Windows.

1988 Bryan Molloy and Klaus Schmiegel invented a class of aryloxyphenylpropylamines which included fluoxetine hydrochloride. It was the active ingredient in Eli Lilly's new drug, Prozac, the world's most widely used antidepressant.

1989 Tim Berners-Lee, a British scientist at CERN, a particle physics laboratory in Switzerland, developed a system to ease the sharing of databases and information. In 1990, he created the hypertext transfer protocol (HTTP) to allow computers to communicate over the internet. He also designed the Uniform Resource Locator (URL) to give sites addresses on the internet and invented a browser program to retrieve hypertext documents called the world wide web (WWW).

1993 The Global Positioning System came into being after the United States Air Force launched the last one of a network of 24 NAVSTAR satellites into orbit over the earth. This worldwide space-based navigation system was originally developed for military uses but GPS devices are now ubiquitous and are the basis for SatNav systems in motor vehicles among many other applications.

2003 The Human Genome Project completed its task of mapping the complete genetic blueprint of the human body. America, in the guise of the National Institutes of Health and the Department of Energy, and Britain's Wellcome Trust Sanger Institute, did almost all the work in this international project to determine the DNA sequences of the human genome.

Some notable patents

Invention	Year patented	Who by
Cotton gin	1794	Eli Whitney
Mechanical reaper	1834	Cyrus Hall McCormick
Revolver with interchangeable parts	1836	Samuel Colt
Screw propeller	1838	John Ericsson
Telegraph	1840	Samuel Morse
Rubber vulcanisation	1844	Charles Goodyear
Manner of buoying vessels	1849	Abraham Lincoln
Electric fire alarm	1852	Moses Gerrish Farmer
Beehive	1852	Lorenzo Lorraine Langstroth
Cylinder-pin tumbler lock	1861	Linus Yale Jr
Stock ticker	1863	Edward Calahan
Cast steel plough	1865	John Deere
Steam generator	1867	George Babcock/ Stephen Wilcox
Typewriter	1868	Christopher Sholes
Dynamite	1868	Alfred Nobel
Breech-loading firearm	1879	John Moses Browning
Statue of Liberty	1879	Auguste Bartholdi
Machine for making flat-bottom paper bags	1879	Margaret E. Knight
Alternating current	1886	William Stanley
Punch-card tabulator	1889	Herman Hollerith
Automatic telephone-exchange	1891	Almon Brown Strowger
Breakfast cereal	1896	John Harvey Kellogg
Internal-combustion engine	1898	Rudolf Diesel
Asprin	1900	Felix Hoffmann
Electric railway	1901	Granville T. Woods
Air conditioner	1906	Willis Haviland Carrier
Flying machine	1906	Orville and Wilbur Wright
Automobile	1911	Henry Ford
X-ray tube	1916	William D. Coolidge
Diving suit	1921	Harry Houdini
Traffic signal	1923	Garrett A. Morgan
Paint and stain/process of producing same	1925	George Washington Carver

Invention	Year patented	Who by
Climbing rose (first plant patented)	1931	Henry F. Bosenberg
Electrophotography (Xerox)	1939	Chester F. Carlson
Flourescent lamp	1939	Edmund Germer
Polyurethane	1942	William E. Hanford/ Donald F. Holmes
Television receiver	1948	Louis W. Parker
Rotor control mechanism for helicopter	1954	Charles Kaman
Oral contraceptive	1954	Frank B. Colton
Heart-lung machine	1955	John Gibbon
Nuclear fission	1955	Enrico Fermi
Pulse transfer controlling devices (magnetic core memory forerunner)	1955	An Wang
Video tape recording	1955	Charles P. Ginsburg
Random Access Memory (RAM)	1956	Jay W. Forrester
Polypropylene Plastics	1958	Robert Banks/Paul Hogan
Laser	1960	Arthur Shawlow/ Charles Townes
Safety belt	1962	Nils I. Bohlin
Optical fibres	1972	Donald Keck/Robert Maurer/Peter Schultz
Magnetic resonance imaging (MRI)	1974	Raymond B. Damadian
Knee implant prothsesis	1975	Ysidro M. Martinez
Catalytic converter	1975	Irwin Lacham/ Ronald Lewis
Ethernet	1977	Robert Metcalfe
Genetic engineering	1980	Herb Boyer/Stan Cohen
Feedback control	1985	Amar Bose
Transgenic non-human mammals (first animal patent – "The mouse that went to Harvard")	1988	Philip Leder
DNA sequencing	1992	Lloyd Smith/Leroy Hood/ Michael Hunkapiller/ Tim Hunkapiller
Optical character recognition	2001	Raymond Kurzweil
System for distributed task execution (internet protocol)	2003	Robert Kahn/Vinton Cerf/ David Ely

Sources: United States Patent and Trademarks Office; National Inventors' Hall of Fame

Business etiquette tips

Even in an increasingly globalised world in which the rules of etiquette have become fuzzier and tolerance of foreigners who show no awareness of them has become greater, it still helps to know what matters to some people in the places you visit. Here are some guidelines.

Business cards

In Asia and East Asia, the giving and receiving of business cards is a formal affair. Offer your card with both hands, and accept graciously those you are handed (do not shove them into a pocket).

In Japan, have a business card (a *meishi*) with you at all times. Failure to offer one signals that you are not interested in pursuing the relationship.

When visiting China or Japan, have your business cards printed in English on one side and Chinese or Japanese on the other. Cards should be presented with the Japanese or Chinese side facing up.

In India, it is usual to include academic qualifications on business cards.

Names and titles and status

In Japan, although things are changing, be cautious about calling people by their first name; first names are often restricted to family and very close friends. In general, it's best to couple someone's last name with "san" (for example, Tanaka-*san*); this works for both men and women.

Chinese names appear in a different order from those in the West. The family name is followed by the generational name and then a given name. The generational and given names are usually separated by a hyphen. Some Chinese people use the initials of their generational and given names, hence Lee Cheng-kwan can be known as C. K. Lee or Mr Lee. However, many people adopt an English first name or nickname to make it easier for westerners to address them. Some of these adopted names are a little odd – so don't be surprised if you run into Ivan Ho in Hong Kong.

Germans like to be called by titles, such as doctor or professor, and will prove much friendlier if you appear to appreciate their educational credentials.

The same is true in India, where job titles and professional qualifications are important in pinpointing status, which in turn indicates which office tasks are too lowly for an individual to carry out.

When entering a taxi in Japan, the most important person sits in the middle with an acolyte on either side.

In business negotiations, expect the representatives of a traditional Chinese firm to enter the room in order of seniority.

Communication, attitudes and greetings

In Japan don't raise your voice; brash westerners are perceived to be intimidating and gauche. Speak slightly more slowly than you would normally do, but not obviously so. Similarly, strong handshakes are considered aggressive.

Falling asleep in meetings or presentations is not uncommon in China and Japan. Closed eyes can also be a sign of concentration. Periods of silence during meetings and conversations are considered useful rather than uncomfortable.

In Thailand, a simple bow of the head is preferable to a handshake. The traditional "wai" (hands in prayer position while bowing) is best avoided for fear of breaching the rules of etiquette.

Like many Germans, Berliners tend to be earnest and

business etiquette tips *continued*

straightforward. It is best to say exactly what you mean and to keep attempts at humour out of business meetings. Irony can be taken the wrong way. And in other countries it is easy for jokes to be lost in translation.

In keeping with their political system, the Swiss are experts at consensus building, and will happily debate an issue until all parties are satisfied.

Good manners mean that a Mexican will sometimes be evasive to avoid disappointing. "Maybe", "probably", "I think so", and "I'll have to check" often mean "no".

Your Russian counterparts may insist that they understand something, when this is not actually the case. Moreover, they sometimes have a tendency to say things they think you want to hear.

If doing business in France, remain polite and cordial during a first meeting and keep in mind that the French tend to be suspicious of early friendliness. Many French consider effusive smiles to be *de trop*. A polite nod of the head will win you more respect.

Germans are quite likely to draw attention to deficiencies in your products or services if they do not correspond to your claims. This is simply because they see nothing wrong in pointing out facts.

At the end of a meeting or presentation, Germans often signal their approval or thanks by gently rapping their knuckles on the tabletop instead of applauding.

Americans favour a direct "tell us how it is" approach and Canadians respond to rationality and logic, even though they may, initially at least, be more reserved than their neighbours to the south.

Brazilians pay more attention to the person they are

negotiating with than the company and take time over negotiations when they get round to discussing business.

In big countries such as the United States and Canada, expect big differences in attitudes and behaviour from region to region – from New York via Oklahoma to California, and from Newfoundland via Francophone Quebec to British Columbia. And be prepared for regional differences in smaller countries too; in Italy and England much is made of the north-south divide, though in England it is traditionally the north that is considered less sophisticated than the south, while in Italy the reverse is the case.

When bidding farewell to a group of Indian colleagues, take time to address each person individually.

In China, *"Bu fangbian"* ("It is not convenient") is a polite way of saying that something is impossible or very difficult.

Deadlines and punctuality

In Germany and Switzerland and other countries such as China, always try to be on time or, if possible, early to appointments, and arrange for meetings or interviews well in advance. In Spain, by contrast, do not be offended if your contact turns up 15 or 20 minutes late for a meeting.

In the Arab world do not be surprised to be kept waiting for a meeting. This reflects a different attitude to time rather than discourtesy or calculation. Also be prepared for long meetings to be interrupted to answer the call to prayer.

In Japan, don't expect an immediate response to anything. Decisions are usually made collectively, and answers typically take much longer than in western companies. Once a decision is taken in Japan, however, the machine rolls forward smoothly and action is speedy.

business etiquette tips *continued*

In France, the quality of a product and the persuasiveness of an argument are far more important than the setting of deadlines.

No-nos

In Arab countries, male business travellers should not flirt with local women.

In Japan, do not leave your chopsticks standing upright in a bowl of rice: this resembles a Buddhist funerary custom.

When in Russia, don't shake hands through a doorway, light a cigarette from a candle, bring an even number of flowers, or whistle indoors.

Don't boast about your past when visiting California. Here, your pedigree counts for less than your next big idea.

In Hong Kong blinking at someone is considered impolite.

Many Singaporeans interpret strong eye contact as aggressive. In meetings, expect to see downward glances, especially from those lower in status. Pounding one fist into the palm of the other hand is a gesture to avoid as many people perceive it to be obscene. And the "arms akimbo" position – standing tall with your hands on your hips – is typically perceived as an angry and aggressive posture.

Eating and drinking

Breakfast meetings are rare in London. Most Brits subscribe to Oscar Wilde's claim that "only dull people are interesting at breakfast".

Wolfing down a sandwich at work confirms the worst French stereotypes of Anglo-Saxons. Lunch, usually a sit-down affair, is treated as a break from the office, and conversation over food is rarely work-related. To refuse wine at a business lunch would be permissible, but to refuse it at a dinner could be considered rude.

In Russia, always hand in your coat at the cloakroom when visiting a restaurant – draping it over the back of your chair is frowned upon.

When in Italy, order an espresso after eating. Topping off a meal with a frothy cappuccino would be unthinkable to a native.

In Japan, never blow your nose on the *oshibori* (a tightly rolled hot towel).

According to German superstition, if you don't look into another person's eyes when clinking glasses, seven years of bad sex will follow.

No Russian drinks vodka without *zakuski* (snacks) or a sniff of some black bread after each shot to help soak up the alcohol.

Social drinking is common in Mexico, where you can expect a boozy lunch and possibly a visit to a strip club to celebrate closing a deal.

In New York, business lunches tend to be dominated by work matters; the focus is not on the food and drink. Smoking (now banned in all restaurants and bars) is usually seen as a sign of weakness, not sophistication. The liquid lunch is a rarity: most New Yorkers stick to sparkling mineral water.

Toasts are important in Russia. Drink to international friendship, the success of an enterprise, or any other heart-warming goal.

Personal face and space

No-one likes to lose face in public but never underestimate the importance of "saving face" in Asia

business etiquette tips *continued*

and East Asia. Causing embarrassment and loss of "face" can scupper the best-laid business plans. Face is also particularly important in South America.

Tactile displays of emotion (back slaps, hugs) and kissing on both cheeks are quite acceptable among men in Saudi Arabia and the Gulf.

Strict Muslim men will not shake hands with women they are not related to. As an alternative, press your palm lightly over your heart.

Personal space is not highly regarded in China: expect people to get quite close to you, though in business gatherings the only contact beyond shaking hands is likely to be when your host may take your arm to show you the way.

Public displays of affection or prolonged body contact would be inappropriate in Japan and Korea.

Sartorial tips

Italians have a tendency to notice shoes straight away – keep yours shiny and in good shape.

Women travellers should dress conservatively in the Middle East (long sleeves and skirts below the knees).

In Latin American cities, high heels, short skirts and plunging necklines are quite acceptable for women.

Shoes are not worn inside Japanese houses or temples. There will be an assortment of slippers for guests to choose from. Leave your shoes (toes pointing towards the exit) at the designated spot and enter the main room. When entering a *tatami* room, remove your slippers.

In informal Israel, do not be surprised to see executives in sandals.

Sports

Many Germans consider chat about sport the preserve of the uneducated.

But in sports-mad Australia, it helps to know who recently won the big boat racing, rugby league football and cricket matches.

Before your business meetings in South Africa, brush up on the latest rugby or cricket triumph or failure of the Springboks. Soccer is also increasingly talked about as a result of the decision to host the 2010 World Cup in the country.

Yes and no

In Bulgaria and parts of Greece and Turkey, nodding and shaking the head have the opposite meanings they do in the rest of the world.

The Japanese avoid saying "no". "Yes" (*hai*) generally means "Yes, I hear what you are saying".

Indians and Singaporeans also dislike saying "no". Body language will often provide more clues than what is actually said. Phrase your questions to avoid a yes/no reply.

> **Some regard private enterprise as if it were a predatory tiger to be shot. Others look upon it as a cow that they can milk. Only a handful see it for what it really is – the strong horse that pulls the whole cart**

Winston Churchill,
British statesman

> **The chief business of the American people is business**

Calvin Coolidge,
former American president